Praise for Meditation For Dummies

"*Meditation For Dummies* is a smart idea whose time has come. If you're looking for an easy-to-follow yet comprehensive introduction to the practice of meditation, you've definitely come to the right place."
— John Gray
Author of *Men Are From Mars, Women Are From Venus*

"*Meditation For Dummies* is a useful guidebook filled with clear instructions and helpful hints to get you started and keep you on track."
— Deepak Chopra, Creative Director, The Chopra Center for Well Being
Author of *The Path to Love*

"Stephan Bodian is a shining light in the fields of meditation, yoga and consciousness. *Meditation For Dummies* is a simple yet very rich compilation of the nitty-gritty information you need to begin or deepen a meditation practice that will work for you, bringing you enhanced creativity, peace of mind, and healing."
— Joan Borysenko, Ph.D.
Author of *A Woman's Book of Life* and *Minding the Body, Mending the Mind*

"Stephan Bodian has given us an intelligent, humorous, and absolutely delightful entry into the world of meditative inquiry. His writing is jargon-free, and his suggested exercises are clear, practical, and easily followed. *Meditation For Dummies* is a wonderful travel guide to inner space. Don't stay home without it."
— Rabbi Rami Shapiro, Temple Beth Or, Miami, Florida
Author of *Wisdom of the Jewish Sages* and *Minyan*

"*Meditation For Dummies* is a . . . brilliantly clear roadmap to your true home, your natural heart, your shining mind. Stephan Bodian speaks from long experience to share the path that ends suffering and frees the heart for flight."
— Stephen Levine
Author of *A Year to Live, Meetings at the Edge: Healing into Life and Death,* and *Who Dies?*

Meditation Checklist

The Basic Amenities

❏ Meditation cushion, bench, or favorite chair

❏ Quiet, tidy spot, preferably reserved for meditation

❏ Regular time slot, if possible

❏ Loose-fitting, comfortable clothing

❏ Phone turned off, answering machine volume down low

❏ Comfortable sitting position

❏ Favorite meditation technique(s)

Optional Items

❏ Stretches to prepare your body for sitting

❏ Altar of special objects, pictures, candles, or incense

❏ Warm sweater or shawl (if you tend to get cold)

❏ Hallway or path for walking meditation, if you wish

❏ Meditation teacher to consult in case you get stuck or want to go deeper

Ten Tips for Getting the Most from Your Meditation

Meditate regularly — preferably every day.

Check out the different techniques, choose one, and stick with it — for a few weeks or months at least.

Set aside a quiet niche where you can meditate undisturbed.

Find a comfortable sitting position — and be sure to gently straighten your spine.

Decide beforehand how long you're going to meditate — and then follow through, no matter how restless or bored you become.

Begin by briefly connecting with your desire or motivation to meditate.

Take a few deep breaths before you start and consciously relax your body on the exhalation.

Drop any expectations about what you're supposed to be achieving or experiencing, and just be, exactly as you are.

Be patient, kind, and gentle with yourself.

As much as possible, extend the qualities of mind and heart you develop in your meditation to every area of your life.

Ten Benefits of a Regular Meditation Practice

Reduced tension, anxiety, and stress

Lower blood pressure and cholesterol levels

Stronger focus and concentration

Clearer thinking and less emotional turmoil

Greater creativity and enhanced performance at work and play

Increased self-understanding and self-acceptance

More joy, love, and spontaneity

Greater intimacy with friends and family members

Deeper sense of meaning and purpose

Glimpses of a spiritual dimension of being

...For Dummies: Bestselling Book Series for Beginners

Meditation For Dummies®

Meditation Lingo

Awareness. The core faculty or quality (which you can develop like a muscle when you meditate) of being present, open, and attentive.

Beginner's mind. An open mind, free from preconceptions and expectations; the best attitude to take toward meditation.

Chakras. Centers of spiritual and emotional energy (generally seven in number) located in a line from the base of your spine to the crown of your head.

Concentration. Awareness that's focused on a particular object or activity; a key ingredient in meditation.

Contemplation. Meditation in which you reflect on a particular issue, experience, or spiritual truth in order to gain greater insight and understanding.

Essential being (also known as pure being, true nature, spirit, or soul). The deeper truth inside you that underlies your personality and your habitual patterns and can be accessed through the practice of meditation.

Flow. An enlivening, deeply enjoyable state of being that develops through concentration when you immerse yourself completely in an activity.

Lovingkindness. Unconditional love and care for the welfare of oneself and others; can be cultivated and deepened in meditation.

Mantra. A meaningful word or phrase that you can repeat again and again in meditation to help facilitate relaxation, stress-reduction, peace of mind, and spiritual unfolding.

Mindfulness. The practice of being deliberately present and aware from moment to moment; a core meditation technique that can be applied to every activity and situation.

Penetrating insight. Direct, experiential understanding of how your mind works, developed in meditation, which allows you to change your habitual reactive patterns — and reduce your stress in the process.

Soft spot. The tender place inside your heart, beneath all the toughness and defensiveness, where you feel love and compassion (as well as sadness and hurt).

Visualization. A form of meditation in which you imagine a particular quality, energy, object, or being in order to achieve a particular purpose, such as healing or performance enhancement.

Zafu. A round, firm, plump cushion used for meditating on the floor.

Ten Popular Meditation Techniques

Here's a brief list of ten of the most commonly practiced techniques:

- ✔ Repeating a meaningful word or phrase, known as a *mantra*
- ✔ Following or counting your breaths
- ✔ Paying attention to the sensations in your body
- ✔ Cultivating love, compassion, forgiveness, and other healing emotions
- ✔ Concentrating on a geometric shape or other simple visual object
- ✔ Visualizing a peaceful place or a healing energy or light
- ✔ Reflecting upon inspirational or sacred writings
- ✔ Gazing at a picture of a holy being or saint
- ✔ Contemplating the beauty to be found in nature, art, or music
- ✔ Bringing mindful awareness to the present moment

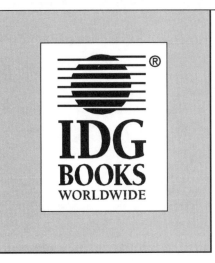

MEDITATION
FOR
DUMMIES®

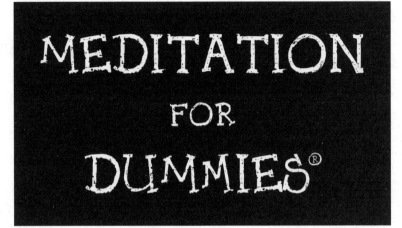

MEDITATION FOR DUMMIES®

by Stephan Bodian

Foreword by Dean Ornish, M.D.
Author of *Dr. Dean Ornish's Program
for Reversing Heart Disease*

x

IDG Books Worldwide, Inc.
An International Data Group Company

Foster City, CA ◆ Chicago, IL ◆ Indianapolis, IN ◆ New York, NY

Meditation For Dummies®

Published by
IDG Books Worldwide, Inc.
An International Data Group Company
919 E. Hillsdale Blvd.
Suite 400
Foster City, CA 94404
www.idgbooks.com (IDG Books Worldwide Web site)
www.dummies.com (Dummies Press Web site)

Library of Congress Catalog Card No.: 99-60185

ISBN: 0-7645-5116-7

Printed in the United States of America

10 9 8 7 6 5 4 3 2 1

1B/RR/QS/ZZ/IN

Distributed in the United States by IDG Books Worldwide, Inc.

Distributed by Macmillan Canada for Canada; by Transworld Publishers Limited in the United Kingdom; by IDG Norge Books for Norway; by IDG Sweden Books for Sweden; by Woodslane Pty. Ltd. for Australia; by Woodslane (NZ) Ltd. for New Zealand; by Addison Wesley Longman Singapore Pte Ltd. for Singapore, Malaysia, Thailand, and Indonesia; by Norma Comunicaciones S.A. for Colombia; by Intersoft for South Africa; by International Thomson Publishing for Germany, Austria and Switzerland; by Distribuidora Cuspide for Argentina; by Livraria Cultura for Brazil; by Ediciencia S.A. for Ecuador; by Ediciones ZETA S.C.R. Ltda. for Peru; by WS Computer Publishing Corporation, Inc., for the Philippines; by Contemporanea de Ediciones for Venezuela; by Express Computer Distributors for the Caribbean and West Indies; by Micronesia Media Distributor, Inc. for Micronesia; by Grupo Editorial Norma S.A. for Guatemala; by Chips Computadoras S.A. de C.V. for Mexico; by Editorial Norma de Panama S.A. for Panama; by Wouters Import for Belgium; by American Bookshops for Finland. Authorized Sales Agent: Anthony Rudkin Associates for the Middle East and North Africa.

For general information on IDG Books Worldwide's books in the U.S., please call our Consumer Customer Service department at 800-762-2974. For reseller information, including discounts and premium sales, please call our Reseller Customer Service department at 800-434-3422.

For information on where to purchase IDG Books Worldwide's books outside the U.S., please contact our International Sales department at 317-596-5530 or fax 317-596-5692.

For information on foreign language translations, please contact our Foreign & Subsidiary Rights department at 650-655-3021 or fax 650-655-3281.

For sales inquiries and special prices for bulk quantities, please contact our Sales department at 650-655-3200 or write to the address above.

For information on using IDG Books Worldwide's books in the classroom or for ordering examination copies, please contact our Educational Sales department at 800-434-2086 or fax 317-596-5499.

For press review copies, author interviews, or other publicity information, please contact our Public Relations department at 650-655-3000 or fax 650-655-3299.

For authorization to photocopy items for corporate, personal, or educational use, please contact Copyright Clearance Center, 222 Rosewood Drive, Danvers, MA 01923, or fax 978-750-4470.

About the Author

Stephan Bodian has been meditating for nearly as long as he's been shaving or driving a car. Although he had some early practice gazing out of his crib and later hanging out with the trees in his backyard, he caught the bug in high school when he came across the word "Zen" in a novel by Beat writer Jack Kerouac. Stephan proceeded to read all the books he could find on Zen — which in those days filled a small shoe box — and attempted to follow the rather cryptic instructions he found there, though without much luck. He also had a history teacher who turned him on to the wonders of Indian philosophy.

In college, Stephan minored in Asian studies and began meditating regularly during his senior year — at last! (He even managed to graduate — with a B.A. in English literature from Columbia University.) While his friends were heading off to do graduate work at other East Coast schools, Stephan decided to go to Stanford because there was a Zen center nearby. He spent most of the '70s meditating and teaching others how to do the same. Ordained a monk in 1974, he spent two years as director of a small Zen center in San Diego before putting aside his robes in 1982 to pursue a master's degree in psychology — and a more ordinary life.

In 1984 Stephan became editor-in-chief of *Yoga Journal,* an award-winning magazine devoted to yoga, meditation, and holistic health. During his ten-year tenure there, he also found time to put together a book of his interviews of famous visionaries and healers entitled *Timeless Visions, Healing Voices*, as well as an anthology of writings from the magazine, *Living Yoga* (with Georg Feuerstein). He has written frequently on meditation and spiritual themes and continues to teach workshops on meditation and on the integration of meditation in everyday life.

Currently, Stephan practices as a psychotherapist at the San Francisco Center for Meditation and Psychotherapy and at his office in Marin County, California, where he guides his clients in using meditative techniques for inner exploration and healing. He's also the host of a Web site (www.meditationsource.com) offering user-friendly meditation instruction, information, books, tapes, supplies, and access to meditation workshops, retreats, and phone counseling services. (If you don't have a modem [or a computer, for that matter!], you can call him at 415-451-7133.)

ABOUT IDG BOOKS WORLDWIDE

Welcome to the world of IDG Books Worldwide.

IDG Books Worldwide, Inc., is a subsidiary of International Data Group, the world's largest publisher of computer-related information and the leading global provider of information services on information technology. IDG was founded more than 30 years ago by Patrick J. McGovern and now employs more than 9,000 people worldwide. IDG publishes more than 290 computer publications in over 75 countries. More than 90 million people read one or more IDG publications each month.

Launched in 1990, IDG Books Worldwide is today the #1 publisher of best-selling computer books in the United States. We are proud to have received eight awards from the Computer Press Association in recognition of editorial excellence and three from Computer Currents' First Annual Readers' Choice Awards. Our best-selling ...For Dummies® series has more than 50 million copies in print with translations in 31 languages. IDG Books Worldwide, through a joint venture with IDG's Hi-Tech Beijing, became the first U.S. publisher to publish a computer book in the People's Republic of China. In record time, IDG Books Worldwide has become the first choice for millions of readers around the world who want to learn how to better manage their businesses.

Our mission is simple: Every one of our books is designed to bring extra value and skill-building instructions to the reader. Our books are written by experts who understand and care about our readers. The knowledge base of our editorial staff comes from years of experience in publishing, education, and journalism — experience we use to produce books to carry us into the new millennium. In short, we care about books, so we attract the best people. We devote special attention to details such as audience, interior design, use of icons, and illustrations. And because we use an efficient process of authoring, editing, and desktop publishing our books electronically, we can spend more time ensuring superior content and less time on the technicalities of making books.

You can count on our commitment to deliver high-quality books at competitive prices on topics you want to read about. At IDG Books Worldwide, we continue in the IDG tradition of delivering quality for more than 30 years. You'll find no better book on a subject than one from IDG Books Worldwide.

John Kilcullen
Chairman and CEO
IDG Books Worldwide, Inc.

Steven Berkowitz
President and Publisher
IDG Books Worldwide, Inc.

VIII WINNER
Eighth Annual Computer Press Awards ≥1992

IX WINNER
Ninth Annual Computer Press Awards ≥1993

X WINNER
Tenth Annual Computer Press Awards ≥1994

XI WINNER
Eleventh Annual Computer Press Awards ≥1995

IDG is the world's leading IT media, research and exposition company. Founded in 1964, IDG had 1997 revenues of $2.05 billion and has more than 9,000 employees worldwide. IDG offers the widest range of media options that reach IT buyers in 75 countries representing 95% of worldwide IT spending. IDG's diverse product and services portfolio spans six key areas including print publishing, online publishing, expositions and conferences, market research, education and training, and global marketing services. More than 90 million people read one or more of IDG's 290 magazines and newspapers, including IDG's leading global brands — Computerworld, PC World, Network World, Macworld and the Channel World family of publications. IDG Books Worldwide is one of the fastest-growing computer book publishers in the world, with more than 700 titles in 36 languages. The "...For Dummies®" series alone has more than 50 million copies in print. IDG offers online users the largest network of technology-specific Web sites around the world through IDG.net (http://www.idg.net), which comprises more than 225 targeted Web sites in 55 countries worldwide. International Data Corporation (IDC) is the world's largest provider of information technology data, analysis and consulting, with research centers in over 41 countries and more than 400 research analysts worldwide. IDG World Expo is a leading producer of more than 168 globally branded conferences and expositions in 35 countries including E3 (Electronic Entertainment Expo), Macworld Expo, ComNet, Windows World Expo, ICE (Internet Commerce Expo), Agenda, DEMO, and Spotlight. IDG's training subsidiary, ExecuTrain, is the world's largest computer training company, with more than 230 locations worldwide and 785 training courses. IDG Marketing Services helps industry-leading IT companies build international brand recognition by developing global integrated marketing programs via IDG's print, online and exposition products worldwide. Further information about the company can be found at www.idg.com.   1/24/99

Dedication

This book is dedicated to the great meditation masters and teachers in every culture and age, who continue to show us the way through their wise and compassionate example; and to you, dear reader: May the practice of meditation bring you the peace, health, and happiness you seek!

Author's Acknowledgments

I would like to express my appreciation to all the colleagues, teachers, and friends who contributed to the creation of this book. First, I'd like to thank my agent, Carol Susan Roth, for sending the project my way. Thanks also to the great folks at IDG, who really know how to make a book happen: executive editor Tami Booth, whose enthusiasm for the project never flagged; project editor Melba Hopper, keen-eyed yet always diplomatic; Jon Malysiak, for diligently tracking endorsements; and the rest of the gang, whose names remain unknown to me, who contributed in innumerable ways to creating the book you hold in your hands.

Special thanks to Dean Ornish, M.D., whose research has helped to change the face of modern medicine, for so graciously offering to write the foreword; and to technical advisor Eleanor Criswell, Ed.D., professor of psychology at Sonoma State University, past president of the Association for Humanistic Psychology, and author of *How Yoga Works,* who has generously supported and critiqued my work over the past 16 years.

I have had the inestimable good fortune to study with some great meditation teachers. Without them, this book would never have been written, and I feel immeasurable gratitude for their generosity and dedication. Any wisdom that shines through these pages has been kindled by their patient instruction. Deep bows especially to Shunryu Suzuki Roshi and Kobun Chino Otogawa Roshi; to Chogyam Trungpa Rinpoche and Drubwang Tsoknyi Rinpoche; and to my beloved "root teacher," Jean Klein, who pointed directly to the heart of meditation.

I would also like to thank the other Western writers and teachers whose work has inspired and informed my own: Joan Borysenko, Pema Chodron, Jon Kabat-Zinn, Jack Kornfield, Joel Levey, Stephen Levine, Byron Katie Rolle, and Suzanne Segal.

On a day-to-day level, I relied on the love and support of my friends and family. Barbara Green listened lovingly and helped ease my worried mind; Katie Darling buoyed my spirits when they sagged; my Thursday morning group (heart friends all) offered spiritual and emotional sustenance; and John Prendergast (who encouraged me to do the book when I had my doubts) and old Zen buddy Roy Wiskar read portions of the manuscript and provided useful and supportive feedback. Finally, I would like to thank Caroline Palden Alioto, whose friendship and wise counsel helped make it all possible.

Publisher's Acknowledgments

We're proud of this book; please register your comments through our IDG Books Worldwide Online Registration Form located at http://my2cents.dummies.com.

Some of the people who helped bring this book to market include the following:

Acquisitions and Editorial

Project Editor: Melba D. Hopper

Executive Editor: Tammerly Booth

Acquisitions Coordinator: Karen Young

General Reviewer: Eleanor Criswell

Associate Permissions Editor:
Carmen Krikorian

Editorial Manager: Mary C. Corder

Media Development Manager:
Heather Heath Dismore

Editorial Coordinator:
Maureen Kelly

Editorial Assistants: Paul Kuzmic, Donna Love

Production

Project Coordinator: Regina Snyder

Layout and Graphics: Angela F. Hunckler, Brent Savage, J. Tyler Connor, Michael A. Sullivan, Brian Torwelle

Special Art: Pam Tanzey (Illustrator)

Proofreaders: Kelli Botta, Rebecca Senninger, Ethel M. Winslow, Janet M. Withers

Indexer: Sherry Massey

Special Help

Jon Malysiak, Suzanne Thomas

General and Administrative

IDG Books Worldwide, Inc.: John Kilcullen, CEO; Steven Berkowitz, President and Publisher

IDG Books Technology Publishing: Brenda McLaughlin, Senior Vice President and Group Publisher

Dummies Technology Press and Dummies Editorial: Diane Graves Steele, Vice President and Associate Publisher; Mary Bednarek, Director of Acquisitions and Product Development; Kristin A. Cocks, Editorial Director

Dummies Trade Press: Kathleen A. Welton, Vice President and Publisher; Kevin Thornton, Acquisitions Manager

IDG Books Production for Dummies Press: Michael R. Britton, Vice President of Production and Creative Services; Cindy L. Phipps, Manager of Project Coordination, Production Proofreading, and Indexing; Kathie S. Schutte, Supervisor of Page Layout; Shelley Lea, Supervisor of Graphics and Design; Debbie J. Gates, Production Systems Specialist; Robert Springer, Supervisor of Proofreading; Debbie Stailey, Special Projects Coordinator; Tony Augsburger, Supervisor of Reprints and Bluelines

Dummies Packaging and Book Design: Patty Page, Manager, Promotions Marketing

♦

The publisher would like to give special thanks to Patrick J. McGovern, without whom this book would not have been possible.

♦

Contents at a Glance

Table of Contents

Foreword

. . . .

*T*he title of this book is a little misleading, because learning to meditate was one of the smartest decisions I ever made.

Meditation is power. Whatever you do, meditation can help you to do it better.

For example, my colleagues and I demonstrated, for the first time, that the progression of even severe coronary heart disease often can reverse when people go on my program of comprehensive lifestyle changes. Although many people believe that this program is based primarily on diet, meditation is actually an equally important part of it.

So — why don't more people meditate?

In *Meditation For Dummies,* Stephan Bodian helps dispel many of the most common misconceptions about meditation.

Many people view meditation as:	**In fact, meditation is:**
Boring	Interesting
Esoteric	Familiar
Ascetic	Sensual
Unproductive	Extremely productive
Difficult	Natural
Wimpy	Powerful

Meditation is the practice and process of paying attention and focusing your awareness. When you meditate, a number of desirable things begin to happen — slowly, at first, and deepening over time. As I described in *Love & Survival*:

First, *when you can focus your awareness, you gain more power.* When you concentrate any form of energy, including mental energy, you gain power. When you focus your mind, you concentrate better. When you concentrate better, you perform better. You can accomplish more, whether in the classroom, in the board room, or in the athletic arena. Whatever you do, you do it more effectively when you meditate. It is for this reason that spiritual teachers and texts often caution that one should begin the practice of meditation only in the context of other spiritual practices and disciplines that help develop compassion and wisdom to use properly this increased power.

Second, *you enjoy your senses more fully.* Although people sometimes view or use meditation as an ascetic experience to *control* their senses, meditation also can *enhance* your senses in ways that are profoundly sensual. Anything that you enjoy — food, sex, music, art, massage, and so on — is greatly enhanced by meditation. When you pay attention to something, it's a lot more enjoyable. Also, you don't need as much of it to get the same degree of pleasure, so you are more likely to enjoy without excess.

When you keep a wall around your heart to armor and protect it from pain, you also diminish your capacity to feel pleasure. When your life is in a continual rush, you may miss exquisite pleasures that exist from moment to moment. Attention spans get shorter. The need for stimulation continually increases just to feel *anything.* Meditation increases awareness and sensitivity; as such, it can be an antidote to numbness and distraction.

Third, *your mind quiets down and you experience an inner sense of peace, joy, and well-being.* When I first learned to meditate and began getting glimpses of inner peace, this experience changed my life. It redefined and reframed my experience. Before, I thought peace of mind came from getting and doing; now, I understand that it comes from *being.* It is our true nature to be peaceful until we disturb it.

This is a radically different concept of where our happiness and our well-being come from. In one of life's great paradoxes, not being aware of this truth, we often end up disturbing our inner peace while striving to get or to do what we think will bring that same peace to us.

Fourth, *you may directly experience and become more aware of the transcendent interconnectedness that already exists.* You may have a direct experience of God or the universal Self, whatever name you may give to this experience.

Meditation is simple in concept but difficult to master. Fortunately, you don't have to master mediation to benefit from it. You just have to practice. No one ever really masters it completely, but even a few steps down that road can make a meaningful difference. It is the *process* of meditation that makes it so beneficial, not how well you perform.

In my research studies, most of the participants reported much greater difficulty practicing meditation than exercising or maintaining their diet. Why? You have to eat; it's just a question of what you eat. Meditation, on the other hand, is not part of most people's daily routine or experience. Exercise is more familiar to people, and also there is a macho quality to exercise — you're out there really doing something, whereas meditation still has what some of our research participants at first called the "wimp factor." From outward appearances, it looks as if you're not doing anything when you meditate. In fact, meditation is a powerful, active process.

There are many different types of meditation. It is found in all cultures and in all religions all over the world — because it works. Truth is truth. While the forms vary, certain principles almost always are found.

This attitude of paying attention can help transform everything we do into a form of meditation. Whatever we do with concentration and awareness becomes meditation.

As the editor of *Yoga Journal* for many years, Stephan Bodian has had the opportunity to become familiar with many different approaches to meditation and yoga. He has distilled the best of these here and gently leads you step by step to discover a form and style of meditation that works best for you.

Meditation For Dummies. Smart. Very smart.

Dean Ornish, M.D.
Founder, President, & Director, Preventive Medicine Research Institute
Clinical Professor of Medicine, University of California, San Francisco
Author, *Love & Survival* and *Dr. Dean Ornish's Program for Reversing Heart Disease*
Sausalito, California, November 26, 1998

Introduction

E veryone seems to want to know how to meditate these days. From Baby Boomers to Generation-Xers, anxious teens to aging retirees, harried housewives to hurried executives, heart attack sufferers to weekend athletes, more and more people are seeking solutions for the stressful, time-urgent, overstimulated lives we lead. Since the media and mainstream medicine have failed to provide satisfying answers, we're turning in increasing numbers to time-honored practices like meditation for proven remedies to cure life's ills.

Well, I have great news: Meditation works. Whether you're seeking greater focus to get your job done more efficiently, less stress and more peace of mind, or a deeper appreciation of the beauty and richness of life, the simple practice of sitting down and turning your attention inward can do wonders. I know — I've been practicing meditation and teaching it to others for more than 25 years.

To tell you the truth, you can learn the basics of meditation in five minutes. Just sit in a comfortable position, straighten your back, breathe deeply, and follow your breath. It's as simple as that! If you do it regularly, you'll find that it won't be long before you're feeling more relaxed and enjoying life more.

Simple though it may be, meditation also has tremendous subtlety and depth, if you're interested in pursuing it further. It's a lot like painting — you can buy your materials, take a few lessons, and have a fun time applying paint to paper. Or you can attend classes at your local adult ed or community college, specialize in a particular medium in art school, and make painting a central part of your life. In meditation, as in art, you can keep it simple — just get up every day and sit quietly for five or ten minutes — or you can explore the subtleties to your heart's content. It all depends on your needs, your intentions, and your level of interest and passion.

About This Book

As a teacher of meditation, I've always been hard-pressed to come up with a single book that teaches the basics, provides a comprehensive overview of techniques and practices, and offers guidance in going deeper. Global surveys generally ignore the nuts and bolts — what to focus on, how to sit, what to do about your crazy mind. Books that teach you how to meditate tend to offer just a few techniques. And those that show you how to explore the rich inner world of meditation often have a sectarian spiritual perspective that limits the breadth of their presentation. (In other words, you'd have to be a Buddhist or a yogi or a Sufi to know what they're talking about.)

Unlike any other book I've come across, this one covers all the bases. If you're looking for simple, easy-to-follow meditation instructions, you'll find state-of-the-art guidance here, filled with helpful tips from seasoned meditators and time-honored wisdom from the great teachers of old. If you want to get an overview of the meditation field before you zero in on a particular method or teaching, you'll catch a glimpse of the primary approaches available these days. If you've been meditating in a particular way and want to expand your horizons to include other techniques, you'll be pleased to discover that this book features dozens of different meditations for a variety of purposes, drawn from a range of sources and traditions. And if you just want to understand why other people meditate — your partner, your friends, the guy in the office next to yours — jump on board! You'll discover whole chapters on why people meditate and how you can benefit too.

The best thing about this book, in my humble estimation, is that it's fun to read. Meditation doesn't have to be a dull or somber affair. Quite the contrary; the whole point of meditating in the first place is to lighten up and experience more peace and joy in your life. So, forget those stereotypes of the uptight Zen monk or the reclusive navel-gazer! You can learn everything you could ever want to know about meditation and enjoy yourself in the process.

How to Use This Book

This book is many things at once: an instructional manual, a survey course, and a guidebook for deeper exploration. Feel free to read it from cover to cover, if you wish, or just browse until you find the chapters that appeal to you. Throughout the book, you'll find meditations and exercises you can experiment with and enjoy.

Depending on your interests and needs, you can also use this book in a number of specific ways:

✔ To gain a better understanding of what meditation really is and what it has to offer, begin with Part I, where all your questions will be answered and all your problems solved. (That will be $75, please!)

✔ To find a crash course in the practice of meditation, head for Part II, where you'll discover everything you need to know, from how to sit still and focus your mind and where and when to meditate to what kind of gear you'll need and how to use it.

✔ For expert guidance in dealing with the issues that may arise when you've been meditating for a while, turn to Part III.

✔ To get an overview of the meditation field, try Chapter 3 for a historical survey and Chapter 13 for a description of the different approaches to cultivating spirituality.

✔ To locate a meditation for a specific purpose or need, check out the chapter with the appropriate title. Or turn to The Part of Tens (Part V) for lists of the best all-purpose meditations.

How This Book Is Organized

Although I designed this book so it can be read cover to cover — some people still do that, don't they? — I also made sure that you can find what you're looking for easily and quickly. Each part covers a different phase of your encounter with meditation.

Part I: Getting Acquainted

If you don't know a thing about meditation, you'll probably want to start here. You'll discover what meditation is (and isn't), where it comes from, and how you can use meditation to reduce your stress, improve your health, and enhance your feelings of peace and well-being. This part also introduces you to the devious workings of your own mind (in case you hadn't already noticed) — and explains how meditation helps to keep you calm and focused.

Part II: Getting Started

Here's where you actually learn how to sit down and work with your mind (and heart)! Just in case you're intimidated by the prospect of being quiet and turning inward, I provide easy-to-follow instructions that lead you through the process gently, step by step. I include a separate chapter on all the little details that most meditation books take for granted — such as how to keep your back (more or less) straight without getting uptight and what to do with your eyes and hands — and one on stretching and preparing your body for sitting. You can even meditate lying down, if you prefer.

Part III: Troubleshooting and Fine-Tuning

Once you start meditating regularly, you'll find that questions and even problems arise from time to time. You may wonder how to put all the pieces together in a way that's uniquely suited to your needs. Or you may encounter distractions you don't know how to deal with, like recurring fantasies or difficult emotions. (For example, "How can I possibly get my mind to stop playing the same Beastie Boys tune over and over?") You may even have an occasional *aha!* experience and long to use your meditation to get answers to spiritual questions. This part covers the fine points and hot spots of practice.

Part IV: Meditation in Action

It's one thing to calm your mind and open your heart in the privacy of your room, but quite another to practice meditation throughout your day, with your boss (or your clients), your partner, your kids, and the person in the car in front of you. This part shows you how to extend the benefits of meditation to every area of your life and includes a special chapter on using meditation for healing and performance enhancement.

Part V: The Part of Tens

I tend to gravitate to the end of a book first, which is why I love lists like these. In this part, you find answers to the most frequently asked questions about meditation and a distillation of the best all-purpose meditations.

Part VI: Appendix

If you're not sure what to do next when you finish this book, or you want to find out more about a particular technique or approach to meditation, or you just want to contact other people to meditate with, check out this annotated list of meditation organizations, centers, and books.

Icons Used in This Book

 These brief exercises offer a refreshing pause from your hectic life. They're designed to lead you out of your head and into the here-and-now.

 When you see this icon, prepare to stop what you're doing, take a few deep breaths, and start meditating. It's your chance to savor the real thing!

 If I haven't said it before, I should have — it's important information that bears repeating.

 This wise guy shows you where to look for musings of a more philosophical nature.

If you want your meditations to be easier and more effective, follow this tidbit of insider advice.

People have been meditating for thousands of years. Here's some of the cool stuff they've learned, in the form of an anecdote or story.

Feedback, Please

The author and publisher of this book would love to hear from readers. To contact the publisher (or authors of other *...For Dummies* books), visit the publisher's Web site at www.dummies.com, send an e-mail to info@idgbooks.com, or send paper mail to IDG Books Worldwide, Inc., 7260 Shadeland Station, Suite 100, Indianapolis, IN 46256. To get in touch with me, check out my Web site at www.meditationsource.com, send an e-mail to info@meditationsource.com, or send a real live letter to Stephan Bodian, P.O. Box 45, Fairfax, CA 94978.

Part I
Getting Acquainted

The 5th Wave   By Rich Tennant

"Here's a tip — if you hear yourself snoring,
you're meditating too deeply."

In this part . . .

You find out everything you could possibly want to know about meditation to get you interested, motivated, and, ultimately, started. Did you realize that meditation has an illustrious multicultural history? That regular practice offers dozens of scientifically proven benefits, from reduced stress and lower blood pressure and cholesterol levels to greater empathy and enhanced creativity? Or that the real cause of suffering and stress is not what happens to you, but how your mind responds? Well, read on! You also have an opportunity to explore for yourself what brings you to meditation — and what you hope to get out of it.

Chapter 1

What Meditation Is — and Isn't

The great thing about meditation is that it's actually quite simple. Just sit down, be quiet, turn your attention inward, and focus your mind. That's all there is to it, really. (See the sidebar "Meditation: It's easier than you think.") Then, why, you may be wondering, do people write so many books and articles about meditation — including detailed books like this one? Why not just offer a few brief instructions and forget about all the verbiage?

Say that you're planning to take a long trip by car to some picturesque location. You could just jot down the directions and follow them one by one. After a few days, you'd probably get where you want to go. But you'll enjoy the trip more if you have a travel guide to point out the sights along the way — and you may feel more secure if you carry a troubleshooting manual to tell you what to do when you have problems with your car. Perhaps you'd like to take some side trips to scenic spots or even change your itinerary entirely and get there by a different route — or a different vehicle!

In the same way, you can consider the practice of meditation to be a journey of sorts — and the book you hold in your hands to be a travel guide. This chapter provides an overview of your trip, offers some alternative routes to your destination, explains the basic skills you need to know to get you there — and points to some detours that may advertise the same benefits but that don't really deliver.

Meditation: It's easier than you think

Meditation is simply the practice of focusing your attention on a particular object — generally something simple, like a word or phrase, a candle flame or geometrical figure, or the coming and going of your breath. In everyday life, your mind is constantly processing a barrage of sensations, visual impressions, emotions, and thoughts. When you meditate, you narrow your focus, limit the stimuli bombarding your nervous system — and calm your mind in the process.

To get a quick taste of meditation, follow these instructions. (For more complete meditation instructions, see Chapter 6.)

1. **Find a quiet place and sit comfortably with your back relatively straight.**

   If you tend to disappear into your favorite chair, find something a bit more supportive.

2. **Take a few deep breaths, close your eyes, and relax your body as much as you can.**

   If you don't know how to relax, you may want to check out Chapter 6.

3. **Choose a word or phrase that has special personal or spiritual meaning for you.**

   Here are some examples: "there's only love," "don't worry, be happy," "trust in God."

4. **Begin to breathe through your nose (if you can), and as you breathe, repeat the word or phrase quietly to yourself.**

   You can whisper the word or phrase, subvocalize it (that is, move your tongue as though saying it, but not aloud), or just repeat it in your mind. If you get distracted, come back to the object of your meditation.

   As an alternative, you can follow your breath as it comes and goes through your nostrils, returning to your breathing when you get distracted.

5. **Keep the meditation going for five minutes or more; then slowly get up and go about your day.**

How did you feel? Did it seem weird to say the same thing or follow your breath over and over? Did you find it difficult to stay focused? Did you keep changing the phrase? If so, don't worry. With regular practice and the guidance of this book, you'll gradually get the knack.

Of course, you could easily spend many fruitful and enjoyable years mastering the subtleties and complexities of meditation. But the good news is, the basic practice is actually quite simple, and you don't have to be an expert to do it — or to enjoy its extraordinary benefits.

Embarking on the Journey of Meditation

No doubt you picked up this book because you're searching for something more in life — more peace of mind, more energy, more well-being, more meaning, more happiness, more joy. You've heard about meditation, and you wonder what it has to offer. To continue the journey metaphor, you could say that the practice of meditation begins where you are and ends up taking you where you want to be.

Being an adventurous sort, I like to think of it as a climb up a mountain. You've seen snapshots of the summit and from the bottom, you can barely glimpse the summit through the clouds. But the only way to get there is up — one step at a time.

Different paths up the same mountain

Imagine that you're getting ready to climb this mountain. (If you live in the Netherlands or the midwestern United States, get out your *National Geographic* for this one!) How are you going to get to the top? You could take some climbing lessons, buy the right gear, and inch your way up one of the rocky faces. Or you could choose one of the many trails that meander up the mountain and take a leisurely hike to the summit. (Of course, you could always cheat and drive your car, but that would ruin my metaphor!)

Although they all end up at the same place, every trail has its unique characteristics. One may take you on a gradual ascent through forests and meadows, whereas another may head steeply uphill over dry, rocky terrain. From one, you may have vistas of lush valleys filled with flowers; from another, you may see farmland or desert.

Depending on your energy and your motivation, you may choose to stop at a picnic spot en route and while away a few hours (or a few days) enjoying the peace and quiet. Hey, you might enjoy it so much that you decide not to climb any farther. Perhaps you'd rather climb one of the smaller peaks along the way instead of going all the way to the top. Or you may prefer to charge to the summit as quickly as you can without bothering to linger anywhere.

Well, the journey of meditation has a great deal in common with climbing a mountain. You can aim for the top, or you can just set your sights on some grassy knoll or lesser peak halfway up the slope. Whatever your destination, you can have fun along the way and reap the benefits of just breathing deeply and exercising muscles you didn't even know you had.

People have been climbing the mountain of meditation for thousands of years in different parts of the world. (For more on the history of meditation, see Chapter 3.) As a result, topographic maps and guidebooks abound, each with their own unique version of how to make your way up the mountain — and their own recommendations for how to hike and what to carry. (To get a sense of the range of meditation materials available these days, just check out the shelves of your local bookstore.)

Traditionally, the guidebooks describe a spiritual path involving a set of beliefs and practices, often secret, that have been passed down from one generation to the next. (See the sidebar "Meditation's spiritual roots.") In recent decades, however, Western researchers and teachers have distilled meditation from its spiritual origins and now offer it as a remedy for a variety of twenty-first century ills. (For more on the benefits of meditation, see Chapter 2.)

Although the maps and books may describe the summit differently — some emphasize the vast open spaces, others pay more attention to the peace or exhilaration you feel when you get there, and some even claim that there's more than one peak — I happen to agree with the ancient sage who said: "Meditation techniques are just different paths up the same mountain."

Here are a few of the many techniques that have been developed over the centuries:

- Repetition of a meaningful word or phrase, known as a *mantra* (see Chapters 3 and 13)

- Mindful awareness of the present moment (for more on *mindfulness,* see Chapters 6 and 15)

- Following or counting your breath (see Chapter 6)

- Paying attention to the flow of sensations in your body (see Chapter 6)

- Cultivation of lovingkindness, compassion, forgiveness, and other healing emotions (see Chapter 10)

- Concentration on a geometric shape or other simple visual object

- Visualization of a peaceful place or a healing energy or entity (see Chapter 16)

- Reading and reflection upon inspirational or sacred writings (see Chapter 13)

- Gazing at a picture of a holy being or saint

- Contemplation of nature

- Chanting praises to the Divine

Throughout this book, you find opportunities to experiment with many of these techniques, as well as detailed guidance in the practice of one in particular — *mindfulness* — beginning with your breath and then extending your meditation to every moment of your life.

The view from the summit — and from other peaks along the way

When you reach the summit of the meditation mountain, what do you see? If we can trust the reports of the meditators and mystics who have climbed the mountain before us, we can declare with some confidence that the top of the mountain harbors the *source* of all love, wisdom, happiness, and joy. Some people call it spirit or soul, true nature or true self, the ultimate truth or the ground of being (or just being itself). Others call it God or the Divine or the Holy Mystery, or simply the One. There are nearly as many names for it as people who experience it. And some spiritual traditions consider it so sacred and powerful that they hesitate to give it a name.

As for the *experience* of reaching the summit, seasoned meditators use words like enlightenment (from ignorance), awakening (from a dream), liberation (from bondage), freedom (from limitation), and union (with God or being).

An old saying likens all these words and names to fingers pointing at the moon. If you pay too much attention to the finger, you risk missing the beautiful moon, which is the reason for pointing the finger in the first place. Ultimately, you need to experience the moon — or in this case the summit — for yourself.

Meditation's spiritual roots

Although many ordinary folks are meditating these days (including, quite possibly, people you know), the practice wasn't always so readily available. For centuries, monks, nuns, mystics, and wandering ascetics preserved it in secret, using it to enter higher states of consciousness and ultimately to achieve the pinnacle of their particular path.

Highly motivated laypeople with time on their hands could always learn a few techniques. But the rigorous practice of meditation remained a sacred pursuit limited to an elite few who were willing to renounce the world and devote their lives to it. (See Chapter 3 for more on the history of meditation.)

How times have changed! From Beat Zen in the '50s and the influx of Indian yogis and swamis in the '60s to the current fascination with Buddhism, meditation has definitely become mainstream, and its practical benefits are applauded in every medium, both actual and virtual. (Have you ever checked out the Web sites devoted to meditation?)

Meditation has been studied extensively in psychology labs and reduced to simple formulas like the Relaxation Response. Yet it has never entirely lost its spiritual roots. In fact, the reason meditation works so effectively is that it connects you with a spiritual dimension, which different commentators give different names, but I like to call simply *"being."*

Of course, you may have no interest in lofty states and experiences like enlightenment or union. Perhaps you bought this book simply because you want to reduce your stress or enhance your healing process or deal with your emotions. Forget about the Holy Mystery — a little more clarity and peace of mind would suit you just fine, thank you very much!

Well, the truth is, you're going to follow the same path no matter how high up the mountain you want to go. The basic instructions remain the same — but you get to choose your destination. Among the most popular stopping places and promontories en route to the summit are the following:

- ✔ Stronger focus and concentration
- ✔ Reduced tension, anxiety, and stress
- ✔ Clearer thinking and less emotional turmoil
- ✔ Lower blood pressure and cholesterol
- ✔ Support in kicking addictions and other self-defeating behaviors
- ✔ Greater creativity and enhanced performance in work and play
- ✔ Increased self-understanding and self-acceptance
- ✔ More joy, love, and spontaneity
- ✔ Greater intimacy with friends and family members
- ✔ Deeper sense of meaning and purpose
- ✔ Glimpses of a spiritual dimension of being

As you can see, these way-stations are actually major destinations in their own right, and all of them are well worth reaching. (For more on the benefits of meditation, see Chapter 2.) You may be quite content to stop halfway up the mountain, once you've reduced your stress, improved your health, and experienced greater overall well-being. Or you may feel inspired to push on for the higher altitudes that the great meditators describe.

The taste of pure mountain water

To elaborate this mountain metaphor a bit, imagine that there's a spring at the summit that gushes forth the pure *water of being* and never runs dry. (Depending on your orientation, you may prefer to call it the water of grace or spirit or unconditional love.) Those who make it to the top get to dive into the pool that surrounds the spring and immerse themselves completely in the water. In fact, some even merge with the water and become identical with being itself. (Don't worry, you won't merge if you don't want to!)

But you don't have to climb all the way to the top to enjoy the pure *taste of being.* The water flows down the mountain in streams and rivulets and nourishes the fields and towns below. In other words, you can taste *being* everywhere, in everything, because being is the essence that keeps life going at every level. Until you start meditating, though, you may not know what being tastes like.

When you meditate, you get closer to the source of the water and learn how to recognize its taste. (Depending on their personalities and where they are on the mountain, people use different terms to describe the water's taste, such as calm, peace, well-being, wholeness, clarity, and compassion.) It doesn't matter where you're headed or where you stop on your way up the mountain; you still get to dip your hands in the water of being and taste it for yourself. Then you can begin to find the taste of being wherever you go!

There's no place like home — and you're already there!

Now that I've constructed the metaphor of the mountain, I'm going to knock it down with one sweep of my hand — like a wave washing away a castle in the sand. Yes, the journey of meditation requires steady effort and application like a climb up a mountain. (For more on effort and discipline, see Chapter 9.) But that metaphor hides some important paradoxes:

- ✔ For one thing, the summit doesn't exist in some faraway place outside you; it exists in the depths of your being — some traditions say in the heart — and awaits your discovery. (See the sidebar "Discovering the treasure in your own house" later in this chapter.)

- ✔ For another thing, you can approach the summit in an instant; it doesn't necessarily take years of practice. While meditating, for example, when your mind settles down and you experience a deep peace or tranquillity or sense your interconnectedness with all beings or feel an upsurge of peace or love, you're tasting the sweet water of *being* right from the source inside you. And these moments inform and nourish you in ways you can't possibly measure.

- ✔ Besides, the mountain metaphor suggests a progressive, goal-oriented journey, whereas, in fact, the point of meditation is to set aside all goals and striving and just *be.* As the title of the recent best-seller by stress-reduction expert Jon Kabat-Zinn puts it, "Wherever you go, there you are." Or as Dorothy says in *The Wizard of Oz,* "There's no place like home" — and the truth is, like Dorothy, you're always already there!

TRADITIONAL WISDOM

Discovering the treasure in your own house

In the Jewish tradition, they tell a story that has its counterparts in all the world's great meditative teachings. Simon, a simple tailor, fantasizes night and day about the great treasure he will one day find when he leaves his little village and his family home and ventures forth into the world. Late one night, with a few belongings on his back, he sets off on his travels.

For years, Simon wanders from one great city to another, making his living mending clothes, searching for the treasure he knows belongs to him. But all the people he asks about the treasure have problems of their own and are unable to help him.

One day he comes upon a psychic known far and wide for her extraordinary abilities. "Yes," she says, "there is indeed a vast treasure that belongs to you and you alone." Hearing this, Simon's eyes light up with excitement. "I will tell you how to find it," she continues, giving Simon complex directions that he meticulously records.

When she comes to the end of her instructions and describes the very street and house where this treasure is allegedly buried, Simon can't believe his ears. For this is the very home he had left years before when setting out on his quest.

Quickly he thanks the psychic, stuffs the directions in his pocket, and hurries back in the direction from which he came. And lo and behold, much to his surprise, he does indeed find a vast and unfathomable treasure buried beneath the hearth in his own house.

The point of this story is obvious: Though we may wander in search of inner peace and experiment with all kinds of meditative practices, the peace and love and wisdom we seek are inevitably here all along, hidden within our own hearts.

Of course, you're not going to give up all your doing and striving instantaneously and just be, even when you meditate. That's something you work up to slowly by practicing your meditation and gradually focusing and simplifying until you're doing less and less while you meditate — and *being* more and more. The following are a few of the stages you may pass through on the path to just being:

- ✔ Getting used to sitting still
- ✔ Developing the ability to turn your attention inward
- ✔ Struggling to focus your attention
- ✔ Being distracted again and again

- Becoming more focused
- Feeling more relaxed as you meditate
- Noticing fleeting moments when your mind settles down
- Experiencing brief glimpses of stillness and peace

And here's perhaps the greatest paradox of all: If you practice meditation diligently, you may eventually come to relpize that you've never left home, even for an instant.

Becoming aware of your awareness

Most of the time, you probably don't pay much attention to your awareness. Yet the truth is, it's crucial to everything you do. When you watch TV, study for an exam, cook a meal, drive around the block, listen to music, or talk with a friend, you're being aware or paying attention. Before you begin to meditate in a formal way, you may find it helpful to explore your own awareness.

First, notice what it's like to be aware. Are there times in your life when you're not aware of anything? Now, complete this thought: "I am aware of. . . ." Do this again and again and notice where your awareness takes you.

Do you tend to be more aware of internal or external sensations? Do you pay more attention to thoughts and fantasies than to your moment-to-moment sensory experiences? Notice whether a preoccupation with mental activity diminishes your awareness of what's happening right here and now.

Next, pay attention to whether your awareness tends to focus on a particular object or sensation or tends to be more expansive and inclusive. You may find that your awareness resembles a spotlight that flows from object to object. Notice how your awareness flows without trying to change it.

Does it shift quickly from one thing to another, or does it move more slowly, making contact with each object before moving on? Experiment with speeding up and slowing down the flow of awareness, and notice how that feels.

You may discover that your awareness is drawn again and again to certain kinds of objects and events, but not to others. Where does your awareness repeatedly wander? Which experience does it seem to selectively avoid?

Now, experiment with gently directing your awareness from one focus to another. When you pay attention to sounds, you may notice that you momentarily forget about your hands or the discomfort in your back or knees. Try to focus on one object of attention for as long as you can. How long can you remain undistracted before your mind skips to the next thing?

Interesting journal idea ✗

Developing Awareness: The Secret to Meditation

If, as the old saying goes, a journey of a thousand miles begins with a single step, then the journey of meditation begins with the cultivation of *awareness,* or *attention.* In fact, awareness is the mental muscle that carries you along and sustains you on your journey, not only at the start but every step of the way. No matter which path or technique you choose, the secret of meditation lies in developing, focusing, and directing your awareness. (Incidentally, attention is just slightly focused awareness, and I use the two terms more or less interchangeably throughout this book. See the sidebar "Becoming aware of your awareness.")

To get a better sense of how awareness operates, consider another natural metaphor: light. You may take light for granted, but unless you've developed the special skills and heightened sensitivity of the blind, you can barely function without it. (Have you ever tried to find something in a pitch-dark room?) The same is true for awareness: You may not be aware that you're aware, but you need awareness to perform even the simplest tasks.

You can use light in a number of ways. You can create ambient lighting that illuminates a room softly and diffusely. You can focus light into a flashlight beam to help you find things when the room is dark. Or you can take the very same light and concentrate it into a laser beam so powerful that it can cut through steel or send messages to the stars.

Likewise, in meditation, you can use awareness in different ways. To begin with, you can increase your powers of awareness by developing *concentration* on a particular object. (For a brief list of meditation objects, see the section "Different paths up the same mountain" earlier in this chapter.)

Then, when you've stabilized your concentration, you can, through the practice of *receptive* awareness, expand your awareness — like ambient light — to illuminate the full range of your experience. Next, you can concentrate even further in order to *cultivate* positive emotions and mind-states. Or you can use awareness to investigate your inner experience and *contemplate* the nature of existence itself. These four — *concentration, receptive awareness, contemplation,* and *cultivation* — constitute the major uses of awareness throughout the world's great meditative traditions.

Building concentration

To do just about anything well, you need to *focus* your awareness. The most creative and productive people in every profession — for example, great athletes, performers, businessmen, scientists, artists, writers — have the ability to block out distractions and completely immerse themselves in their work. If you've ever watched Michael Jordan drive to the basket or Meryl Streep transform herself into the character she's portraying, you've witnessed the fruits of total *concentration*.

Some people have an innate ability to concentrate, but most of us need to practice to develop it. Buddhists like to compare the mind to a monkey — constantly chattering and hopping about from branch to branch, topic to topic. Did you ever notice that most of the time, you have scant control over the whims and vacillations of your monkey mind, which may space out one moment and obsess the next? When you meditate, you calm your monkey mind by making it *one-pointed* rather than scattered and distracted.

Many spiritual traditions teach their students concentration as the primary meditation practice. Just keep focusing your mind on the mantra or the symbol or the visualization, they advise, and eventually you will attain what is called *absorption,* or *samadhi.*

In absorption, the sense of being a separate "me" disappears, and only the object of your attention remains. Followed to its natural conclusion, the practice of concentration can lead to an experience of union with the object of your meditation. If you're a sports enthusiast, this object could be your tennis racket or your golf club; if you're an aspiring mystic, the "object" could be God or being or the absolute.

Even though you may not yet know how to meditate, you've no doubt had moments of total absorption, when the sense of separation disappears: gazing at a sunset, listening to music, creating a work of art, looking into the eyes of your beloved. When you're so completely involved in an activity, whether work or play, that time stops and self-consciousness drops away, you enter into what psychologist Mihaly Csikszentmihalyi calls *flow.* In fact, Csikszentmihalyi claims that activities that promote flow epitomize what most of us mean by enjoyment. Flow can be extraordinarily refreshing, enlivening, and even deeply meaningful — and it is the inevitable result of unbroken concentration.

Opening to receptive awareness

The great sages of China say that all things comprise the constant interplay of *yin* and *yang* — the feminine and masculine forces of the universe. Well, if concentration is the yang of meditation — focused, powerful, penetrating — then *receptive awareness* is the yin — open, expansive, welcoming.

Where concentration disciplines, stabilizes, and grounds the mind, receptive awareness loosens and extends the mind's boundaries and creates more interior space, enabling you to familiarize yourself with the mind's contents. Where concentration blocks extra stimuli as distractions to the focus at hand, receptive awareness embraces and assimilates every experience that presents itself.

Most meditations involve the interplay of concentration and receptive awareness, although some more advanced techniques teach the practice of receptive awareness alone. Just be open and aware and welcome to what-ever arises, they teach, and ultimately you will be "taken by truth." Followed to its conclusion, receptive awareness guides you in shifting your identity from your thoughts, emotions, and the stories your mind tells you to your true identity, which is being itself. (For more on thoughts, emotions, and stories, see Chapter 5.)

Of course, if you don't know how to work with attention, these instructions are impossible to follow. That's why most traditions prescribe practicing concentration first. Concentration, by quieting and grounding the mind (enough so that it can open without being swept away by a deluge of irrelevant feelings and thoughts), provides a solid foundation on which the practice of meditation can flourish.

Using contemplation for greater insight

Although concentration and receptive awareness provide enormous ben-efits, ultimately it's insight and understanding — of how the mind works, how you perpetuate your own suffering, how attached you are to the outcome of events, and how uncontrollable and fleeting these events are — that offer freedom from suffering. And in your everyday life, it's creative thinking — free from the usual limited, repetitive patterns of thought — that offers solutions to problems. That's why *contemplation* is the third key component that transforms meditation from a calming, relaxing exercise to a vehicle for freedom and creative expression.

After you've developed your concentration and expanded your awareness, you eventually find that you have access to a more penetrating insight into the nature of your experience. You can use this faculty to explore your inner terrain and gradually understand and undermine your mind's tendency to cause you suffering and stress (see Chapters 5 and 11). If you're a spiritual seeker, you can use this faculty to inquire into the nature of the self or to reflect upon the mystery of God and creation. And if you're a person with more practical concerns, you may ponder the next step in your career or relationship or contemplate some seemingly irresolvable problem in your life.

Cultivating positive, healing states of mind

Some meditations aim to open the heart and develop certain life-affirming qualities like compassion, lovingkindness, equanimity, joy, or forgiveness (see Chapter 10). On a more practical level, you can use meditation to cultivate a proactive, healthy immune system or to develop poise and precision in a particular sport. For example, you can visualize killer T-cells attacking your cancer or imagine yourself executing a dive without a single mistake (see Chapter 16). These are the kinds of meditations I've chosen to call *cultivation*.

Where contemplation aims to investigate, inquire, and ultimately see deeply into the nature of things, cultivation can help you transform your inner life by directing the concentration you develop to strengthen positive, healthy mind-states and withdraw energy from those that are more reactive and self-defeating.

Mindfulness: Meditation as a way of life

Although I provide a variety of different techniques for your enjoyment and exploration, this book offers as its primary approach what the Buddhists call *mindfulness* — ongoing attention to whatever arises moment to moment.

Based on my years of experience and training, I've found that mindfulness, which blends concentration and receptive awareness, is one of the simplest techniques for beginners to learn and also one of the most readily adaptable to the busy schedules most of us face. After all, if you're like me, you're primarily concerned with living a more harmonious, loving, stress-free life, not lifting off into some disembodied spiritual realm divorced from the people and places you love.

In fact, the beauty, belonging, and love you seek are available right here and now — you only need to clear your mind and open your eyes, which is precisely what the practice of mindfulness is intended to teach! When you pay attention to your experience from moment to moment, you keep waking up from the daydreams and worries your mind fabricates and returning to the clarity, precision, and simplicity of the present, where life actually takes place.

The great thing about mindfulness is that you don't have to limit your practice to certain places and times — you can practice waking up and paying attention wherever you happen to be, at any time of the day or night.

Other Journeys That Masquerade as Meditation

Now that you have an overview of the meditative journey, take a look at some paths that superficially resemble meditation but lead you in an altogether different direction. Of course, every activity can become a meditation if you do it with awareness or concentration. For example, you can wash the dishes or drive the car or talk on the phone meditatively. (For more on how to do this, see Chapter 15.) But certain activities become confused with meditation in the popular imagination, whereas they may have a totally different intent. Some people claim that reading the newspaper or watching their favorite sitcom qualifies as meditation — well, who am I to judge?

Here are some ersatz meditations that certainly have their place in the repertory of leisure pursuits but don't generally offer the benefits of meditation:

- **Thinking:** In the West, the term "meditation" has frequently been used to refer to a kind of focused reflection on a particular theme, as when you say, "I'm going to meditate on this problem for a while." Although higher-order contemplation or inquiry plays a part in some meditation techniques, it bears little resemblance to the often tortured, conflicted process that usually passes for thinking. Besides, thinking tires you out, whereas meditation refreshes you and perks you up.

- **Daydreaming:** Daydreaming and fantasy offer their own unique pleasures and rewards, including occasional problem-solving and a momentary escape from difficult or tedious circumstances. But rather than leaving you feeling more spacious and more connected with being, as meditation does, daydreaming often embroils you more actively in the drama of your life.

- **Spacing out:** Sometimes spacing out involves a momentary gap in the unbroken stream of thoughts and feelings that flood your awareness, a kind of empty space in which nothing seems to be happening except being itself. Such genuine "spacing out" lies at the heart of meditation and can be deliberately cultivated and extended. Alas, most spacing out is just another form of daydreaming!

- **Repeating affirmations:** This common new-age practice — a contemporary version of what used to be called positive thinking — purports to provide an antidote to your negative beliefs by replacing them with positive alternatives. Generally, however, the negativity is so deeply rooted that the affirmations merely skim the surface like froth on the ocean and never really penetrate to the depths, where your core beliefs reside.

✔ **Self-hypnosis:** By progressively relaxing your body and imagining a safe, protected place, you can lull yourself into an open, suggestible state known as a *light trance*. Here you can rehearse upcoming performances, rerun past events to get a more positive outcome, and reprogram your brain using affirmations. Although self-hypnosis differs from mindfulness meditation — the primary approach taught in this book, emphasizing ongoing attention to the present moment — it's actually quite similar to the healing and performance enhancement techniques offered in Chapter 16.

✔ **Praying:** Ordinary or petitionary prayer, which calls on God for help or asks for something, can be performed meditatively but has little in common with meditation as I've been describing it. However, contemplative prayer, also known as *orison* — the yearning of the soul for union with the Divine — is actually a form of concentrated contemplation whose focus is God.

✔ **Sleeping:** Refreshing though it may be, sleep is not meditation — unless you happen to be an expert yogi who meditates in your sleep. Research shows that the brain waves generated during sleep are significantly different from those generated during meditation. Of course, meditators often find themselves falling asleep — and then, as one of my teachers used to say, sleep well! (For more on sleepiness in meditation, see Chapter 12.)

Eating a piece of fruit

For this "in the moment" exercise, imagine that you've just arrived from another planet and have never experienced an orange before.

1. **Place an orange on a plate and close your eyes.**

2. **Set aside all thoughts and preconceptions, open your eyes, and see the fruit as though for the first time.**

   Notice the shape, the size, the color, the texture.

3. **As you begin to peel the orange, notice how it feels in your fingers, the contrast between the flesh and the peel, the weight of the fruit in your hand.**

4. **Slowly raise a piece of the orange to your lips and pause a moment before eating.**

   Notice how it smells before you begin.

5. **Open your mouth, bite down, and feel the texture of its soft flesh and the first rush of juice into your mouth.**

6. **Continue to bite and chew the orange, remaining aware of the play of sensations from moment to moment.**

   Imagining that this may be the first and last orange you will ever eat, let each moment be fresh and new and complete in itself. Notice how this experience of eating an orange differs from your usual way of eating a piece of fruit.

Chapter 2
Why Meditate?

In This Chapter

▶ Taking a close look at how life fails to live up to your expectations

▶ Tallying the high price of constant, rapid change

▶ Using meditation as a remedy for 21st-century ills like stress, anxiety, and alienation

▶ Cataloguing the many benefits of meditation

*I*f you're like me, you want to know what you're going to get for your time and energy before you commit to an activity. I mean, why pump the Stairmaster for an hour or puff and grunt through an aerobics class if you can't expect to slim down, beef up, and increase your stamina? Or why put aside an evening each week to attend a gourmet cooking class if you're not going to end up making dynamite fettucine or duck a l'orange?

The same is true for meditation. Why spend 10 or 15 or even 20 minutes of your hard-earned free time each day to follow your breath or repeat the same phrase again and again when you could be jogging, spacing out in front of the tube, or surfing the Net? Because of the innumerable benefits, that's why!

But before delving into these benefits, this chapter explores some of the problems that meditation can help resolve. You know the old expression "If it ain't broke, don't fix it." Well, the reality is that many of us find that our lives are "broke" in some pretty significant ways. After all, you bought this book for a reason or two. Now it's time to find out what some of those reasons may be.

How Life Drives You — to Meditate

Although you may be reluctant to admit it, at least publicly, life doesn't always live up to your expectations. As a result, you suffer — from stress, disappointment, fear, anger, outrage, hurt, or any of a number of other unpleasant emotions. Meditation teaches you how to relate to difficult circumstances and the tensions and emotions they evoke with balance, equanimity, and compassion. But before I describe the positive solutions that meditation has to offer — and rest assured, there are plenty — I'd like to take you on a whirlwind tour of the problems they're intended to solve.

The myth of the perfect life

In my years as a psychotherapist and meditation teacher, I've noticed that many people suffer because they compare their lives to some idealized image of how life is supposed to be. Cobbled together from childhood conditioning, media messages, and personal desires, this image lurks in the shadows and becomes the standard to which every success or failure, every circumstance or turn of events, is compared and judged. Take a moment to check out yours.

Perhaps you've spent your life struggling to build the American dream — two kids, house in the suburbs, brilliant career, what Zorba the Greek called the "full catastrophe." After all, that's what your parents had (or didn't have), and you decided that you owed it to them and to yourself to succeed. Only now you're juggling two jobs to save the money for a down payment, the marriage is falling apart, and you feel guilty because you don't have enough time to spend with the kids.

Or maybe you believe that ultimate happiness would come your way if you could only achieve the perfect figure (or physique). The problem is, diets don't work, you can't make yourself adhere to exercise regimens, and every time you look in the mirror, you feel like passing out. Or perhaps your idea of earthly nirvana is the perfect relationship. Unfortunately, you're approaching 40, you still haven't met Mr. or Ms. Right, and you scour the personals while secretly fearing that you must have some horrible social disease.

Whatever your version of the perfect life — perfect vacations, perfect sex, perfect health, even perfect peace of mind or total freedom from all tension and stress — you pay a high price for holding such high expectations. When life fails to live up to those expectations, as it inevitably does, you end up suffering and blaming yourself. (Take it from me — I've fallen into this trap myself again and again!) If only you had made more money, spent more time at home, been a better lover, gone back to school, lost those extra pounds . . . the list is endless. No matter how you slice it, you just don't measure up.

Or perhaps you're among the elite few who manage to get everything you want. The problem is, you eventually find yourself becoming bored and wanting more — or you spend every spare moment struggling to protect or control what you have.

The great meditative traditions have a more humane message to impart. They teach that the ideal earthly life is a myth. As an old Christian saying puts it, "Man proposes, God disposes." Or, in the words of a popular joke, "If you want to make God laugh, tell her your plans." These traditions remind us that far more powerful forces are at work in the universe than you and I. You can envision and intend and strive and attempt to control all you want — and ultimately even achieve some modicum of success. But the truth is, in the long run, you and I have only the most limited control over the circumstances of our lives! (For more on letting go, see Chapter 9.)

When things keep falling apart

Because it runs counter to everything you've ever been taught, you may have a difficult time accepting the basic spiritual truth that you and I have only limited control over the events in our lives. After all, isn't the point of life to go out and "just do it," as the Nike ads urge? Well, yes, you need to follow your dreams and live your truth; that's a crucial part of the equation.

But when life turns around and slaps you in the face, as it sometimes does, how do you respond? (Look at the Olympic skiers who spend years in training only to have their hopes for a medal wiped out in an instant by bad weather or a patch of ice!) Or when it levels you completely and deprives you of everything you've gained, including your confidence and your hard-won self-esteem — where do you go for succor and support? How do you deal with the pain and confusion? What inner resources do you draw upon to guide you through this frightening and unknown terrain? Consider the following story.

One day a woman came to see the Buddha (the great spiritual teacher who lived several thousand years ago in India) with her dead child in her arms. Grief-stricken, she had wandered from place to place, asking people for medicine to restore him to life. As a last resort, she asked the Buddha if he could help her. "Yes," he said, "but you must first bring me some mustard seed from a house in which there has never been a death."

Filled with hope, the woman went from door to door inquiring, but no one could help her. Every house she entered had witnessed its share of deaths. By the time she reached the end of the village, she had awakened to the realization that sickness and death are inevitable. After burying her son, she returned to the Buddha for spiritual instruction. "Only one law in the universe never changes," he explained, "that all things change and all things are impermanent." Hearing this, the woman became a disciple and eventually, it is said, attained enlightenment.

Of course, life offers far more than sickness and death; it also presents us with moments of extraordinary love, beauty, wonder, and joy. But like the woman in the story, we in the West — and the United States especially — tend to deny the dark side of life. We relegate our old and dying to nursing homes, ignore our homeless, restrict our impoverished minorities to ghettoes, and confine our mentally ill and developmentally challenged to hospitals and asylums, while plastering our billboards and magazines with the smiling faces of youth and prosperity.

The fact is, life is a rich and perplexing interplay of light and dark, success and failure, youth and age, pleasure and pain — and, yes, life and death. Circumstances change constantly, apparently falling apart one moment, only to come together the next. As the contemporary Zen teacher Shunryu Suzuki puts it, everything is constantly "losing its balance against a background of perfect balance."

The key to your peace of mind lies not in your circumstances, but in how you respond to them. As the Buddhists say, suffering is wanting what you don't have and not wanting what you do have, while happiness is precisely the opposite: enjoying what you have and not hungering for what you don't have. This concept doesn't mean that you must give up your values, dreams, and aspirations — only that you need to balance them with the ability to accept things as they are.

Meditation gives you an opportunity to cultivate acceptance by teaching you to reserve judgment and to open to each experience without trying to change or get rid of it. Then, when the going gets rough, you can make use of this quality to ease your ruffled feathers and maintain your peace of mind. (If you want to find out how to accept things the way they are, turn to Chapters 6 and 11.)

Dealing with the postmodern predicament

Of course, it's news to no one that circumstances change constantly — certainly pundits and sages have purveyed this truth for ages. But at no time in history has change been as pervasive and relentless — or affected our lives so deeply — as during the past 10 or 15 years. Watching the evening news or reading a paper, we're flooded with statistics and images of violence and famine, environmental depredation, and economic instability, all depicting a world that seems to be coming increasingly unstitched.

On a more personal level, you may have lost your job because of corporate downsizing, ended a relationship because your lover was shipped off to another state, been a victim of a violent crime, or lost a bundle in a volatile market. Perhaps you spend your spare time figuring out how to stay one step ahead in a competitive work environment. Or you may simply lie awake each night worrying about when the tidal wave of change will finally reach you and sweep you away. Does any of this sound familiar?

TRADITIONAL WISDOM

Appreciating impermanence

In his book *Thoughts Without a Thinker*, psychiatrist Mark Epstein recounts this teaching by the Thai meditation master Achaan Chaa. "You see this goblet?" Achaan Chaa asks. "For me this glass is already broken. I enjoy it; I drink out of it. It holds my water admirably, sometimes even reflecting the sun in beautiful patterns. If I should tap it, it has a lovely ring to it. But when I put this glass on the shelf and the wind knocks it over or my elbow brushes it off the table and it falls to the ground and shatters, I say, 'Of course.' When I understand that this glass is already broken, every moment with it is precious."

Sociologists call this period the *postmodern era,* when constant change is becoming a way of life and time-honored values and truths are being rapidly dismantled. How do you navigate your way through life when you no longer know what's true and you're not even sure how to find out? Do you search for it on the Web or somehow glean it from the latest pronouncements of media soothsayers and corporate CEOs?

Despite the unarguable advantages of all the electronic gadgets that have become indispensable since the 1980s, you may have noticed that the faster you communicate, the less you really connect with others in a rich and meaningful way. A cartoon reprinted in *Newsweek* sums it up well: Entitled "A '90s Vacation," it shows a family on a beach, each person using his or her own personal electronic device: Mom's on the phone, Dad's on the Internet, one child is picking up a fax, another is responding to his beeper, a third is checking her voice mail — and they're all oblivious to one another!

Such relentless change exacts a steep emotional and spiritual price, which we tend to deny in our collective attempt to accentuate the positive and deny the negative. Here are a few of the negative side effects of life in the postmodern age:

✔ **Anxiety and stress:** When the ground starts shifting beneath your feet, your first reaction as you attempt to regain your stability may be anxiety or fear. This gut-level response has been programmed into our genes by millions of years of living on the edge. These days, unfortunately, the tremors never stop, and small fears accumulate and congeal into ongoing tension and stress. Your body may feel perpetually braced against the next onslaught of difficulties and responsibilities — which makes it virtually impossible to relax and enjoy life fully. By relaxing your body and reducing stress, meditation can provide a much-needed antidote.

✔ **Fragmentation:** Most Americans once lived, shopped, worked, raised their kids, and spent their leisure time in the same community. They encountered the same faces every day, worked the same job for a lifetime, stayed married to the same person, and watched their children raise their own children just down the block. Now we often shuttle our kids off to school or daycare and commute long distances to work, while checking our messages on the cell phone. On the way home, we may stop by the mall, and we may spend our evenings surfing the Net. We change jobs and partners more frequently than ever, and when our children grow up, they often move to another state — or another country! Although we may not be able to stay the tide of fragmentation, we can use meditation to connect us with a deeper wholeness that external circumstances can't disturb.

✔ **Alienation:** When our lives appear to be made up of disconnected puzzle pieces that don't fit together, no wonder we wind up feeling completely stressed out. Despite the statistics that herald prosperous times, many people work at marginal jobs that pay the bills but fail to connect them to a deeper sense of value or purpose. According to an article in *American Demographics* magazine, more people are flocking to small towns in an attempt to recapture a sense of community, and fewer and fewer are voting in each election, apparently because they believe that they have little power to change things. Never before, it seems, have human beings felt so alienated, not only from their work and their government, but also from others, themselves, and their own essential being — and most of us don't have the skills or the know-how to reconnect! By bridging the chasm that separates us from ourselves, meditation can help to heal our alienation from others and the world at large.

✔ **Loneliness and isolation:** With people moving from place to place more frequently and families fragmenting and scattering across the globe, you're less and less likely to have regular contact with the people you know and love — and even if you do, you may be too busy to relate in a mutually fulfilling way. Recently, I heard a radio ad arguing that since family dinners are clearly a thing of the past, why not purchase Family Net — a separate cell phone for mom, dad, and the kids — so that the family can keep in touch! Again, you may not be able to stem the forces that keep us apart. But you can use meditation to turn every moment together into "quality time."

✔ **Depression:** When we feel lonely, alienated, stressed out, and disconnected from a deeper source of meaning and purpose, it's no wonder that some people end up feeling depressed. In a nation where Prozac is a household word, millions of people take mood-altering chemicals each day to keep from feeling the pain of postmodern life. Meditation can connect you with your own inner source of contentment and joy that naturally dispels the clouds of depression.

TRADITIONAL WISDOM

Accepting things the way they are

In the Zen tradition, they tell the story of a poor farmer who lost his only horse. His friends and neighbors bemoaned his plight, but he seemed unperturbed. "We'll see," he said with an enigmatic smile.

Several days later, his horse returned with a pack of five wild stallions that had joined it along the way. His neighbors rejoiced in his good fortune, but he did not appear to be excited. "We'll see," he said again.

The following week, while attempting to ride and tame one of the stallions, his beloved, only son fell and broke his leg. The ever-solicitous neighbors were beside themselves with grief,

but the farmer, though he comforted and cared for the boy, did not seem to be concerned about the future. "We'll see," he mused.

At the end of the month, the local warlord arrived in the farmer's village to conscript all the healthy young men to fight in the latest campaign. But the farmer's son . . . well, you can imagine the rest of the story.

In case you hadn't noticed, life's a roller-coaster ride, and you can't control the ups and downs. If you want to hold on to your lunch — and your sanity — you need to learn how to maintain your peace of mind.

✔ **Stress-related illness:** From tension headaches and acid indigestion to heart disease and cancer, the steady rise in stress-related illness reflects our collective inability to cope with the instability and fragmentation of our times — and fuels a billion-dollar healthcare industry that at times only masks the deeper problems of fear, stress, and disorientation. As numerous scientific studies have shown, the regular practice of meditation can actually reverse the onslaught of many stress-related ailments. (See the section "How to Survive the 21st Century — with Meditation" later in this chapter.)

70-80% dr's visits are related to stress

Four popular "solutions" that don't really work

REMEMBER

Before I leave the litany of postmodern woes and suggest some solutions that actually work, I'd like to offer a quick look at a few popular approaches to handling stress and uncertainty that create more problems than they solve.

✔ **Addiction:** By distracting people from their pain, encouraging them to set aside their usual concerns and preoccupations, and altering brain chemistry, addictions mimic some of the benefits of meditation. Unfortunately, addictions also tend to fixate the mind on an addictive substance or activity — drugs, alcohol, sex, gambling, and so on — making it even more difficult for people to be open to the wonders of the moment or to connect with a deeper dimension of being. Besides, most addictions involve a self-destructive lifestyle that ultimately intensifies the problems the addict was attempting to escape.

✔ **Fundamentalism:** By advocating simple, one-dimensional answers to complex problems, offering a sense of meaning and belonging, and repudiating many of the apparent evils of postmodern life, fundamentalism — be it religious or political — provides a refuge from ambiguity and alienation. Alas, fundamentalists divide the world into black and white, good and bad, us and them, which only fuels the fires of alienation, conflict, and stress in the world at large.

✔ **Entertainment:** When you feel lonely or alienated, just turn on the tube or head to your local multiplex and take in the latest offering. That will calm your anxiety or soothe your pain — or will it? In addition to providing entertainment, the media seemingly create community by connecting us with other people and the events around us. But you can't have a heart-to-heart conversation with a TV celebrity or hug your favorite movie star. Besides, the media (intentionally or not) manipulate your emotions, fill your mind with the ideas and images of the popular culture, and focus your attention outside yourself — rather than give you the opportunity to find out what you really think, feel, and know.

✔ **Consumerism:** This bogus solution to life's ills teaches that wanting and having more is the answer — more food, more possessions, more vacations, more of every perk that plastic can buy. As you may have noticed, however, the thrill fades fast, and you're quickly planning your next purchase — or struggling to figure out how to pay the credit card bill that arrives like clockwork at the end of the month. Need I say more?

How to Survive the 21st Century — with Meditation

Now for the good news! As I mentioned earlier in this chapter, meditation offers a time-honored antidote to fragmentation, alienation, isolation, stress — even stress-related illnesses and depression. Although it won't solve the external problems of your life, it does help you develop inner resilience, balance, and strength to roll with the punches and come up with creative solutions.

To get a sense of how meditation works, imagine for a moment that your body and mind are a complex computer. Instead of being programmed to experience inner peace, harmony, equanimity, and joy, you've been programmed to respond to life's inevitable ups and downs with stress, anxiety, and dissatisfaction. But you have the power to change your programming. By putting aside all other activities, sitting quietly, and attuning yourself to the present moment for 10 or 15 minutes each day, you're developing a whole new set of habitual responses and programming yourself to experience more positive emotions and mind-states. (For more on the actual practice of meditation, see Chapters 6 and 10.)

Of course, if you find it distasteful to think of yourself as a computer, you can picture life as an ocean, with the constant ups and downs you experience as the waves that churn and roil on the water's surface. When you meditate, you dive beneath the surface to a quiet place where the water is calmer and more consistent.

Whatever your favorite metaphor, the point is that meditation provides a way of transforming stress and suffering into equanimity and ease. In this section, you get to see how meditators have been reaping the remarkable benefits of meditation for millennia — and how you can, too!

Advanced technology for the mind and heart

Traditionally, the Western world has emphasized external achievement, and the East has valued inner development. The great scientific and technological advances of the past 500 years originated in the West, while yogis and roshis in the monasteries and ashrams of Asia were cultivating the inner arts of meditation. (See Chapter 3 for more about the history of meditation.) Now, the currents of East and West and North and South have joined and are intermingling to form an emerging global culture and economy. As a result, we can apply the inner "technology" perfected in the East to balance the excesses of the rapid technological innovations perfected in the West!

Like master computer programmers, the great meditation masters throughout history developed the capacity to program their bodies, minds, and hearts to experience highly refined states of being. While we in the West were charting the heavens and initiating the industrial revolution, they were chalking up some pretty remarkable accomplishments of their own:

✔ Penetrating insights into the nature of the mind and the process by which it creates and perpetuates suffering and stress

✔ Deep states of ecstatic absorption in which the meditator is completely immersed in union with the Divine

✔ The wisdom to discriminate between relative reality and the sacred dimension of being

✔ Unshakable inner peace that external circumstances can't disturb

✔ The cultivation of positive, beneficial, life-affirming mind-states, such as patience, love, kindness, equanimity, joy, and — especially — compassion for the suffering of others

✔ The ability to control bodily functions that are usually considered involuntary, such as heart rate, body temperature, and metabolism

✔ The capacity to mobilize and move vital energy through the different centers and channels of the body for the sake of healing and personal transformation

✔ Special psychic powers, such as *clairvoyance* (the ability to perceive matters beyond the range of ordinary perception) and *telekinesis* (the ability to move objects at a distance without touching them)

Of course, the great meditators of the past used these qualities to seek liberation from suffering, either by withdrawing from the world into a more exalted reality or by achieving penetrating insights into the nature of existence. Yet the meditation technology they developed — which has become widely available in the West in the past few decades — can be used by the rest of us in ordinary, everyday ways to yield some extraordinary benefits.

The mind-body benefits of meditation

Although the earliest scientific studies of meditation date back to the 1930s and 1940s, research into the psychophysiological effects of meditation took off in the 1970s, fueled by a burgeoning interest in Transcendental Meditation (TM), Zen, and other Eastern meditation techniques. Since then, more than 1,000 studies have been published in English. In the book *The Physical and Psychological Effects of Meditation* (first published in 1988 and revised and updated in 1997), Michael Murphy and coauthor Steven Donovan sifted through these studies and synthesized the data.

Murphy, author of the best-seller *Golf in the Kingdom,* has pioneered the exploration of human potential since he cofounded Esalen Institute in Big Sur, California, in 1962. (Esalen is generally acknowledged as the birthplace of the human potential movement.) Donovan, former president and CEO of Esalen, directed the Institute's Study of Exceptional Functioning. Based on the results of the studies they surveyed, Murphy and Donovan came up with the following mind-body benefits of meditation.

Tuning in to your body

Like Mr. Duffy in James Joyce's novel *Ulysses,* most of us "live a short distance" from our bodies. The following meditation, which has counterparts in yoga and Buddhism, helps re-establish contact with the body by drawing attention gently from one part to another. Because it cultivates awareness and also relaxes the muscles and internal organs, it makes a great preamble to more formal meditation practice. Allow at least 20 minutes to complete.

1. **Lie on your back on a comfortable sur-face — but not too comfortable unless you plan to fall asleep.**

2. **Take a few moments to feel your body as a whole, including the places where it con-tacts the surface of the bed or floor.**

3. **Bring your attention to the toes of your right foot.**

   Allow yourself to feel any and all sensa-tions in this area. If you don't feel any-thing, just feel "not feeling anything." As you breathe, imagine that you're breath-ing into and out of your toes. (If this feels weird or uncomfortable, just breathe in your usual way.)

4. **When you're done with your toes, move on to the sole, heel, top of foot, and ankle in turn, feeling each part in the same way that you felt your toes.**

   Take your time. The point of this exer-cise is not to achieve anything, not even

relaxation, but to be as fully present as possible wherever you are.

5. **Gradually, move up your body, staying at least three or four breaths with each part.**

   Follow this order: lower right leg, right knee, right thigh, right hip, left toes, left foot, lower left leg, left thigh, left hip, pel-vis, lower abdomen, lower back, solar plexus, upper back, chest, shoulders; now focus on the fingers, hands, and arms on both sides, and then on the neck and throat, chin, jaws, face, back of the head, and top of the head.

   By the time you reach the top of your head, you may feel as though the boundaries between you and the rest of the world have become more fluid — or have melted away entirely. At the same time, you may feel silent and still — free of your usual restlessness or agitation.

6. **Rest there for a few moments; then gradu-ally bring your attention back to your body as a whole.**

7. **Wiggle your toes, move your fingers, open your eyes, rock from side to side, and gen-tly sit up.**

8. **Take a few moments to stretch and reac-quaint yourself with the world around you before standing up and going about your day.**

Physiological benefits:

✔ Decreased heart rate during quiet meditation

✔ Lower blood pressure in normal and moderately hypertensive individuals

✔ Quicker recovery from stress

✔ Increase in alpha rhythms (slow, high amplitude brain waves that correlate with relaxation)

✔ Enhanced synchronization (that is, simultaneous operation) of the right and left hemispheres of the brain (which positively correlates with creativity)

✔ Reduced serum cholesterol levels

✔ Decreased consumption of energy and need for oxygen

✔ Deeper, slower breathing

✔ Muscle relaxation

✔ Reduction in the intensity of pain

Psychological benefits:

✔ Increased empathy

✔ Enhanced creativity and self-actualization

✔ Heightened perceptual clarity and sensitivity

✔ Reductions in both acute and chronic anxiety

✔ Complement to psychotherapy and other approaches in the treatment of addiction

Promoting the benefits of meditation

Although Western researchers have been studying the benefits of meditation for more than 50 years, three people in particular have helped popularize the practice by demonstrating how it can cause measurable improvement in a broad range of health concerns.

✔ **Herbert Benson and the Relaxation Response:** A cardiologist and professor of medicine at Harvard Medical School, Benson pioneered the field of mind-body medicine with the publication of his best-seller *The Relaxation Response* in 1975. Based on his study of TM practition-ers, the book identifies a natural reflex mechanism that can be triggered by 20 minutes of daily meditation practice involving a quiet environment, repetition of a sound or phrase, a receptive attitude, and a comfortable sitting position — a kind of generic TM!

Once initiated, this reflex apparently induces relaxation, reduces stress, and counteracts the fight-or-flight response. In subsequent studies, Benson found that the Relaxation Response had a beneficial effect on hypertension, headaches, heart disease, alcohol consumption, anxiety, and PMS.

✔ **Jon Kabat-Zinn and Mindfulness-Based Stress Reduction:** Since 1979, when he established the Stress Reduction Clinic at the University of Massachusetts Medical Center, Kabat-Zinn and his colleagues have trained thousands of patients with a variety of health problems in the fundamentals of Buddhist mindfulness meditation and mindful hatha yoga. Outcome studies indicate that the eight-week program, which involves formal classes, home-study, and a one-day meditation workshop, helps participants reduce the stress that contributes to their illness and teaches them how to extend the benefits of mindfulness into every area of their lives.

Featured in the PBS series "Healing and the Mind" with Bill Moyers, Kabat-Zinn's program has been duplicated in clinics, schools, and workplaces across the country.

✔ **Dean Ornish and the Opening Your Heart Program:** In a landmark study published in the *Journal of the American Medical Association,* Ornish, who is a physician and the director of the nonprofit Preventive Medicine Research Institute, showed that patients can actually reverse their heart disease through fundamental lifestyle changes, without the use of surgery or cholesterol-lowering drugs. Although his program also emphasizes the health benefits of a low-fat diet, exercise, and hatha yoga, Ornish teaches that the key to healing the heart lies in opening the heart — and that meditation is a crucial component in this process because it helps to free us from our habitual patterns of stress and emotional reactivity.

Eleven More Great Reasons to Meditate

You don't have to join some cult or get baptized or bar mitzvahed to enjoy the benefits of meditation. And you don't have to check out of your everyday life and run off to a monastery in the Himalayas. You simply need to practice your meditation regularly without trying to get anywhere or achieve anything. Like interest in a money-market account, the benefits just accrue by themselves. These benefits include:

✔ **Awakening to the present moment:** When you rush breathlessly from one moment to the next, anticipating another problem or hungering for another pleasure, you miss the beauty and immediacy of the present, which is constantly unfolding before your eyes. Meditation teaches you to slow down and take each moment as it comes — the sounds of traffic, the smell of new clothes, the laughter of children, the worried look on an old woman's face, the coming and going of your breath. In fact, as the meditative traditions remind us, only the present moment exists anyway — the past is just a memory and the future a fantasy, projected on the movie screen of the mind right now.

✔ **Making friends with yourself:** When you're constantly struggling to live up to images and expectations (your own or someone else's) or racing to reinvent yourself to survive in a competitive environment, you rarely have the opportunity or the motivation to get to know yourself just the way you are. Self-doubt and self-hatred may appear to fuel the fires of self-improvement, but they're painful — and besides, they contribute to other negative mind-states, such as fear, anger, depression, and alienation, and prevent you from living up to your full potential. When you meditate, you learn to welcome every experience and facet of your being without judgment or denial. In the process, you begin to treat yourself as you would a close friend, accepting (and even loving) the whole package, the apparent weaknesses and shortcomings as well as the positive qualities and strengths.

✔ **Connecting more deeply with others:** As you awaken to the present moment and open your heart and mind to your own experience, you naturally extend this quality of awareness and presence to your relationships with family and friends. If you're like the rest of us, you tend to project your own desires and expectations onto the people close to you, which acts as a barrier to real communication. But when you start to accept others the way they are — a skill you can cultivate through the practice of meditation — you open up the channels for a deeper love and intimacy to flow between you.

✔ **Relaxing the body and calming the mind:** As contemporary health researchers have discovered — and traditional texts agree — mind and body are inseparable, and an agitated mind inevitably produces a stressed out body. As the mind settles, relaxes, and opens during meditation, so does the body — and the longer you meditate (measured both in minutes logged each day and in days and weeks of regular application), the more this peace and relaxation ripples out to every area of your life, including your health.

✔ **Lightening up:** Perhaps you've noticed that nonstop thinking and worrying generate a kind of inner claustrophobia — fears feed on one another, problems get magnified exponentially, and the next thing you know, you're feeling overwhelmed and panicked. Meditation encourages an inner mental spaciousness in which difficulties and concerns no longer seem so threatening and constructive solutions can naturally arise — as well as a certain detachment that allows for greater objectivity, perspective, and, yes, humor. That mysterious word _enlightenment_ actually refers to the supreme "lightening up"!

✔ **Experiencing focus and flow:** When you're so fully involved in an activity that all sense of self-consciousness, separation, and distraction dissolves, you've entered what psychologist Mihaly Csikszentmihalyi calls a state of _flow_ (see Chapter 1). For human beings, this total immersion constitutes the ultimate enjoyment — and provides the ultimate antidote to the fragmentation and alienation of postmodern life. No doubt you've experienced moments like these — playing a sport, creating a work of art, working in the garden, making love. Athletes call it "the zone." Through meditation, you can discover how to give the same focused attention to — and derive the same enjoyment from — every activity.

✔ **Feeling more centered, grounded, and balanced:** To counter the escalating insecurity of life in rapidly changing times, meditation offers an inner groundedness and balance that external circumstances can't destroy. When you practice coming home again and again — to your body, your breath, your sensations, your feelings — you eventually grow to realize that you're always home, no matter where you go. And when you make friends with yourself, embracing the dark and the light, the weak and the strong, you no longer get thrown off-center by the "slings and arrows" of life.

✓ **Enhancing performance at work and play:** Studies have shown that basic meditation practice alone can enhance perceptual clarity, creativity, self-actualization, and many of the other factors that contribute to superior performance. In addition, specific meditations have been devised to enhance performance in a variety of activities, from sports to schoolwork (see Chapter 16).

✓ **Increasing appreciation, gratitude, and love:** As you begin to open to your experience without judgment or aversion, your heart gradually opens as well — to yourself and others. You can practice specific meditations for cultivating appreciation, gratitude, and love (see Chapter 10) — or you may find, as so many meditators have before you, that these qualities arise naturally when you can gaze at the world with fresh eyes, free from the usual projections and expectations.

✓ **Aligning with a deeper sense of purpose:** When you practice making the shift from doing and thinking to being (see Chapter 1), you discover how to align yourself with a deeper current of meaning and belonging. You may get in touch with personal feelings and aspirations that have long remained hidden from your conscious awareness. Or you may connect with a more universal source of purpose and direction — what some people call the *higher self* or *inner guidance*.

✓ **Awakening to a spiritual dimension of being:** As your meditation gradually opens you to the subtlety and richness of each fleeting but irreplaceable moment, you may naturally begin to see through the veil of appearances to the sacred reality at the heart of things — and you eventually may come to realize (and this one could take lifetimes!) that the very same sacred reality is actually who you are in your own heart of hearts. This deep insight — what the sages and masters call "waking up from the illusion of separation" — cuts through and ultimately eliminates loneliness and alienation and opens you to the beauty of the human condition.

Getting into the habit

Take a habit that you wish you could break but can't. Maybe it's smoking, drinking coffee, or eating junk food. The next time you do it, instead of spacing out or daydreaming, turn it into a meditation. Pay close attention as you draw the smoke into your lungs, for example, or chew the French fries. Notice how your body feels. Whenever your mind drifts off, notice where it goes — you may have favorite fantasies that accompany this habit — and then gently bring it back to your experience.

Don't try to stop or change the habit; just do it as usual, except this time you're doing it with full awareness. The next time you indulge the habit, notice how you feel. Has your attitude changed in any way? What are you aware of this time that you weren't aware of before?

Chapter 3

Where Meditation Comes From

*W*hen you think of meditation, do you envision an Asian monk or yogi in loincloth or robe, sitting cross-legged in deep concentration? Well, meditation was definitely refined in the temples, caves, and monasteries of the East and Near East — and fortunately for you and me, it has made its way West over the past 100 years or so. But meditation also appears, though less conspicuously and in slightly different form, in the Judeo-Christian tradition. Did you know, for example, that many of the biblical prophets meditated? Or that Jesus engaged in some form of meditation when he retreated to the desert for 40 days?

Meditation dates back to our earliest ancestors, who gazed in wonder at the night sky, crouched in bushes for hours waiting for game, or sat in reverie beside communal fires. Because meditation involves a shift from thinking and doing to just *being* (see Chapter 1 for more about "being"), our fore-bears had a headstart on you and me. After all, their lives were simpler, their thinking more rudimentary, and their connection to nature and the sacred far stronger.

Although you can certainly practice meditation without knowing where it comes from, tracing its development grounds it in a historical and spiritual context. So, join me for a brief overview of meditation's evolution as a *sacred practice* in various parts of the world.

Shamans: The first great meditators

Long before the time of the Buddha or the great Indian yogis, shamans in hunter-gatherer cultures throughout the world used meditative practices to enter altered states of consciousness, known as *trances*. Focusing their minds through drumming or rhythmic chanting, dancing in simple, repetitive steps, and sometimes using hallucinogenic plants, these powerful spiritual figures (both men and women) left their bodies and journeyed to the "world of the spirits." They then brought back sacred wisdom, healing abilities, magical powers, and spirit blessings for the sake of the tribe.

Cave paintings dating back at least 15,000 years depict figures lying on the ground in meditative absorption. Scholars have determined that these figures were shamans journeying in trance to ask the spirits for a successful hunt. Other cave paintings from a similar period show shamans who transformed into animals — a typical practice that continues to this day. (Depending on your belief system, you may be inclined to dismiss such experiences as figments of an overactive imagination. But the shamans and their followers have no doubt that such journeys and transformations actually occur.)

Though shamanism declined with the shift from hunting and gathering to farming, shamans still act as healers, guides for the dead, and intermediaries between humans and spirits in parts of Siberia, North America, Mexico, South America, Africa, Australia, Indonesia, and Asia. In recent years, through the writings of Carlos Castaneda, Michael Harner, and Joseph Campbell, more and more Westerners have taken an interest in shamanism — and some have even become accomplished shamans themselves.

The Indian Connection

You can find meditation's deepest roots in India, where *sadhus* (wandering holy men and women) and *yogis* have cultivated the practice in one form or another for more than 5,000 years. Attribute it to the climate, which slows the pace of life, or to the monsoon, which forces people to spend more time indoors, or just to the unbroken line of meditators over the ages. Whatever the reasons, India provided the fertile soil in which the meditative arts flourished and from which they spread both East and West.

The earliest Indian scriptures, the *Vedas*, don't even have a word for meditation, but the Vedic priests performed elaborate rites and chants to the gods that required tremendous concentration. Eventually, these practices evolved into a form of prayerful meditation that combined the use of breath control and devotional focus on the Divine. (See Chapter 1 for more on focus.) The deeper they delved, the more these priests realized that the worshipper and the object of worship, the individual being and the divine being itself, are one and the same — a profound insight that continued to inspire and instruct spiritual seekers through the ages.

From the garden of Vedic and post-Vedic spirituality sprouted three of India's best-known meditative traditions: *yoga, Buddhism,* and *tantra.*

Classical yoga: The path of blissful union

When you think of yoga, do you picture people twisting and stretching their bodies into challenging poses? Even if you practice hatha yoga yourself, what you may not know is that such "poses" are just one component of the traditional path of classical yoga, which includes breath control and meditation. (For a comprehensive introduction to yoga, check out *Yoga For Dummies* by Georg Feuerstein and Larry Payne, published by IDG Books Worldwide, Inc.)

SPIRITUAL STUFF

The art of the mantra

As Herbert Benson, M.D., explains in his ground-breaking book *The Relaxation Response,* the meditative repetition of a mantra tends to calm the mind and relax the body. But the earliest practitioners of mantra had more spiritual intentions, such as invoking the power of a particular deity, cultivating and strengthening positive qualities, or achieving union with divine reality.

Though the term *mantra* (meaning "mind protection") derives from the Sanskrit, the practice appears in one form or another in virtually every religion. Sufis repeat the phrase *La ila'ha, il'alahu* ("There is nothing but God"), Christians say the "Our Father" or the prayer of the heart ("Lord Jesus Christ have mercy on me"), Buddhists intone sacred invocations like *om mani padme hum* or *namu amida butsu,* and Hindus repeat one of the many praises or names of God.

Essentially, mantras are sounds infused with numinous or spiritual power by a teacher or a tradition. When you repeat a mantra — either aloud, under your breath, or mentally (actually considered the most potent method) — you resonate with a particular spiritual frequency and with the power and blessings the sound has accumulated over the years.

The practice of mantra focuses and stabilizes the mind and protects it from unwanted distractions. For this reason, mantra recitation often accompanies more formal meditation practices. To experiment with mantra, just choose a word or phrase with deep personal or spiritual meaning for you. (Traditionally, you would receive a particular mantra directly from your teacher.) Then sit quietly and repeat it again and again, allowing your mind to rest on the sound and the feeling it evokes. When your mind wanders, just come back to your mantra.

The practitioner of classical yoga aims to withdraw from the material world, which is considered illusory, and merge with the formless but ultimate reality of consciousness. After preparing the body with *asanas* (the familiar hatha yoga poses), cultivating refined energy states through various breathing practices, and excluding all external distractions, the yogi focuses on an intermediate object, such as a *mantra* (repetition of a meaningful word or phrase) or a sacred symbol, and then on consciousness itself. Finally, the yogi arrives at a state known as *samadhi,* where all traces of separation dissolve and the yogi blissfully unites with consciousness.

Compiled and codified by Patanjali (a sage of the second century A.D.), the philosophy and practices of classical yoga gave rise to numerous and, at times, competing schools over the centuries. Most of the yogis and swamis who have taught in the West trace their lineage to classical yoga.

Early Buddhism: The roots of mindfulness meditation

The historical Buddha was a Hindu prince who, according to the traditional account, renounced his luxurious life to find answers to the mystery of suffering, old age, and death. After practicing asceticism and yoga for many years, he decided that rejecting the world and mortifying the flesh would not lead to the understanding he sought. Instead, he sat down under a tree and began looking deeply into his own mind. After seven days and nights of intensive meditation, he woke up to the nature of existence — hence the name *Buddha,* or "the awakened one."

The Buddha taught that we suffer because we cling to the false belief that (1) things are permanent and can be relied upon for happiness and (2) we have an abiding *self* that exists independently of other beings and makes us who we are. Instead, he taught that everything changes constantly — our minds, our emotions, our sense of self, and the circumstances and objects in the external world.

To be free from suffering, he counseled, we must liberate ourselves from ignorance and eliminate fear, anger, greed, jealousy, and other negative mind-states. The approach he prescribed involves both practices for working with the mind and guidelines for living in the world in a virtuous and spiritual way.

Meditation lies at the heart of the historical Buddha's approach. The practice of meditation he taught, known as *mindfulness,* involves wakeful attention to our experience from moment to moment.

Here are the four traditional foundations of mindfulness:

- Awareness of the body
- Awareness of feelings
- Awareness of thoughts and mind-states
- Awareness of the laws of experience (the relationships between what we think and what we experience)

Departing from the other teachers of his day, who generally recommended withdrawing from the world to seek ecstatic union with the Divine, the Buddha taught the importance of gaining direct insight into the nature of existence and into how the mind creates suffering. He likened himself to a physician who offers medicine to heal wounds, rather than a philosopher who provides abstract answers to metaphysical questions.

Indian tantra: Finding the sacred in the world of the senses

Many Westerners associate the word "tantra" with traditional sexual practices that have been adapted to appeal to a popular audience. However, *tantra* developed in the early centuries A.D. as a major form of Indian spiritual practice and thought. Believing that absolute reality and the relative world of the senses are inseparable, *tantrikas* (practitioners of tantra) use the senses — including the practice of ritual sex — as gateways to spiritual realization. Needless to say, such an approach has its pitfalls; whereas yoga and Buddhism can veer toward life-denial, tantra can be confused with sensual indulgence.

Tantric meditation frequently involves practices for awakening the *kundalini shakti,* believed to be a powerful energy associated with the divine feminine that resides at the base of the spine. Once stimulated, the shakti rises through an energetic channel located in the spine and activates and opens each of the seven energy centers, or *chakras,* in its path. These centers, which vibrate at different frequencies and are associated with different physical and psychological functions, are located at the perineum, the genitals, the solar plexus, the heart, the throat, the forehead, and the crown of the head, respectively. (For more on chakras, turn to Chapter 12.) Ultimately, the shakti may erupt through the crown chakra in a burst of ecstasy. At this point, the practitioner realizes his or her identity with the Divine, while still fully contained in a physical body.

To the Roof of the World — and Beyond

Before it left India for good at the end of the first millennium A.D., Buddhism went through significant changes. The early teachings developed into what we now call Theravada — the dominant approach in Sri Lanka and Southeast Asia, emphasizing a progressive path to liberation largely limited to monks and nuns. At the same time, another major current emerged that preached the ideal of the *bodhisattva* — the person who dedicates his or her life to liberating others. Known as the Mahayana ("the great vehicle"), this second major branch of Buddhism was more egalitarian and offered the possibility of enlightenment to everyone, whether lay or monastic.

From India, wandering monks and scholars transported Mahayana Buddhism over the Himalayas (the "roof of the world") to China and Tibet. There it mingled with indigenous spiritual teachings, set down roots, and evolved into a number of different traditions and schools, most notably Ch'an ("Zen" in Japanese) and Vajrayana Buddhism, which took the practice of meditation to new heights.

Ch'an (Zen): The sound of one hand clapping

You've no doubt read about the Zen masters who whacked their disciples with a stick or bellowed instructions at the top of their lungs. But you may not realize that Zen is a unique blend of Mahayana Buddhism (which as I just mentioned is egalitarian) and the native Chinese tradition known as Taoism (which emphasizes the seamless and undivided nature of life, known as the Tao). (Although Indian monks began transporting Buddhism to China in the early centuries A.D., Zen did not emerge as a separate current until the seventh or eighth century.) Zen departed radically from traditional Buddhism by emphasizing direct, wordless transmission of the enlightened state from master to disciple — sometimes through behavior that by ordinary standards would be considered eccentric or even bizarre.

While the other traditions of Buddhism increasingly focused on scriptural study, Zen cut through the metaphysical underbrush and said: just sit! Meditation became the primary means for dismantling a lifetime of attachment to the material world and realizing what the Zen masters call *Buddha nature,* the innate wisdom that exists within each of us.

Zen also introduced those seemingly unsolvable riddles known as *koans* — for example, "What is the sound of one hand clapping?" or "What was your original face before your parents were born?" By totally immersing himself in the koan, the monk could ultimately see into the nature of existence — what the Zen masters called *satori.*

In Japan, Zen developed some of its notorious samurai intensity and gave rise to the austere, pristine aesthetic that has made rock gardens and brush paintings so typical of Japanese culture. From Japan, of course, Zen made its way to North America, encountered the Beat generation of the 1950s, and set the stage for the recent explosion of interest in meditation. (For more on Zen in North America, see the section "The Americanization of Meditation" later in this chapter.)

Vajrayana Buddhism: The way of transformation

Like China (where Buddhism encountered Taoism), Tibet had its indigenous religion, called Bonpo, which included magical practices designed to appease the local spirits and deities. When the great Indian master Padmasambhava brought Buddhism from India to Tibet in the seventh century A.D., he first had to conquer the hostile spirits that resisted his efforts. Ultimately, these spirits were incorporated into Tibetan Buddhism as protectors and allies in an elaborate pantheon that included various Buddhas and *dakinis* (awakened women).

Tibetan Buddhists believed that the historical Buddha taught simultaneously at different levels, depending on the needs and abilities of his disciples. The most advanced teachings, they said, were kept secret for centuries and ultimately conveyed to Tibet as the *Vajrayana* ("the diamond way"). In addition to traditional mindfulness meditation, this approach incorporated elements of Indian tantra and involved powerful practices for working with energy. Instead of eliminating negative emotions and mindstates like anger, greed, and fear, as traditional Buddhism recommends, the Vajrayana teaches practitioners how to transform negativity directly into wisdom and compassion.

Meditation in Tibetan Buddhism also employs *visualization* — the active use of the imagination to invoke potent spiritual forces that fuel the process of spiritual realization.

From the Middle East to the Rest of the West

Although meditation in the Judeo-Christian and Islamic traditions had its own independent development, meditators in the Middle East may have been influenced by the practices of their counterparts in India and Southeast Asia (see the earlier sections of this chapter). Historians do have evidence that traders and pilgrims traveled between the two regions constantly, and Buddhist monks appeared in Rome in early Christian times! There's even the rumor, buoyed by some interesting historical coincidences, that Jesus may have learned how to meditate in India. While Indian meditators — following the ancient insight that *atman equals Brahman* ("I and the ground of being are one") — turned their attention progressively inward, seeking the sacred in the depths of their own being, Western thinkers and theologians pointed to a God that purportedly exists outside the individual. At the same time, mystics in the West wrestled with the paradox that God is both inside and outside, personal and transcendent.

Meditation in the Western religions usually takes the form of prayer — that is, direct communion with God. But the meditative prayer of the monks and mystics differs from ordinary prayer, which often includes complaints and requests. Instead, meditative prayer approaches God with humility and devotion, contemplates His divine qualities, and invites His presence into the heart of the meditator. Ultimately, the goal is to surrender the individual self completely in union with the Divine.

Christian meditation: Practicing contemplative prayer

The Christian equivalent of meditation, known as *contemplative prayer,* dates back to Jesus himself, who fasted and prayed in the desert for 40 days and nights. In contemplation, says Father Thomas Keating, whose "centering prayer" has helped revitalize interest in Christian meditation, you open your awareness and your heart to God, the ultimate mystery, who dwells in the depths of your being, beyond the reach of the mind. (See the sidebar "Centering prayer" for more about the practice taught by Father Keating.)

After the time of Jesus, the first great Christian meditators were the desert fathers of Egypt and Palestine in the third and fourth centuries, who lived largely in solitude and cultivated awareness of the divine presence through constant repetition of a sacred phrase. Their direct descendants, the monks, nuns, and mystics of medieval Europe, developed the contemplative practice of repeating and ruminating over a scriptural passage (not to be confused with thinking about or analyzing it!) until its deeper significance revealed itself to the mind. Both of these practices, explains Father Keating, hark back to Jesus's admonition, "When you pray, go into your closet, your innermost being, and bolt the door."

In the Eastern Orthodox Church of Greece and Eastern Europe, monks have long engaged in a similar practice combining *prostrations* (full-body bows) with the repetition of the Jesus prayer ("Lord Jesus Christ have mercy on me, a sinner") until all practices drop away to reveal a deep interior silence filled with love and bliss.

MEDITATION

Centering prayer

Developed in the past few decades by Father Thomas Keating, a Catholic priest, and based on traditional Christian sources, *centering prayer* is a contemplative practice that opens the mind and heart to the divine presence. Unlike a mantra, which is designed to clarify or calm the mind, centering prayer purifies the heart to become a vehicle for God's transformative grace. Instead of repeating it again and again like a mantra, you hold it in your awareness as an object of contemplation.

Here are the instructions for practicing centering prayer, as given by Father Keating (whose words appear in quotation marks):

1. Choose a "sacred word as a symbol of your intention to consent to God's presence and action within."

2. **Settle comfortably, and silently introduce the sacred word.**

   When your attention wanders, gently bring it back.

3. **Stay with the same word during the period of contemplation.**

Some people may prefer to "turn inwardly toward God as if gazing upon him," without words. In any case, the same guidelines apply. When we open to God, says Father Keating, we find that God is "closer than breathing, closer than thinking, closer than choosing — closer than consciousness itself."

In recent years, many Christian ministers and monastics have been influenced by the Hindu and Buddhist teachers who have appeared in the West in increasing numbers. (See the section "The Americanization of Meditation" later in this chapter.) In response, some have adapted Eastern practices to the needs of Christian audiences. Others, like Father Keating, have delved into their own contemplative roots and resuscitated practices that had become dusty with disuse.

Meditation in Judaism: Drawing closer to God

According to Rami Shapiro, rabbi of Temple Beth Or in Miami, Florida, and author of *Wisdom of the Jewish Sages,* mystical interpreters of the Bible have found evidence of meditation dating back to Abraham, the founder of Judaism. The Old Testament prophets apparently entered into altered states of consciousness through fasting and ascetic practices, and mystics in the first few centuries A.D. meditated on a vision of the prophet Ezekiel.

But the first formal Jewish meditation, says Shapiro, centered on the Hebrew alphabet, which was considered the divine language through which God created the world. "If you could see into the alphabet," explains Shapiro, "you could see into the source of creation and thereby become one with the creator Himself."

Like practitioners in all the God-centered religions, Jewish meditators have traditionally used sacred phrases or verses from scripture as mantras to bring them closer to God. As one great Hasidic master used to say of the phrase *r'bono shel olam* ("master of the universe"), if you just repeat it continuously, you will achieve union with God. And it is precisely this union that Jewish meditation intends to induce.

Like Christianity, Judaism has been inspired by Eastern influences in recent years to revive its own meditative traditions. Rabbis like Shapiro (who practices Zen meditation) and David Cooper (who trained in Buddhist mindfulness meditation) are creating a Jewish meditative renaissance by forging a new synthesis of ancient techniques from East and West.

MEDITATION

Contemplating the stars

In his book *Jewish Meditation*, Rabbi Aryeh Kaplan describes a traditional technique based on the biblical verse "Lift your eyes on high and see who created these [stars], the One who brings out their host by number, He calls them all by name . . ." (Isa. 40:26):

1. **On a clear night, lie or sit comfortably out of doors, gazing up at the stars.**

2. **While repeating a mantra, focus your attention on the stars as though you are probing them to reveal the mystery behind them.**

You can use the traditional Jewish mantra *r'bono shel olam* to help you deepen your concentration and your sense of the sacred. Or feel free to use a mantra of your own choosing.

As Rabbi Kaplan puts it, you are "calling to God in the depths of the heavens, seeking to find Him beyond the stars, beyond the very limits of time and space."

3. **Remain absorbed in your contemplation for as long as you wish.**

According to Rabbi Kaplan, this meditation "can bring a person to an overwhelmingly deep spiritual experience."

Toward the one

To prepare for more advanced meditative practices, Sufis often begin with a *darood* — the recitation of a sacred phrase coordinated with the breath. The American-born Sufi master Samuel Lewis, who died in 1971, taught the following exercise:

1. **Start to walk in a rhythmic fashion and synchronize your breathing with your pace — four steps for each inhalation and four steps for each exhalation.**

2. **As you walk, repeat the phrase "toward the one" — one syllable per step with a silent space on the fourth step.**

   Walking develops and strengthens the rhythm of the breath.

3. **Continue for as long as you like, with wholehearted attention.**

"The Sufi practices living in the breath 24 hours a day," says Shabda Kahn, a Sufi teacher who studied with Lewis.

Meditation among the Sufis: Surrendering to the Divine with every breath

Since the time of the prophet Mohammed in the seventh century A.D., Sufis have worn the garments of Islam. But, according to the American-born Sufi teacher Shabda Kahn, their roots go back much further, beyond Mohammed or Buddha or other famous teachers, to the first awakened person. Sufis claim to be a fellowship of mystical seekers whose sole purpose is to realize the Divine in their own hearts. The forms of Sufism varied from century to century and teacher to teacher and from one geographical location to another, but the basic teaching is the same: There is nothing but God.

Meditation in Sufism generally takes the form of chanting a sacred phrase, either silently or out loud, while breathing deeply and rhythmically — a practice known as *zikr*, "remembrance of the Divine." Kahn explains that Sufis retranslate the biblical beatitude "Blessed are the poor in spirit" to "Blessed are those who have a refined breath." Once the Sufi cultivates and refines the breath, he or she can use it as a method for surrendering to the divine presence in each moment — with every breath.

The Americanization of Meditation

If you hark back to the counterculture of the 1960s and '70s to find the first seeds of meditation on American soil, you may be surprised to learn that the roots go far deeper. Some of the earliest settlers transplanted Eastern ideas when they fled to the colonies, seeking freedom for their particular brand of Christianity. And many of the framers of the Declaration of Independence and the U.S. Constitution — men like Thomas Jefferson and Benjamin Franklin — belonged to secret fraternities informed by the mystical teachings of Sufism and Judaism.

Transcendentalism and Theosophy: 1840 – 1900

The first major influx of Eastern teachings began in the 1840s and '50s, when Transcendentalists like Emerson and Thoreau read Hindu scriptures in English translations of German adaptations from the Sanskrit! While Thoreau, whose ideas on civil disobedience were influenced by Eastern philosophy, withdrew to Walden Pond to meditate in nature, his good friend Emerson was blending German idealism, Yankee optimism, and Indian spirituality to formulate his version of the Transcendentalist credo. In the process, he transformed the Hindu *Brahman* (the divine ground of being) into a more universal concept that he called the *Oversoul*.

Later in the century, the Theosophists — members of a largely Western movement, led by the Russian-born Madame Blavatsky, who adapted and popularized Indian spiritual thought — made Hindu meditation texts available to the ordinary reader, and followers of the New Thought movement practiced guided visualizations and mantra meditations adapted from Eastern sources.

But the landmark meditation event of the nineteenth century turned out to be the World Parliament of Religions, an international gathering of religious leaders and teachers held in Chicago in 1893. For the first time, Asian masters presented their teachings directly to Westerners on American soil. Following the conference, several of the masters (including the Indian sage Swami Vivekananda and the Japanese Zen teacher Soyen Shaku) toured the U.S. lecturing to interested audiences.

Yoga and Zen prepare the soil: 1900 – 1960

In the decades following the World Parliament, the Zen monk Nyogen Senzaki continued Soyen Shaku's work of sowing the seeds of meditation in the New World, and Swami Paramananda, a disciple of Swami Vivekananda, established centers where curious Americans could practice meditation and hear sophisticated Indian spiritual teachings. (The Vedanta Society, which grew up around the work of swamis Vivekananda and Paramananda and their disciples, continues to flourish in the United States and Europe.) In the 1920s, the Indian yogi Paramahansa Yogananda settled in the U.S., and his work gradually blossomed into the Self-Realization Fellowship, which today boasts followers throughout the Western world.

Perhaps the best-known spiritual teacher to arrive during this period was J. Krishnamurti, who settled in southern California in the 1940s and attracted the English writers Aldous Huxley and Christopher Isherwood. Although Krishnamurti (who was groomed from childhood to be a world teacher by the Theosophists) shunned formal meditation and religious dogma in favor of dialogue and self-inquiry, Huxley and Isherwood helped to popularize the great Hindu scriptures.

By the 1950s, Zen began to significantly influence the American counterculture. While the poet Gary Snyder (who later won the Pulitzer Prize for his book *Turtle Island*) was off studying Zen in Japan, his friend and Beat colleague Jack Kerouac wrote novels that popularized Buddhist concepts such as *dharma, karma,* and *satori.* Also in the '50s, the great Japanese scholar D.T. Suzuki began teaching Zen at Columbia University in New York City, where his audiences included the young Thomas Merton, novelist J.D. Salinger, composer John Cage, and psychoanalysts Erich Fromm and Karen Horney. About the same time, the books of former Episcopal priest and Zen aficionado Alan Watts — including *The Way of Zen* and *Psychotherapy East and West* — became popular sellers.

REMEMBER

Spirituality or religion?

Polls cited in *Newsweek* indicate that more and more Americans consider themselves spiritual but not necessarily religious. You may be one of many who have given up their childhood creed, but feel drawn, nevertheless, to spiritual questions and practices. You may find organized religion too limited by its rituals and belief systems, too focused on archaic symbols and stories, and not sufficiently concerned with supporting you in your search for direct spiritual experience.

Religions generally begin with a vital spiritual impulse — look at the lives of Jesus or Mohammed or Buddha — but often grow rigid over the centuries like an old tree and lose touch with their living essence — which is, after all, what spirituality is all about.

Genuine spirituality keeps resurfacing within religions, however, as an esoteric undercurrent. The establishment may view it with skepticism or even scorn but allow it to flourish as long as it doesn't threaten the status quo. Judaism has its kabbalists and Hasids, Islam its Sufis, Buddhism its Zen masters and forest monks, Christianity its Franciscans and Carmelites.

If you want a sense of meaning and belonging that comes from viewing your life in a broader metaphysical and historical context, conventional, name-brand religion may be your cup of tea. But if you want to awaken to the meaning of life and seek the inner transformation afforded by the practice of meditation or some other spiritual discipline, you're better off ferreting out one of the esoteric undercurrents within the religious mainstream — or simply following a meditative practice that offers the possibility of direct spiritual experience but has no affiliation with traditional religion. (For more on spiritual practices, see Chapter 13.)

Meditation reaches Main Street: 1960 – present

In the 1960s, a unique cluster of events set the stage for the mainstreaming of meditation. Many Baby Boomers, who were now reaching young adulthood, began experimenting with altered states of consciousness by using so-called mind-expanding drugs like marijuana and LSD. At the same time, the war in Vietnam prompted a national backlash among a sizable segment of the population and helped forge a counter-culture opposed in many ways to the status quo. Popular music fueled the fires of discontent and touted the benefits of "tuning in, turning on, and dropping out" — words that in another time, place, and context might have referred to renouncing the world in favor of the monastic life. And political unrest in Asia (including shock waves from Vietnam and the Chinese takeover of Tibet) combined with the spirit of the times to bring a new wave of spiritual teachers to the New World.

From the standpoint of meditation, perhaps the landmark event of this era was the conversion of the Beatles to the practice of Transcendental Meditation (TM), which prompted thousands of their young fans to begin meditating, too. (Over the years, the TM movement has taught millions of Westerners how to meditate and has pioneered research revealing the mind-body benefits of meditation.) As psychedelics lost their luster, more and more people who had looked to drugs to provide meditative experiences like peace and insight turned to the real thing — and some even took refuge in the yoga communities and Zen centers constructed by their newfound teachers.

Native American meditation

When I describe the "Americanization" of meditation, I'm revealing my cultural bias. Clearly, Native Americans have been meditating here for tens of thousands of years. In addition to shamans, who play a special role in the life of the tribe (see the sidebar "Shamans: The first great meditators"), Native American boys and girls often mark the transition from childhood to adulthood by spending three or four days meditating alone in a sacred spot. By fasting, praying, focusing their mind, and opening their senses, they solicit dreams or visions that bring them special wisdom or power and help them contact their guardian spirits. As adults, Native Americans may also meditate alone in nature when they need spiritual sustenance or answers to important life questions. In addition, the practice of moment-to-moment mindfulness has always been an essential ingredient of traditional Native American life.

Since the 1970s, a new generation, with the savvy to translate the teachings for their brothers and sisters, has emerged in the West as sanctioned teachers of Eastern spiritual disciplines. As Alan Watts anticipated (in his book *Psychotherapy East and West*), the field of psychotherapy has been particularly open to Eastern influences — perhaps because psychotherapy, like meditation, purports to offer a solution for suffering. As a result, American spiritual teachers often couch their messages in language that appeals to proponents of "personal growth."

At the same time, scientific researchers like Herbert Benson, Jon Kabat-Zinn, and Dean Ornish have pioneered the mainstreaming of meditation (see the sidebar "Promoting the benefits of meditation" in Chapter 2), and books on meditation and related topics regularly appear on *The New York Times* best-seller list. In one six-month period recently, *Time* magazine ran a cover story on the growing popularity of Buddhism, and *Newsweek* ran covers featuring the faces of Ornish and best-selling author and meditation expert Deepak Chopra. Without doubt, meditation has emerged as a mainstream American practice!

Playing with gravity

1. **Sit in a chair and take a few moments to become aware of how gravity acts on your body.**

2. **Notice the weight of your legs and hips against the chair.**

3. **Stand up and notice how gravity pulls you toward the earth.**

4. **Begin walking and, with each step, pay attention to the tug of gravity against your feet.**

5. **Look around and consider how all these objects are held in place by gravity — and how you move through a field of gravity like a fish swimming through water.**

   This mysterious force is everywhere, even though you may not see or comprehend it.

6. **Continue to be aware of this invisible but powerful field as you go about your day.**

Chapter 4

Laying the Foundation: Motivation, Attitude, and Beginner's Mind

. . . .

In This Chapter

▶ Recognizing and maintaining "beginner's mind"

▶ Finding out what motivates you to meditate

▶ Checking out five basic motivational styles

▶ Deepening your meditation by cultivating an "attitude"

. . . .

As an effective practice for reprogramming your mind and opening your heart, meditation has no parallel. But traditionally meditation never stands alone — it's always accompanied by an emphasis on motivation and attitude, that is, on the qualities of mind that fuel the fires of meditation and keep you going when the going gets tough.

Some meditation teachers may urge you to take a vow to dedicate your meditation to the well-being of others, rather than hoarding all the goodies for yourself. Others may ask you to consider your deepest aspirations or intentions or attitudes — what one Zen master calls your "inmost request." Whatever the term used to describe it, you need to look deeply into your own mind and heart to clarify the reasons that motivate you to meditate. Then you can consult this motivation when the practice becomes boring and uneventful — which it inevitably does.

My teenage nephew aspires to become a professional baseball player. Despite the odds, he might just make it — he's a six-foot-five left-hander with a mean fastball and the work ethic of a winner. Recently, he asked me to teach him how to meditate so he can pitch with more poise and composure. Then there's my thirtysomething cousin with a Harvard MBA, who works at a prestigious East Coast investment firm. When we talked by phone the other day, he wondered whether meditation could help relieve the unremitting stress that comes with his job.

A close friend in her fifties who was just diagnosed with breast cancer wants to learn how to meditate in order to deal with her fear and facilitate her healing. And one of my therapy clients asked for meditation instruction to help quiet her mind so she can get a clearer picture of the recurring patterns of thinking and acting that disrupt her life and make her unhappy.

You may be driven to meditate by pain or suffering or desperation of some kind, or you may simply be dissatisfied with the quality of your life — the level of stress, the lack of enjoyment, the speed and intensity. Whatever your story, you need to be sufficiently motivated if you're ever going to take the trouble to change your routine, slow down, and turn your attention inward for 15 or 20 minutes each day. In this chapter, you have an opportunity to face your unique brand of dissatisfaction — and cultivate the motivation that keeps you meditating, week after week.

Beginning (And Ending) with Beginner's Mind

Ultimately, the great meditation teachers advise that the best attitude to take toward meditation is an open mind, completely free from all preconceptions and expectations. One of my first meditation teachers, Zen master Shunryu Suzuki, calls this *beginner's mind* — and he counsels that the goal of meditation is not to accumulate knowledge, learn something new, or achieve some special state of mind, but simply to maintain this fresh, uncluttered perspective.

"If your mind is empty, it is always ready for anything; it is open to everything," he writes in his book *Zen Mind, Beginner's Mind.* "In the beginner's mind, there are many possibilities; in the expert's mind, there are few." As the title of his book suggests, Suzuki teaches that beginner's mind and Zen mind — the awake, clear, unfettered mind of the enlightened Zen master — are essentially the same. Or, as another teacher puts it, "The seeker is the sought; the looker is what he or she is looking for!"

Needless to say, it's easier to talk about beginner's mind than it is to maintain or even recognize it. But that's precisely the point — the "don't know mind" of the beginner can't conceptualize or identify beginner's mind, just as the eye can't see itself, even though it is the source of all seeing. No matter which meditation technique you choose, try to practice it with the innocent, open, "don't know" spirit of beginner's mind. In a sense, beginner's mind is the *non-attitude* underlying all attitudes, the *non-technique* at the heart of all successful techniques.

SPIRITUAL STUFF

Your end is your beginning

It's one of the great mysteries of meditation that you inevitably end up where you began. Like Simon in the sidebar "Discovering the treasure in your own house" in Chapter 1, you ultimately find that the treasure was hidden under your own hearth all along — and the path you follow only serves to lead you home again. As T. S. Eliot puts it in his poem "Four Quartets," "The end of all our exploring/ Will be to arrive where we started/ And know the place for the first time."

To clarify this mystery, the Tibetans make a distinction between the *ground,* the *path,* and the *fruition.* The confused, busy, suffering mind, they say, has within it the peace, love, and happiness you seek — the ground or basis for awakening. But the clouds of negativity (doubt, judgment, fear, anger, attachment) that obscure this ground — which is who you really are in your heart of hearts — have become so thick and impenetrable that you need to embark on the path of meditation to clear away the clouds and bring you closer to the truth.

When you finally recognize your essential being — the moment of fruition — you realize that it has always been right here, where and who you already are, nearer than your own heart, more immediate than your breath. This essential being is identical to what the Zen folks call *beginner's mind.*

Here are the characteristics of beginner's mind:

- **Openness to whatever arises:** When you welcome your experience in meditation without trying to change it, you align yourself with being itself, which includes everything — light and dark, good and bad, life and death — without judgment or aversion.

- **Freedom from expectations:** When you practice beginner's mind, you encounter each moment with fresh eyes and ears. Instead of meditating to achieve some future goal, you sit with the confidence that the open, ready awareness you bring to it ultimately contains all the qualities you seek, such as love, peace, happiness, compassion, wisdom, and equanimity.

- **Spacious and spontaneous mind:** Some teachers liken beginner's mind to the sky — though the clouds may come and go, the boundless expanse of sky is never damaged or reduced in any way. As for spontaneity, Jesus summed it up when he said, "You must become as little children to enter the kingdom of heaven." Free from expectations and open to whatever arises, you naturally respond to situations in a spontaneous way.

Empty your cup

There's an old Zen story about a scholar who visited a famous Zen master to inquire into the meaning of Zen. The scholar asked question after question but was so full of his own ideas that he rarely gave the master an opportunity to answer.

After about an hour of this one-sided dialogue, the master asked the scholar if he wanted a cup of tea. When the scholar held out his cup, the master filled it but just kept on pouring.

"Enough," the scholar cried out. "The cup is full. It won't hold any more."

"Yes," replied the master, "and so is your mind. You can't learn Zen until you empty your cup."

✔ **Original, primordial awareness:** A famous Zen *koan* (provocative riddle) goes like this: "What was your original face before your parents were born?" This koan points to the ineffable, primordial quality of mind, which predates your personality and even your physical body. Perhaps beginner's mind should really be called beginningless mind!

What Motivates You to Meditate?

We don't talk much in our culture about motivation — unless it's deficient or missing and we need to amp it up and "get motivated." In your own life, you may be the kind of person who does what comes naturally or does it because it's fun — or exciting or educational or merely interesting. Or perhaps you're the responsible sort who fills her life with obligations and spends her time meeting them.

Whatever your motivational style, you may find, on closer investigation, that the motivation or attitude you bring to an activity has a dramatic impact on your experience of the activity. Take sex, for example. If you do it out of lust or boredom or fear, your sexual pleasure will be permeated by the flavor of the feeling that motivated you. But if you have sex as a heartfelt expression of love for your partner, you may move in the same way, touch the same places, use the same techniques — but you'll have an exponentially different experience.

Reflecting on your life

The great spiritual teachers and meditation masters have always reminded us of the brevity of life. The medieval Christian mystics kept a skull on their desks to remind them of their own mortality. And Buddhist monks and nuns in some Asian countries still meditate in cemeteries to deepen their awareness of impermanence. Whether tomorrow, next year, or many years from now, you and I will eventually die. Remembering this from time to time can help us to clarify life's priorities — and remind us of our reasons for meditating.

Of course, if you find it too depressing to think about dying, by all means feel free to skip this exercise. But you may discover that your initial aversion fades as you open your heart to the preciousness of life. Take ten minutes or more to do this guided meditation (which is adapted from the book *A Path with Heart* by Jack Kornfield):

1. **Sit quietly, close your eyes, and take a few deep breaths, relaxing a little with each exhalation.**

2. **Imagine that you're at the end of your life and death is quickly approaching.**

   Be aware of the tentativeness of life — you could die at any moment.

3. **Reflect on your life as you watch it replay before your eyes like a video.**

4. **As you reflect, choose two things you've done that you feel good about now.**

   They may not be important or life-changing; in fact, they may be simple, seemingly insignificant events.

5. **Look deeply at what makes these moments memorable — at the qualities of mind and heart you brought to them.**

6. **Notice how these memories affect you — what feelings and other memories they stir up.**

7. **In light of these memories, consider how you might live differently if you had your life to live again.**

   What activities would you give more time to than you do now? What qualities of being would you choose to emphasize? Which people would you give more (or less) of your attention?

8. **As you end this exercise and go about your day, notice whether your attitude toward your life has changed in any way.**

Well, meditation is like sex — what you bring to it is what you get! In fact, the meditative traditions suggest that your motivation determines the outcome of your practice as much as the technique you use or the time you spend. Just as clients in Jungian therapy proverbially have Jungian dreams and Freudian clients have Freudian dreams, Christian meditators tend to experience God or Christ, Buddhist meditators see emptiness — and those who seek healing or peace of mind or peak performance tend to get what they came for.

Looking deeply into your own heart

Sit quietly, take a few deep breaths, and set aside some time to inquire into your own heart and mind for answers to these questions:

- What brings me to practice meditation?
- What motivates me to meditate?
- What do I hope to achieve?
- What do I expect to learn?

Set aside the first thoughts that come to mind, look more deeply, and ask the question, "What is the dissatisfaction or suffering that drives me?"

- Do I want to reduce stress and calm my mind?

- Do I want to be happier and more self-accepting?

- Do I seek answers to the deeper, existential questions like "Who am I?" or "What is the meaning of life?"

Perhaps you are even attuned to the suffering of others and aspire to help them before helping yourself. Or maybe you just want to improve your performance at work or be more attentive and loving to your family. Whatever answers you find, just note them down without judgment and refer to them as needed to help keep you motivated.

Spiritual traditions often rank attitudes and motivations as higher or lower, and they generally agree that the motivation to help others before helping oneself is the highest. But we have to begin where we are — and it's more important to be honest with yourself than to pretend to some motivation that you don't genuinely hold. Anyway, the more you meditate, the more you open your heart and reveal your natural, inherent concern for the well-being of others. The following sections cover the five basic motivational styles. Check them out to get a sense of where you stand. Note that the boundaries between these styles are fuzzy at best, and most of us tend to be a blend of a few or all five.

Improving your life

Imagine for a moment that your life's a mess and you're struggling to get it together — so you take up the practice of meditation. You figure meditation will teach you the concentration and self-discipline you need to succeed. Or maybe you have a difficult time in relationships, and you want to calm your mind and even out the emotional rollercoaster so you're not constantly in conflict with others.

Perhaps you suffer from some chronic illness and hope that the regular practice of meditation will reduce your stress and improve your health in general. Or maybe you just want to enhance your performance at work or in sports or learn how to take greater enjoyment from your family, friends, and leisure activities. Whatever the scenario, your primary concern at this level is to fix or improve yourself and your external circumstances — a thoroughly noble intention.

Understanding and accepting yourself

At a certain point in your development, you may get tired of trying to fix yourself — or perhaps you've done such a good job that it's time to move on to the next phase. Here you realize that some patterns can't be changed — or at least struggling to change them just makes them more entrenched — and you decide to shift from "fixing" to self-awareness and self-acceptance. As former Chicago Bulls coach Phil Jackson puts it in his book *Sacred Hoops,* "If we can accept whatever hand we've been dealt, no matter how unwelcome, the way to proceed eventually becomes clear."

I like to compare change to one of those woven Chinese finger puzzles that were popular when I was a kid: The harder you pull, the more stuck you get. But if you move your fingers toward one another — the gesture of self-acceptance — you can free them quite easily. If you're tormented by self-blame, self-doubt, or self-judgment, you may be drawn to meditation as a way of learning to accept and even love yourself.

In my work as a psychotherapist, I've found that mean-spirited self-criticism can wreak havoc in the psyches of otherwise well-balanced people — and the antidote almost inevitably involves self-acceptance, what the Buddhists call "making friends with yourself." When you practice accepting yourself fully, you soften and open your heart, not only to yourself, but ultimately to others as well. (For more on self-acceptance, see Chapters 6, 10, and 11.)

Realizing your true nature

Although you recognize the value of improving or making friends with yourself, you may be spurred to meditation by a desire to penetrate the veils that separate you from the true source of all meaning, peace, and love. Nothing less will satisfy you! Perhaps you're obsessed with one of the great spiritual questions, like "Who am I?" "What is God?" or "What is the meaning of life?" In Zen, they say that such an intense yearning for truth is like a red-hot iron ball lodged in the pit of your stomach — you can't digest it, and you can't spit it out; you can only transform it through the power of your meditation.

Your quest may be motivated by personal suffering, but you're unwilling to stop at self-improvement or self-acceptance and feel impelled to reach the summit of the mountain I describe in Chapter 1 — what the great masters call *enlightenment* or *satori*. When you realize who you essentially are, the separate self drops away and reveals your identity with being itself. This realization, in turn, can have wide-reaching ramifications — including, ironically, a happier and more harmonious life and complete self-love and self-acceptance.

Awakening others

The Tibetan Buddhists teach that all meditators must cultivate the most important motivation of all — to liberate others before liberating themselves. Known as *bodhichitta* ("awakened heart"), this selfless aspiration actually accelerates the meditative process by offering an antidote to the natural human tendency to hoard our own accomplishments and insights and defend our own psychic and spiritual territory. Unless it is suffused by bodhichitta, say the Tibetans, meditation can take us only so far along the path to self-realization.

Expressing your innate perfection

In the Zen tradition, the highest motivation for meditating is not to attain some special state of mind, but to express your innately pure and undefiled "true nature" — what I referred to earlier as *beginner's mind,* or in Chapter 1 as *pure being.* With this motivation, you never leave your own hearth, but sit with the confidence that you already are the peace and happiness you seek. This level of motivation requires tremendous spiritual maturity, but once you have a glimpse of who you really are, you may find yourself moved to meditate in order to actualize and deepen your understanding.

How to Live in Harmony with Your Meditation

Now that you know what motivates you to meditate, you may benefit from a few guidelines for enhancing and deepening your practice. In particular, meditators over the centuries have discovered that how you act, what you think about, and which qualities you cultivate can have an immediate impact on the depth and stability of your meditation.

Every spiritual tradition emphasizes right conduct of some kind — and not necessarily on the basis of rigid notions of right and wrong. When your actions don't jibe with your reasons for meditating — for example, when you're meditating to reduce stress but your actions intensify conflict — your everyday life may be working at cross-purposes with the time you spend on your cushion. (The Hebrew word for sin originally meant "off the mark!") The more you meditate, the more sensitive you become to how some activities support or even enhance your meditation — and others disturb or discourage it.

Of course, there is a never-ending feedback loop between formal meditation and everyday life: How you live affects how you meditate, and how you meditate affects how you live.

With these thoughts in mind, here are ten basic guidelines for living in harmony with the spirit of meditation:

- ✔ **Be mindful of cause and effect:** Notice how your actions — and the feelings and thoughts that accompany them — influence others and your own state of mind. When you flare up in anger or lash out in fear, observe how the ripples can be felt for hours or even days — in the responses of others, in your own body, and in your meditation. Do the same with actions that express kindness or compassion. As the Bible says, "As you sow, so shall you reap."

- ✔ **Reflect on impermanence and the preciousness of life:** Death is real, say the Tibetans; it can come without warning, and this body, too, will one day be food for worms and other earthly creatures. By reflecting on how rare it is to be a human being at a time when physical comforts are relatively plentiful and the practice of meditation and other methods for reducing stress and relieving suffering are so readily available, you may feel more motivated to take advantage of the opportunities you have.

- ✔ **Realize the limitations of worldly success:** Check out the people you know who have achieved the worldly success you aspire to. Are they really any happier than you are? Do they have more love in their lives or more peace of mind? Through meditation, you can achieve a level of inner success that's based on joy and tranquillity rather than material gain.

- ✔ **Practice nonattachment:** This classic Buddhist counsel may seem on first blush like an impossible task. But the point here is not to be indifferent or to disengage from the world, but to notice how attachment to the outcome of your actions affects your meditations — and your peace of mind. What would it be like to act wholeheartedly, with the best of intentions, then let go of struggling to get things to be a certain way?

✔ **Cultivate patience and perseverance:** If nothing else, the practice of meditation requires the willingness to keep on keeping on — call it discipline, diligence, perseverance, or just plain stick-to-itiveness, you'll reap the greatest benefits if you do it regularly, day after day. Besides, the qualities of patience and perseverance translate nicely to every area of life. (For more on effort and self-discipline, see Chapter 9.)

✔ **Simplify your life:** The busier and more complicated your life, the more agitated your mind will be when you meditate — and the greater your stress level. Pay particular attention to all those extra activities you tack on to an already crammed schedule (perhaps to avoid taking a deep breath, hearing your heartbeat, facing your fears, and dealing with other unpleasant feelings like loneliness, emptiness, grief, or inadequacy). If you stop running and listen closely, you may hear the voice of your own inner wisdom.

✔ **Live with honesty and integrity:** When you lie, manipulate, and compromise your core values, you may be able to hide from yourself for a time — until you reach your meditation cushion. Then the proverbial "you know what" hits the fan, and every peccadillo comes back to haunt you. Meditation mirrors you back to you, and what you see may motivate you to actualize more of your positive potential.

✔ **Face situations with the courage of a warrior:** Unlike their battlefield counterparts, "meditation warriors" cultivate the courage to drop their aggression and defensiveness, face their fears, and open their hearts — to themselves and others. Easier said than done, you may say, but meditation will teach you how — and then you need to be willing to follow through in real-life situations. Ultimately, every moment becomes an opportunity to practice. (For more on how to meditate in every moment of life, see Chapter 15.)

✔ **Trust the technology of meditation — and yourself:** It helps to remember that people have been meditating successfully for thousands of years — far longer than they've been using, say, Microsoft Windows or the Power PC. Besides, we're talking low-tech technology here, something anyone can do — like breathing and paying attention. Just trust the technology, follow the instructions — and let go of the results.

✔ **Dedicate your practice to the benefit of others:** As I mentioned earlier, the Tibetans call this dedication bodhichitta ("awakened heart") and regard it as essential for meditation that is life-changing, rather than merely cosmetic. Studies of the impact of prayer on healing, cited in *Healing Words: The Power of Prayer and the Practice of Medicine* by Larry Dossey, M.D., have shown that prayers that request specific results are not nearly as effective as those that ask for the best for all concerned. In other words, the love you take is equal to the love you make!

Looking for the last time

Imagine that you will never see your friends or your loved ones again. Now, follow these steps:

1. Sit quietly, take a few deep breaths, and close your eyes.

2. Let the usual thoughts, feelings, and pre-occupations that surround you disperse like fog on a sunny morning.

3. Look at the objects and people in your field of vision as though for the last time.

   How do they appear to you? How do you feel? What thoughts go through your mind?

4. Consider the beauty and preciousness of this moment, which is the only one you have.

5. Reflect on the recognition that every moment is like this one.

6. As you finish this meditation, let whatever insights you've gained continue to suffuse your experience.

Chapter 5

How Your Mind Stresses You Out and What You Can Do about It

For thousands of years, pundits and sages both East and West have been telling us that our problems originate in our minds. So you won't be surprised if I join the chorus of voices and agree. Yes, they're right, your mind by itself "can make a heaven of hell and a hell of heaven" (as English poet John Milton put it). But how, you may be wondering, can this cute little truism help you when you don't know what to do about it? "Sure, my mind's the problem," you may say, "but I can't exactly have it surgically removed."

You can begin by becoming familiar with how your mind works. As you may have noticed, it's a rather complex assortment of thoughts, ideas, stories, impulses, preferences, and emotions. Without a diagram, it can be as difficult to negotiate as the jumble of wires and hoses under the hood of your car.

Once you have a working knowledge of how it's structured, you can begin to notice how all those thoughts and feelings distort your experience and keep you from achieving the happiness, relaxation, effectiveness, or healing you seek. Then you can discover how meditation can teach you to change all that by focusing and calming your mind, and ultimately by delving more deeply and unraveling the habitual stories and patterns that keep causing you suffering and stress. Who knows, you may not need to have a lobotomy after all!

Taking a Tour of Your Inner Terrain

Because I'm an avid hiker and swimmer, I'm fond of using natural metaphors, which actually lend themselves quite nicely to describing meditation. In Chapter 1, I compare practicing meditation to climbing a mountain. Now I'll turn that metaphor on its head, so to speak, and have you imagine that the journey you're taking is down — to the bottom of a lake. (If you want to picture yourself in a wetsuit and scuba gear, go right ahead.) In fact, the lake I'm referring to is *you* — you're journeying to the depths of your own being.

Sifting through the layers of inner experience

When you meditate, in addition to developing your concentration and calming your mind, you may find yourself delving deeper into your inner experience — and uncovering layers you didn't even know existed. Now, what do you suppose lies at the bottom? The great meditative traditions have different names for it — essence, pure being, true nature, spirit, soul, the pearl of great price, the source of all wisdom and love. The Zen folks call it your original face before your parents were born. You might like to picture it as a spring that gushes forth the pure, refreshing, deeply satisfying water of being without reservation. (For more on this spring, see Chapter 1, where it awaits the climber at the top of the mountain of meditation.)

SPIRITUAL STUFF

Is it higher or deeper?

Spiritual teachers and personal growth advocates have a dizzying fondness for up and down metaphors. Some talk about digging down into your inner experience like a miner, or having profound insights, or feeling or knowing things deeply. Others talk about higher consciousness or transcending the mundane or having a mind like the sky. (I make the best of both worlds by using the two directions more or less interchangeably.)

To some degree, the difference lies in the personal preferences of the particular writer or teacher. But it can also refer to an attitude toward inner experience: If you believe that the wellspring of *being* lies deep inside you, beneath the personal, then you talk about down. If you believe that it exists in the upper echelons of your being or comes down like grace or spirit from above, then you talk about up.

In my humble opinion, if you dive deep enough, you find yourself at the top of the mountain — and if you rise high enough, you find yourself at the bottom of the sea. In the end, it's the same place anyway. Ultimately, in fact, pure *being* has no location — it's everywhere in every one of us all the time.

How to tell the difference between thoughts and feelings

In my work as a psychotherapist, I've found that many people have trouble distinguishing between thoughts and feelings. For example, if I ask "What are you feeling?" they may reply, "I feel like I shouldn't be so open with my partner anymore." Even though this insight begins with the right word, it's actually a judgment, rather than a feeling. Here are a few pointers for telling the difference:

✔ *Feelings* occur as a set of recognizable sensations in your body. When you're angry, for example, you may feel tension in your shoulders and jaw and experience a rush of energy in the back of your head. When you're sad, by contrast, you may feel a heaviness in your chest and heart and a congested feeling in your sinuses and throat. Through meditation, you can discover how to experience your feelings directly as sensations, separate from the thoughts and stories that perpetuate them. (For more on meditating with thoughts and feelings, see Chapter 11.)

✔ *Thoughts* are the images, memories, beliefs, judgments, and reflections that float through your mind and often give rise to your feelings. If you follow the word "feel" with "like," you're probably voicing a thought or a belief, rather than a feeling. You can practice breaking strong feelings down into their component parts by asking: What are the thoughts and images in my mind that keep me feeling the way I do? And what am I actually experiencing in my body right now, aside from my thoughts?

Thoughts not only generate feelings, they often masquerade as feelings (so you won't actually feel the ones you have), attempt to talk you out of your feelings, judge your feelings, or suppress them entirely. The more you can disentangle your thoughts and feelings, the more clearly and consciously you can relate with (and express) your inner experience.

This wellspring of being is who you really are in your heart of hearts — before you became conditioned to believe that you're somehow deficient or inadequate, as so many of us do. It's your wholeness and completeness — before you began to feel separate or lonely or fragmented. It's the deep intuition of being inextricably connected with something larger than yourself and with every other being and thing. And it's ultimately the source of all peace, happiness, joy, and other positive, life-affirming feelings — even though you may think they're caused by outside circumstances. (Of course, people experience this source differently, which explains why there are so many words to describe it.)

Connecting in some way with this source or spring of pure being is actually the point of meditation, whether you're aspiring to become enlightened or just trying to reduce stress, enhance your performance, or improve your life. And meditation will definitely take you there, as I explain later in this chapter. But when you meditate, you also begin to encounter material that seems to come between you and the experience of being, just as you may encounter layers of sediment, algae, fish, and debris on your way to the bottom of a lake. These layers don't pose a problem unless the inner water is turbulent, in which case they can make it difficult to see clearly. (By *turbulence,* I mean a busy, agitated mind or a troubled, frightened, defended heart.) In more or less the order in which you may encounter them in meditation, these layers include:

- ✔ **Mind chatter:** When you turn your attention inward, the first thing you're likely to encounter is the ceaseless chattering of your mind. The Buddhists like to compare the mind to a noisy monkey that swings uncontrollably from thought-branch to thought-branch without ever settling down. Most of the time, you may be so caught up in this chatter that you're not even aware it's happening. It may take the form of reliving the past or rehearsing for the future or trying to solve some problem in the present. Whatever the content, your mind is constantly talking to itself, often spinning a story with you as the hero — or the victim. (Research indicates that a very small percentage of people experience no inner dialogue at all but have only images or feelings instead.)

- ✔ **Intense or recurring emotions:** Just as an action film or a romantic comedy takes you on a rollercoaster ride of emotions, so the *dramas* your mind keeps spinning out evoke their own play of feelings. If you're trying to figure out how to make a killing in the stock market, for example, or ask out that attractive man or woman you just met at work, you may feel fear or anxiety or possibly excitement or lust. If you're obsessing about the injustices or unkindnesses you suffered recently, you may experience sadness, grief, outrage, resentment. Together with these emotions, of course, go a range of bodily sensations, including tension, arousal, contraction in the heart, waves of energy in the belly or the back of the head.

    Some of these feelings may be pleasurable, others unpleasant or even painful. But emotions in themselves don't pose a problem. It's just that as long as you keep reacting to the dramas inside your head, you may be cutting yourself off from others and from deeper, more satisfying dimensions of your being — and you may miss what's really going on around you as well. (For more on working with emotions in meditation, see Chapter 11.)

- ✔ **Grasping and pushing away:** At a somewhat subtler level of experience than thoughts and emotions lurks a perpetual play of like and dislike, attachment and aversion. The Buddhists teach that the key to happiness and contentment lies in wanting what you have and not wanting what you don't have. But often, we're somehow dissatisfied with what we have, while we yearn for what we don't have and struggle to get it. Or we may become deeply attached to what we have and then suffer when time and circumstances change it or take it away. Because change is unavoidable, this tendency to either hold on tight to our experience or push it away can actually cause constant suffering.

✔ **Negative beliefs and life scripts:** Here's another nature metaphor for you. Imagine that your thoughts and emotions and even the dramas that keep running through your brain form the leaves and branches of some inner, subterranean bush or tree. (Think wild and uncontrollable here, like blackberries or bamboo.) What do you suppose constitutes the root, from which the leaves and branches relentlessly spring?

Well, you may be surprised to discover that the root is a cluster of beliefs and stories, many of them negative, that formed as the result of what people — especially significant people like loved ones and friends — have done to you and told you over the years. These beliefs and stories have intertwined over your lifetime into a kind of life script that defines who you think you are and how you view the people and circumstances around you. (I say "surprised" because most of us are clueless when it comes to life scripts — although you may have noticed some resemblance between your life and, say, "As the World Turns" or "ER" or "The Simpsons.")

The point is, your tendency to identify with your life script actually limits your range of possibilities and causes you suffering by acting as a *filter* through which you interpret your life in negative ways. To return to the bush metaphor, you can keep pruning back the branches, but you'll keep living out the same old story until you pull it up by the roots.

✔ **The sense of separation:** Even deeper than your stories — some would say the soil in which the stories grow — lies a feeling of being cut off or separate from life or being itself. Although the meditative traditions teach that separation is actually an illusion and we're inextricably connected to one another, the sense of being separate runs deep indeed. Often it dates back to early childhood experiences, when you were forced by circumstances to separate prematurely from your mother or some other nurturing figure. Sometimes it can be traced to the birth trauma itself, when you had to exchange your placental paradise for a colder, harsher reality. (Or maybe, as some traditions contend, it comes packaged with the embryonic hardware.)

Whatever its origins, this feeling may give rise to a kind of primordial fear: If I'm separate, then I must end at my skin, and everything out there must be *other*. Because these others are often bigger than I am and I have only the most limited control over their actions, then my survival must be at stake — and I need to protect myself at all costs. Life scripts evolve as strategies for surviving in a world of apparent separation, in which others are perceived as potentially unfriendly, withholding, demanding, or rejecting.

Becoming aware of your inner dialogue

Begin this meditation by paying attention to your thoughts. After several minutes, notice what the voices inside your head are telling you. (If you're not aware of any voices, you may want to observe feelings or images instead.) Does one voice predominate, or do several voices vie for your attention? Do they criticize or encourage you? Shame or praise you? Or do they focus primarily on the other people in your life? Do any of the voices argue with one another?

What kind of emotional tone do these voices have? Are they loving and gentle or angry and impatient? Does one voice sound more like you than the others? Do any of them remind you of people in your life, past or present? How do these voices make you feel?

Allow ten minutes for this exercise initially. Once you have the knack of it, you can stop from time to time during the day and pay attention to your inner dialogue. The important point is, you're not your thoughts — and you don't necessarily have to believe the messages they impart.

Discovering how turbulence clouds your mind and heart

Needless to say, when you're experiencing inner turbulence, you may find it difficult to connect with *being* when you sit down to meditate. Sometimes, of course, you may have moments when your mind just settles by itself and you can see all the way down to the bottom of the lake. (To use another nature metaphor, think of those overcast days when the cloud cover suddenly parts and the sun shines through with all its warmth and radiance.) These moments may be marked by feelings of inner peace and tranquillity, upsurges of love and joy, or intimations of your oneness with life. But most of the time, you may feel like you're doing a breaststroke through muddy water.

Well, the turbulence and confusion you encounter when you meditate doesn't suddenly materialize on cue. It's there all along, clouding your mind and heart and acting as a filter that obscures your clear seeing. You may experience it as an inner claustrophobia or density — you're so full of your own emotions and opinions that you have no room for the ideas and feelings of others, or even for any new or unfamiliar ideas and feelings that may well up inside you. Or you may get so caught up in your drama that you're not even aware that you're filtering your experience.

MEDITATION

You are not your thoughts or feelings

Find a quiet spot where you can sit for the next ten minutes. When you're comfortably settled, do the following:

1. **Take a few slow, deep breaths.**

2. **Turn your attention to your thoughts. (If you tend to be an emotional person, you can do the same exercise with your emotions.)**

   Instead of getting caught up in your thoughts (or emotions) as you might usually do, watch them closely, the way an angler watches the tip of a rod or a tennis player watches a ball. If you find your attention wandering, come back to the task at hand.

   At first, your mind may seem like wall-to-wall thoughts or emotions, and you may have difficulty determining where one thought leaves off and the next one begins. You may also find that certain thoughts or emotions keep recurring like popular tunes — for example, repetitive worries or favorite images or fantasies. If you're especially attentive, you may begin to notice that each thought or emotion has its own constituent parts, including a beginning, a middle, and an end.

3. **At the end of the ten minutes, stop and reflect on your experience.**

   Did you experience some "distance" from your thoughts or emotions? Or did you keep losing yourself in the thinking or feeling process?

The point of this exercise is not to see how well you can track your thinking or feeling, but to give you the experience of being the observer of your thoughts. Believe it or not, you're the thinker *not* the thoughts! As you begin to gain some perspective on your thoughts through the practice of meditation, you may find that they start losing the power they once had over you. You can have your thoughts, but they won't have you.

For example, I have a friend, a computer programmer, who received plenty of love and support as a child. Now, as an adult, he thinks of himself as inherently competent and worthy, even though he's no Steve Jobs. As a result, he enjoys his career, experiences only minimal anxiety when he makes work-related decisions, sees others as inherently supportive, and exudes a palpable self-confidence that draws others to him and invites them to trust him.

By contrast, I have another friend, an independent entrepreneur, who has several advanced degrees and has taken countless work-related trainings but who believes deep down that he's inherently unworthy. No matter how hard he works, he can't seem to get ahead. Besides, he doesn't really enjoy his work because he's constantly anxious that he may fail, and he imagines that others are conspiring to undermine or discredit him. In each case, the way my friend views himself and interprets what's going on around him determines whether he's happy or stressed out.

Thinking and feeling with a meditator's mind

In case you're worrying that meditation might stop you from thinking and feeling, here are a few helpful distinctions I picked up from one of my teachers, Jean Klein, author of a number of books, including *Who Am I?* and *The Ease of Being.*

Jean likes to distinguish between ordinary thought and creative thought; functional thought and psychological memory; and emotivity and emotion. (Although he teaches a direct approach to spiritual truth through self-inquiry rather than meditation, I've taken the liberty of applying his insights because I believe they're also relevant to the practice of meditation.)

✔ **Ordinary thought versus creative thought:** When your mind keeps churning out an endless series of thoughts linked together like boxcars on a train, with no spaces between them, you're trapped by your own claustrophobic thinking process and don't have any room for fresh, original thinking or problem solving. But when your mind is completely open and *unfurnished,* as Jean likes to say — a state of mind you can cultivate in meditation — you have plenty of inner space for creative thoughts to bubble up from their source in pure being.

Unlike ordinary thoughts, these thoughts are completely appropriate to the situation at hand.

✔ **Psychological memory versus functional thinking:** The more you meditate, the more you free your mind of *psychological memory,* which is the turbulent, obsessive, self-centered kind of thinking that's generated by your stories and centers on the separate, fragmented person you imagine yourself to be. Instead, your thoughts become primarily functional, arising in response to circumstances and then stopping when they're no longer required.

✔ **Emotivity versus emotion:** Likewise, the powerful, disturbing emotions that sometimes seem to run your life — which Jean Klein calls *emotivity* — are actually rooted in your stories, not in reality, and have little in common with true emotion. Subtler than emotivity and rooted in love, *true emotion* arises naturally from *being* itself in response to situations where the illusory sense of separation has been diminished or dissolved through the practice of meditation — or some other spiritual practice like self-inquiry.

As these examples indicate, it's the inner turbulence and confusion through which we filter and distort our experiences that causes most of our suffering and stress, not the experiences themselves. The good news is that meditation can teach you how to calm the troubled waters of your mind and heart, turn some of your inner claustrophobia into inner spaciousness, and find your way past your filters (or avoid them altogether) so you can experience life more directly — and reduce your stress in the process. But before I describe how meditation does that, I'd like to explain in some detail in the next section how suffering and stress occur in the first place.

The Bad News: How Your Mind Stresses You Out

Recently a friend of mine in her mid-30s decided to ask for a raise. Even though she'd worked with the company as a graphic designer for years and was long overdue for a pay increase, she was overcome with self-doubt. Every day as she drove to work, she would agonize and obsess as conflicting voices and feelings battled it out inside her.

In particular, she kept rehearsing her upcoming conversation with her boss and reviewing all the things she'd done to make her worthy of more money — the projects she'd completed, the successful ads and brochures she'd designed. Sometimes she would emerge from these imaginary conversations feeling triumphant; at other times she would emerge crestfallen and defeated. As she listened to all this mind chatter, her feelings fluctuated wildly, from excited and confident to afraid and uncertain.

At times, she could hear a barely audible voice (sounding suspiciously like her father's) arguing that given her overall ineptitude, she didn't deserve a raise and that she was lucky to have a job at all. In response, she would feel ashamed and hopeless.

Next, an angry, vindictive voice would step in, arguing that her boss was an ungrateful autocrat and she should barge into his office and put him in his place. Then a confident, affirmative voice would remind her how much she had contributed at work and what a fine person she was overall. Finally, a voice that sounded a lot like her mother's would counsel her to stay calm and unruffled and be thankful for whatever crumbs life sent her way.

After nearly a week of intense inner struggle and stress, during which she had difficulty sleeping and could barely function at work, my friend finally made an appointment with her boss. Filled with conflicting emotions, she entered his office — and was immediately offered a raise even larger than the one she had planned to request! As it turned out, all the images, emotions, and ideas her mind and body had churned out over the days leading up to the meeting had no connection with what ultimately happened.

Does any of this sound familiar? Like my friend — indeed, like just about everyone I know, including me! — you may spend much of your time engrossed in the captivating but ultimately illusory scenarios fabricated in the original "fantasy factory" (the one that predates Disney and LucasFilm) — that is, the *neocortex*.

One moment you may be worrying about the future — how am I going to make enough money, orchestrate a great vacation, impress my lover, amuse my kids — and you're lost in a reverie filled with hope and fear. The next moment, you may be obsessed with the past — why didn't I tell the truth, take that job, accept that proposal — and you're overcome with regret and self-recrimination.

And like my friend, you may have noticed, much to your chagrin, that you have remarkably little control over the worrying, fantasizing, and obsessing your mind generates. Instead of having thoughts and feelings, it may often seem that the thoughts and feelings are having you!

The reason these thoughts and feelings seem uncontrollable is that they spring from a deeper story or life script that may be largely unconscious. For example, you may hold the subliminal notion that nothing you do is quite good enough, so you push yourself anxiously to make up for your shortcomings. Or, quite the contrary, you may believe that you deserve more than you're getting, so you're unhappy with what you have. Perhaps you believe that you're inherently unattractive, so no matter how much you compensate, you feel embarrassed and uncomfortable around the opposite sex. Or maybe you see intimate relationships as inherently threatening, so you do all you can to avoid being vulnerable.

Your inner story or drama has a powerful momentum that carries you along, whether you're aware of it or not. Sometimes it may seem like a tragedy, complete with villains and victims. At other times, it may seem more like a comedy, a romance, a fantasy, or a boring documentary. The point is, you're the center around which this drama revolves, and you're often so enthralled by the scenery that you can't really see what's going on outside, in the real world around you.

As a result, you may be constantly acting and reacting excessively and inappropriately, based not on the actual circumstances but on the distorted pictures inside your brain. (If you're like me, you've no doubt had moments when you suddenly woke up, as though from a dream, and realized that you had no idea what the person you were interacting with really meant or felt.) Besides, you risk missing entirely the beauty and immediacy of the present moment as it unfolds.

As I mentioned earlier, it's this inner drama that causes most of your suffering and stress, not the experiences themselves. Not that life doesn't serve you up your share of difficult times and painful situations or that the homeless in American cities or the starving children in Bosnia don't really suffer. But the mind often adds an extra layer of unnecessary suffering to the undeniable hardships of life by interpreting experience in negative or limited ways. (See the sidebar "Distinguishing between suffering, pain, and stress" later in this chapter.) The following sections highlight some of the major ways your mind stresses you out.

Hearts and minds

When I talk about how the "mind" causes suffering and stress, I'm using the term generically to include emotions as well as thoughts — for the two are inseparable. Certain Eastern languages, such as Chinese and Sanskrit, even use the same word to refer to both mind and heart, and many Eastern sages teach that the mind actually resides in the heart center.

When you have a thought about potentially charged situations such as relationships, work, financial problems, or life transitions, you almost invariably have an emotional response — subliminal though it may be. In fact, the field of mind-body medicine has corroborated the view that the mind and body can't really be separated — thoughts give rise to chemical changes in the blood that affect metabolism and immunity, and alterations in blood chemistry, through drugs or environmental toxins or stressors, can change how you think and feel.

Similarly, the stories that run your life consist of complex layers of emotions, beliefs, and physical contraction that can't easily be teased apart. Through the practice of meditation, you can begin to peel back these layers, infuse them with awareness, and gain insight into the patterns that hold them together.

Preoccupation with past and future

Like most minds, yours may flit from past to future and back again — and only occasionally come to rest in the present. When you're preoccupied with what may happen next month or next year, you churn up a range of stressful emotions based on hope, fear, and anticipation that have nothing to do with what's happening right now. And when you're reliving the past — which after all has no existence except as thoughts and images inside your brain — you may bounce from regret to resentment to sadness and grief.

By contrast, when you meditate, you practice bringing your mind back again and again to the present moment, where, as the Persian poet Rumi says, "The only news is that there's no news at all." By returning to the simplicity of the here and now, you can take refuge from the stressful scenarios of your mind. (See the section "Returning to the present moment" later in this chapter.)

Resistance to the way things are

Most of us struggle unhappily to get what we believe we need in order to be happy, while ignoring or actively disliking what we already have. Now, don't get me wrong; I'm not suggesting that you just sit back passively and do nothing to improve your life. But as one of my teachers used to say, the secret to improving your life is first to accept things just the way they are — which is precisely what the practice of meditation can teach. In particular, resistance to the way things are usually comes in one of two flavors: resistance to change and resistance to pain.

Resistance to change

Like it or not, constant change is unavoidable. If you try to resist the current of change by holding on to some image of how things are supposed to be, you're going to suffer because you can't possibly get life to hold still and conform. As the Greek philosopher Heraclitus used to say, "You can't step into the same river twice."

Through meditation, you can discover how to flow with the current by developing an open, flexible, accepting mind. In fact, meditation provides the perfect laboratory for studying change because you get to sit quietly and notice the thoughts and feelings and sensations coming and going. Or you can stiffen up and resist and make the process more painful. Did you ever notice how some people become more crotchety and depressed as they age, while others age gracefully and with a joyful twinkle in their eyes? The difference lies in their ability to adapt to the challenging changes life brings their way.

Resistance to pain

Like change, pain is inevitable — but so, of course, is pleasure. In fact, you can't have one without the other, though most of us would love to have it some other way. When you tighten your belly and hold your breath against the onslaught of pain, be it emotional or physical, you actually intensify it. And when you affix a story to the pain — for example, this shouldn't be happening to me, or I must have done something to deserve this — you just Velcro an extra layer of suffering on top of the pain, which causes your body to tighten and resist even more and only serves to perpetuate the pain rather than relieve it. Through meditation, you can learn to breathe deeply, soften your belly, cut through your story, and relax around your pain. (To discover how to soften your belly, see Chapter 10.) Often, the pain will naturally let go and release — and even when it doesn't, it generally becomes much easier to bear.

Judging and comparing mind

The tendency of your mind to compare you to others (or to some impossible ideal) and to judge every little thing you do as imperfect or inadequate just keeps you anxious, frustrated, and upset. Generally, this tendency originates in your stories or life script, a deeply held cluster of often negative beliefs. (See the bullet "Negative beliefs and life scripts" earlier in this chapter.) After all, if you believe that you're lovable and inherently perfect just the way you are, your mind has nothing to compare you with. When you practice meditation, you can develop the capacity to observe the judgments and comparisons of your mind without identifying with them or mistaking them for truth. (For more on this capacity, see the section "Penetrating your experience with insight" later in this chapter.)

Learned helplessness and pessimism

As numerous psychological studies suggest, your ability to deal with stressful situations largely depends on whether you believe you have the resources necessary to cope. That's right — the *belief* that you have what it takes is perhaps your greatest resource. If your story keeps telling you that you're inadequate, it's just making stressful situations more stressful.

Meditation can teach you coping skills such as focusing and calming your mind; returning to the present moment; and cultivating positive emotions and mind-states that help you avoid negative, distracting thoughts and empower you to deal with difficult circumstances and people. (Refer to the section "The Good News: How Meditation Relieves Stress" later in this chapter.) Ultimately, you can discover how to see beyond your story and make direct contact with the true source of optimism and joy, the wellspring of pure being inside you.

Overwhelming emotions

Although you can't necessarily identify your story, you may be painfully aware of how powerful emotions like anger, fear, longing, grief, jealousy, and desire cloud your mind, torment your heart, and cause you to act in ways you later regret. Initially, meditation won't get rid of these emotions, but it will teach you how to focus and calm your mind and prevent them from distracting you. If you wish, you can then use meditation to help you observe these emotions as they arise without avoiding or suppressing them. Over time, you can develop penetrating insight into the nature of these emotions and their connection to the underlying stories that keep generating them — and ultimately you can investigate these stories and even dismantle them entirely. (For more on meditating with challenging emotions, see Chapter 11.)

Distinguishing between suffering, pain, and stress

Yikes! Who wants to burden their brain with such an unappetizing topic? Yet, the clearer you are about suffering and stress, the more easily you can minimize their impact on your life. With this in mind, you may want to consider the following helpful (and admittedly unofficial) distinctions:

✔ *Pain* consists of direct, visceral experiences with a minimum of conceptual overlays. Your best friend says something mean to you, and you feel a painful constriction in your heart. You hit your thumb with a hammer, and it aches and throbs. You get the flu, and your head feels like someone's squeezing it in a vice. Pain hurts, pure and simple.

✔ *Suffering,* by contrast, is what happens when your mind makes hay with your pain. For example, you decide that because she hurt your feelings, she must secretly hate you, which means that there's something terribly wrong with you . . . and the next thing you know, you're feeling depressed as well as hurt. Or you turn your headache into a sure warning signal of some serious illness, which just heaps a big dose of fear and hopelessness onto an already difficult situation. Suffering, in other words, results from seeing situations through the distorting lens of the story your mind tells you.

✔ The *stress* response is a physiological mechanism for adapting to challenging physical or psychological circumstances. Certain physical stressors, such as extraordinary heat or cold, an extremely loud noise, or a violent attack, will be stressful no matter how your mind interprets them. But the stressful effect of most stressors depends on the spin your mind adds to the situation.

For example, driving to work in heavy traffic, sitting at your desk for eight hours handling paperwork and phone calls, and then driving home may be only mildly stressful on a purely physical level — believe it or not.

But when you're afraid of arriving late, have a conflicted relationship with your boss, feel angry at several of your clients or coworkers, and are still mulling over the argument you had with your spouse or best friend, no wonder you crawl home at the end of the day completely exhausted. Just as your mind can transform pain into suffering, so it can parlay ordinary stressors into extraordinary stress.

Fixation of attention

The tendency of the thinking mind to obsess or fixate on certain thoughts and emotions causes the body to contract in response. Have you ever noticed how tense and anxious you can get when you mentally rehearse the same scenario again and again, even when it's an ostensibly positive one?

By contrast, an alert, open, fluid mind — which you can develop through the regular practice of mindfulness meditation (see Chapter 6) — allows you to flow from experience to experience without getting fixated or stuck. Ultimately, you can practice receptive awareness (see Chapter 1), the spacious, skylike quality of mind that welcomes whatever arises.

Clinging to a separate self

The great meditative traditions teach that the root cause of suffering and stress, which gives rise to your stories, is the belief that you're inherently separate — from others, from the rest of life, and from being itself. Because you feel separate and alone, you need to protect yourself and ensure your survival at all costs. But you have only limited power, and you're surrounded by forces beyond your control. As long as you keep struggling to defend your turf, you're going to keep suffering, no matter how hard you try. Meditation offers you the opportunity to relax your guard, open your awareness, and ultimately catch a glimpse of who you really are, beyond your stories and the illusion of a separate, isolated self.

The Good News: How Meditation Relieves Suffering and Stress

Now for the good news! In case you found all the talk earlier in this chapter depressing, let me reassure you: Your story or drama may masquerade as who you really are — but it's not. Your essential being remains pure and unharmed, no matter how elaborate and compelling your story becomes. Besides, as stubborn and intractable as they may seem, your mind and heart are actually malleable. Through the regular practice of meditation, you can reduce your suffering and stress by stilling and ultimately dissipating the turbulence and confusion inside you. As one ancient Zen master put it, "If your mind isn't clouded by unnecessary things, this moment is the best moment of your life."

To begin with, you can develop the skill of *focusing and concentrating* your mind, which calms it and prevents it from becoming agitated. As your concentration deepens, thoughts and feelings that have been building up inside naturally bubble up and evaporate — a process I like to call *spontaneous release.* Once you've developed strong concentration, you can expand your awareness to include thoughts, feelings, and the deeper patterns and stories that underlie them. Then through the power of *penetrating insight,* you can explore the various layers of inner experience, get to know how they function, and ultimately use this understanding to dismantle the patterns that keep causing you stress.

Developing focus and concentration

So your mind chatters constantly, swirling you up and stressing you out, and you're wondering what you can do to quiet it down. Well, you can begin by practicing a meditation technique that emphasizes concentration, such as following or counting your breaths (see Chapter 6) or reciting a mantra (see Chapter 3). Once you get the knack, you can keep shifting from your inner dialogue to the present moment, wherever you happen to be. And if you're so inclined, you can develop positive qualities that counteract some of the negative tendencies of your mind and heart.

Stabilizing your concentration

If you've ever tried to quiet your mind by preventing it from thinking, you know how hopeless that can be. (See the sidebar "Stop your mind" at the end of this chapter.) But the more you invest your mental energy in a single focus during meditation, the more one-pointed your mind becomes, and the more the distractions recede to the background. Eventually, you can develop the ability to stabilize your concentration on a single focus for minutes at a time, gently returning when your mind wanders off.

With increased one-pointedness comes an experience of inner harmony and stillness, as the sediment in the turbulent lake of your mind gradually settles down, leaving the water clean and clear. This experience is generally accompanied by feelings of calm and relaxation — and occasionally by other pleasurable feelings like love, joy, happiness, and bliss (which incidentally originate at the bottom of the lake, in pure being).

At deeper levels of concentration, you may experience total absorption in the object — a state known as *samadhi*. When this power of focused concentration is directed like a laser beam to everyday activities, you can enter what psychologist Mihaly Csikszentmihalyi calls *flow* — a state of supreme enjoyment in which time stops, self-consciousness drops away, and you become one with the activity itself.

Returning to the present moment

Once you've begun to develop your concentration, you can use it to keep shifting in everyday life away from your inner drama and back to the present moment. You may not eliminate the turbulence, but you can keep seeing beyond it. It's kind of like taking off your sunglasses and looking at things directly — or like opening your eyes wide when you start falling asleep. The more you look past the drama, the more you see the freshness of being itself reflected in what you see. Returning to the present moment again and again forges a trail that allows you to do an end run around your drama and strengthens your direct connection with life. (For more on returning to the present moment, see Chapters 6 and 15.)

Cultivating positive emotions and mind-states

You can also use the concentration you develop to cultivate positive alternatives to agitation, fear, anger, depression, and the other powerful emotions
that arise when you're involved in your story. (In fact, the practice of
cultivation itself can develop your powers of concentration.) These positive
mind-states include lovingkindness, compassion, equanimity, and joy. (For
more on cultivating positive emotions, see Chapter 10.)

Allowing spontaneous release

When you meditate regularly, you start to notice that thoughts and feelings
that have accumulated inside you naturally dissipate like mist rising from
the surface of a lake. You don't have to do anything special to make this
happen — it just occurs naturally as your concentration deepens and your
mind settles down. You may sit to meditate feeling weighted down by
worries or concerns and then get up half an hour later feeling somehow
lighter, more spacious, and more worry-free. Who knows how this mysterious process happens? You might say that meditating is like lifting the lid on
a boiling pot of soup — you create space for the water to evaporate and
relieve the pressure that has been building up inside.

To encourage this process, you can practice meditation techniques that
involve receptive awareness — open, spacious awareness that welcomes
whatever arises. (You'll need to develop your concentration first.) When
your mind's not fixated on a particular object — be it a thought or a memory
or an emotion — but expansive and unattached like the sky, you're no longer
investing energy in your drama, but rather inviting whatever's churning
inside you to unfold and let go.

Penetrating your experience with insight

So far, I've been highlighting concentration and awareness techniques that
teach you how to circumvent your drama, develop alternatives to your
drama, or still your mind so that your drama doesn't disturb you. The
problem is, these techniques still leave your inner stories more or less in
tact, and when your concentration weakens or your lovingkindness wanes,
the same old distracting thoughts and troubling emotions come back to
stress you out!

Through the practice of penetrating insight, you can get to know your
drama, gain an understanding of how it causes suffering, see beyond it —
and eventually free yourself from it entirely.

Put the story down and move on

Two Zen monks were walking along a country road when they came to a stream swollen to a raging torrent by the heavy spring rains. There they found an attractive young woman waiting on the shore, unable to cross.

One of the monks approached the woman and offered to help her. With her consent, he lifted her in his arms and carried her across the stream. Then the two monks continued on their way in silence.

When they got back to the monastery, the monk who had watched his friend carry the woman could not contain himself any longer. "You know we're not supposed to have any contact with females, especially attractive ones. How could you possibly do that?"

"Ah," said the other monk, "I put the woman down hours ago, but you're still carrying her with you."

Becoming aware of your inner experience

When you sit quietly for 10 or 15 minutes and notice your thoughts and feelings, you're making a radical shift in your relationship to your inner experience. (For more on observing thoughts and feelings, see Chapter 11.) Instead of being swept away by the current, you become, for the moment, an observer on the shore, watching the river of your experience flow by. Though the difference may seem inconsequential and you may not feel that you're making any headway, you've actually begun to loosen your story's stranglehold on your life. Gradually, you begin to notice spaces in your mind's chatter, and what once seemed so serious and solid slowly becomes lighter and infused with fresh air. You may find yourself laughing at your tendency to worry and obsess, or perhaps you pause and notice what you're feeling before you react.

As you practice welcoming your experience just as it is, including your judgments and self-criticisms, you may also discover that your attitude toward yourself begins to change in subtle ways. Instead of impatience or contempt, you may begin to notice a certain self-acceptance creeping in as you become more familiar with the repetitive patterns of your mind. Hey, you may even develop a measure of compassion for yourself as you see how self-critical or distracted or frightened you can become.

Becoming aware of your story and how it confuses you

When you meditate regularly and observe your thoughts and feelings, you begin to notice recurring themes and story lines that keep playing in your mind. Perhaps you become aware of the tendency to obsess about all the times people misunderstood you or failed to give you the love you wanted. Maybe you watch yourself comparing yourself to other people and judging yourself better — or worse. Possibly you find yourself fantasizing about the ideal mate, even though you've been happily married for years. Or you may notice that you're constantly planning for the future while ignoring what's happening right here and now.

Whatever your particular patterns may be, you can observe how they keep arising to disturb you and pull you away from the reality at hand — which may be some simple task, like following your breath or reciting your mantra. Gradually, you realize that your story is just that — a story your mind keeps spinning that separates you from others and causes you pain. As John Lennon put it, "Life is what's happening while you're busy making other plans." When you start seeing your story for what it is, you don't allow it to confuse you in the same way anymore.

Changing your story

As you may notice after you meditate for a while, just being aware of your story can begin changing it in subtle (or even not so subtle!) ways. Once you develop a certain distance from your story — knowing at some level that it's just your story, not who you really are — you naturally become less reactive, people respond to you differently, and circumstances shift accordingly. Soon your life is just not the same old story anymore!

Of course, you may already be struggling to change your life by manipulating circumstances or reprogramming your mind with affirmations or positive thinking. But first you have to bring the power of penetrating insight to bear on your habitual patterns and stories; otherwise, healthier perspectives and patterns can't take root, and you just keep running in the same old grooves.

Seeing beyond your story to who you really are

Even though you may become aware of your story, gain some distance from it, and begin to alter it in certain fundamental ways, you may still identify with it until you can catch a glimpse of who you really are, beyond your story.

Such glimpses can take a number of different forms. Perhaps you have unexpected moments of peace or tranquillity, when your thoughts settle down — or even stop entirely — and a sweet silence permeates your mind. Or you may experience a flood of unconditional love that momentarily opens your heart wide and gives you a brief glimpse of the oneness beyond all apparent separation. Or maybe you have a sudden intuition of your inherent interconnectedness with all beings or a sense of being in the presence of something far vaster than yourself. Whatever the insight that lifts you beyond your story, it can irrevocably alter who you take yourself to be. Never again can you fully believe that you're merely the limited personality your mind insists you are.

I can still remember how fresh and clear everything appeared after my first meditation retreat — the colors so vivid, people's faces so radiant — even though I'd spent five days doing nothing but struggle to count my breaths from one to ten without losing my way. I felt as though a bandage had been ripped from my eyes and I could see things clearly for the first time. Everything I encountered seemed to radiate *being,* and I knew as never before that I belonged on this Earth. Of course, the intensity faded after a few days, but I never forgot that first glimpse of *clear seeing,* free from the perceptual filters I'd been carrying around for a lifetime.

Freeing yourself from your story

Once you've caught a glimpse of who you really are, beyond your mind (and even your body), you can keep reconnecting with this deeper level of *being* in your meditations — and in your everyday life as well. To resurrect the metaphor of the lake, you can dive down to the bottom again and again because you know what it looks like and how to find it. (Most approaches to meditation offer the possibility of such a glimpse. For more specific instructions, see Chapter 13.)

Even though your story may continue to play on the video screen of your brain, you can develop the capacity to disengage from it — or even disidentify from it entirely. As a friend of mine put it, you come to realize that the personality is a case of mistaken identity — and that who you are is the vast expanse of being itself, in which your personal thoughts and feelings arise and pass away.

Such a profound realization may take years of meditation to achieve, yet it's always available to you, no matter how long you've meditated — indeed, whether you've ever meditated at all! Many people report laughing uproariously when they finally see that their true nature was right there all along, as plain as the proverbial nose on their face.

Contrary to popular belief, people who learn to integrate this realization and live their understanding in a moment-to-moment way don't become more detached and disengaged from life. Rather, because their story and their sense of separation have lifted like a fog, they actually perceive situations and people with more immediacy and compassion, and they are able to act more appropriately, according to circumstances.

Stopping your mind

Impossible though this task may seem, you can at least attempt to stop your mind and see what happens. Try the following exercise:

1. **Sit quietly and take a few slow, deep breaths.**

2. **For the next five minutes, try to stop thinking.**

   That's right — do whatever you can to keep your mind from generating more thoughts. Try humming to yourself or concentrating on your big toe or recalling a beautiful day in nature. Or just try being as still as you possibly can. Do whatever you think will work for you.

3. **At the end of five minutes, reflect on your experience.**

   How successful were you? Could you actually stop thinking for an extended period of time? Did you find that the struggle to stop thinking just generated more thoughts? This exercise reveals how stubborn and tenacious your thinking mind can be — in case you hadn't noticed.

Part II
Getting Started

"Okay, your posture's very good. Now relax, concentrate, and slowly let go of your cell phone."

In this part . . .

1 lead you (gently) step by step through the process of learning how to meditate. First you experiment with turning your mind inward and developing concentration. Then you explore the practice of mindfulness, which means paying attention to whatever you're experiencing. By the end of this part, you know all the little tricks that make meditation easy and fun, from how to sit still and follow your breath and where and when to meditate to what kind of gear you need and how to use it. If you follow these instructions, you'll be a savvy meditator in no time.

Chapter 6

Meditation 101: Relaxing Your Body and Calming Your Mind

*I*f you're looking for simple, concise meditation instructions, you've come to the right chapter. You can muse forever about meditation's benefits or the nature of the mind, but there's nothing quite like attempting to practice to show you how stubborn and wild the mind can actually be.

As I mention in Chapter 5, the Buddhists like to compare the mind to a monkey that swings uncontrollably from branch to branch — from plan to memory, thought to emotion, sight to sound — without ever settling down in one place. Some contemporary teachers prefer the more domestic analogy of the wayward puppy that keeps wandering impulsively from one place to another, blithely peeing on the carpet wherever it goes. You know what it's like trying to train a puppy — you can't overpower it or subdue it or sit on it until it agrees to obey. Well, the same holds true for your mind. In fact, if you attempt to force your mind to calm down, you just swirl it up even more and end up going nowhere fast, like a puppy chasing its tail!

Instead, the practice of meditation involves gently returning your mind again and again to a simple focus of attention. In this chapter, you have an opportunity to find out how to meditate on your breath — one of the most popular forms of meditation throughout the world's spiritual traditions. You also discover mindfulness techniques for "training your puppy," balancing relaxation and alertness, and extending your meditation to include the full range of sensate experiences.

Paradoxically, the mundane, repetitive, seemingly inconsequential activity of attending to your breath can eventually lead to all the glamorous benefits meditation promises to provide, including reduced stress, enhanced performance, increased appreciation and enjoyment of life, deeper connection with your essential being — even advanced meditative states, such as unconditional love or transformative insights into the nature of existence. But before you get carried away counting your cookies (or your puppy biscuits, as the case may be), you need to take the first step toward the cookie jar.

Turning Your Attention Inward

As the old saying goes, a journey of a thousand miles begins with a single step. In the case of meditation, this simple but essential step involves turning your mind away from its usual preoccupation with external events — or, just as often, with the story it tells you about external events — and toward your inner sensate experience.

If you're like most people, you're so caught up with what's happening around you — the look in other people's eyes, the voices of family and coworkers, the latest news on the radio, the messages appearing on your computer screen — that you forget to pay attention to what's happening in your own mind, body, and heart. In fact, popular culture has been designed to seduce you into searching outside yourself for happiness and satisfaction. In such a confusing and compelling world, even the most rudimentary gesture of self-awareness can seem like a challenge of monumental proportions.

Just take a few minutes right now to turn your mind around and pay attention to what you're sensing and feeling. Notice how much resistance you have to shifting your awareness from your external focus to your simple sensate experience. Notice how busily your mind flits from thought to thought and image to image, weaving a story with you as the central character.

Because these habitual patterns are so deeply rooted, it can take tremendous courage and patience to do something as seemingly innocuous as returning your attention again and again to a basic internal focus like your breath. You may be afraid of what you'll discover if you venture into essentially unknown terrain — or afraid of what you'll miss if you turn inward even for a few moments. But this shift from outer to inner is precisely the simple but radical gesture that meditation requires.

Although I talk about turning inward, the shift I'm suggesting actually has several related dimensions:

✔ **Content to process:** Instead of becoming engrossed in the meaning of what you're sensing or thinking or feeling, you can shift your interest and attention to *how* experiencing occurs — or to the mere fact of experience itself. For example, instead of getting lost in thinking or daydreaming, you can notice how your mind flits from thought to thought — or merely observe that you're thinking. Instead of becoming transfixed by your fear, you can notice how the waves of tension move through your belly — or simply note that you're feeling.

✔ **Outer to inner:** Initially, you need to balance your usual tendency to be so outer-directed by paying particular attention to inner experience. Eventually, you'll be able to bring the same quality of awareness to every experience, whether inner or outer.

✔ **Secondhand to direct:** Even more helpful than inner and outer is the distinction between secondhand experience and direct experience. Secondhand experience has been filtered and distorted by the mind, whereas direct experience is mediated through the senses or some other form of direct awareness. In addition to turning inward, meditation involves turning your attention away from the story your mind spins about your experience and toward the direct experience itself.

✔ **Doing to being:** You spend virtually all your waking hours rushing from one task or project or activity to another. Do you remember what it's like to just *be,* the way you did when you were a baby or a little child, whiling away a summer afternoon just playing or lying in the grass? Meditation gives you the opportunity to make this crucial shift from doing to being.

Relaxing Your Body

As the emerging field of mind-body medicine reminds us — and yogis and sages have been telling us for millennia — your body, your mind, and your heart form one seamless and inseparable whole. When your thoughts keep leaping like the proverbial monkey from worry to worry, your body responds by tightening and tensing, especially in certain key places like the throat, the heart, the solar plexus, and the belly. When the discomfort gets intense enough, you register it as an emotion — fear, perhaps, or anger or sadness.

Because it connects you with your direct experience — and ultimately with a realm of pure being beyond the mind — meditation naturally relaxes your body while it focuses your mind. As a beginner, though, you may not experience this natural relaxation for days or even weeks. So it can be helpful to practice one of the techniques in the following list before you meditate, especially if you tend to be noticeably tense. (If you're one of those rare people who are generally so relaxed that you tend to drift off to sleep at the slightest provocation, you may want to skip this exercise.) Of course, relaxing your body has its own wonderful benefits — but your body won't stay relaxed until you are able to work with your mind.

If you've never deliberately relaxed your body before, start with the meditation in the sidebar "Deep relaxation." Because it takes at least 15 minutes to complete, you probably won't do it each time you meditate, but it does teach you how to relax your body part by part. Once you've practiced this exercise a few times, your body will have a memory of what it's like to be deeply relaxed, and you can then advance to one of the five-minute relaxations listed here. By the way, deep relaxation is a great antidote for insomnia — just practice it in bed and then drift off to sleep!

- ✔ **Shower of relaxation:** Imagine taking a warm shower. As the water cascades across your body and down your legs, it carries with it all discomfort and distress, leaving you refreshed and invigorated.

- ✔ **Honey treatment:** Imagine a mound of warm honey perched on the crown of your head. As it melts, it runs down your face and head and neck, covering your shoulders and chest and arms and gradually enveloping your whole body down to your toes. Feel the sensuous wave of warm liquid draining away all tension and stress and leaving you thoroughly relaxed and renewed.

- ✔ **Peaceful place:** Imagine a safe, protected, peaceful place — perhaps a forest, a meadow, or a sandy beach. Experience the place fully with all your senses. Notice how calm and relaxed you feel here; now, allow that feeling to permeate every cell of your body.

- ✔ **Body scan:** Beginning with the crown of your head, scan your body from top to bottom. When you come to an area of tension or discomfort, gently allow it to open and soften; then move on.

- ✔ **Relaxation response:** Choose a word or brief phrase that has deep spiritual or personal significance for you. Now close your eyes and repeat this sound softly, again and again. (For more detailed instructions on practicing the Relaxation Response, see Chapter 18.)

MEDITATION

Deep relaxation

Here's a meditation you can do any time that you have 15 or 20 minutes to spare and want to shed some of the tension you've accumulated in your busy life. It's also a great way to prepare for the other meditations in this book because it leaves you feeling relaxed, refreshed, and in touch with yourself.

1. **Find a comfortable place to lie down.**

   Take off your shoes, loosen your belt and other tight clothing, and stretch out on your back with your arms resting at your sides, legs slightly apart.

2. **Sense your body as a whole, including the places where it contacts the surface of the bed or floor.**

3. **Close your eyes and bring your awareness to your feet. Wiggle your toes, flex your feet, and then let go of all tension as much as you can, allowing your feet to melt into the floor.**

4. **Shift your awareness to your lower legs, thighs, and hips. Imagine them becoming heavy and relaxed and melting into the floor.**

   If the image of melting doesn't appeal to you, you might try dissolving or sinking or disappearing.

5. **Bring your awareness to your lower abdomen. Imagine all tension draining away, your breath deepening, and your belly opening and softening.**

6. **Bring your awareness to your upper abdomen, chest, neck, and throat, feeling the areas opening and softening.**

7. **Bring your awareness to your shoulders, upper arms, lower arms, and hands. Imagine them becoming heavy and relaxed and melting into the floor.**

8. **Bring your awareness to your head and face. Feel the tension melting away from your face across your head and into the floor.**

9. **Scan your body from head to toe, searching for any remaining areas of tension or discomfort.**

   If you find any, just imagine them relaxing completely.

10. **Experience your body as one field of relaxation, without parts or edges.**

11. **Continue to rest in this way for five or ten minutes more; then very slowly begin to wiggle your fingers and toes, stretch your arms and legs, open your eyes, and gradually come up to a sitting position.**

Check in with yourself and notice how you feel. Do you feel more relaxed? Does your body feel lighter or more expanded? Does the world appear different in any way? Now gently get up and go about your day.

Developing Mindfulness: Awareness of the Here and Now

This chapter highlights an approach to meditation known as *mindfulness* — moment to moment awareness of your experience as it unfolds. Mindfulness combines concentration, or highly focused awareness, and a more receptive awareness that simply welcomes whatever arises. Because mindfulness grows like a house on a foundation of concentration, you'll need to strengthen and stabilize your concentration before you can proceed to the full practice of mindfulness. That's why the initial meditations provided here emphasize focusing on a particular object of concentration — your breath.

Ultimately, the goal of mindfulness meditation is to develop the capacity to be fully present for whatever is occurring right here and now. Once you've stabilized your concentration by focusing on your breath, you can expand your awareness to include the full range of bodily sensations — and eventually you can just welcome whatever presents itself in your field of experience. Though supremely simple, this advanced technique can take years of patient practice to master, but you may have glimpses of a more expanded awareness after only a few weeks of regular meditation.

Letting go of your expectations

When you invest in the stock market or work out at a gym, you expect results — and you keep checking the quotes or the scale to tell you how well you're doing. If you bring the same attitude to meditation, however, you're defeating the purpose — which is to let go of your thoughts altogether and just be present in the here and now. It's one of the great paradoxes of meditation that you can't reap the benefits until you drop all your expectations and accept things the way they are. Then the benefits come back to you a thousandfold.

In the beginning, of course, you're going to keep wondering whether you're doing it right. But don't worry, there's no wrong way to meditate — except perhaps sitting and trying to measure how well you're doing! One day you may feel like you're on top of the world — you're full of energy, your mind is clear, and you can follow your breath with relative ease. "Wow, now I'm getting the hang of it," you think. The next day you're so overwhelmed by thoughts or emotions that you sit for 20 minutes without even noticing your breath. Welcome to the practice of meditation! The point is not to do it right, but just to do it — again and again.

One of my Zen teachers used to compare meditation to walking in the fog on a warm summer day; though you may not pay attention to what's happening, pretty soon you're drenched in dew.

SPIRITUAL STUFF

The meaning of the breath

Traditional cultures identified the breath with the life force that animates all things. For example, the Latin word *spiritus* (the root of both "spirited" and "spiritual"), the Greek word *anima* (from which we derive the word "animated"), the Hebrew word *ruach,* and the Sanskrit word *brahman* may sound quite different, but they have one thing in common — they all mean both breath and spirit or soul. When you follow your breath with awareness, you're not only harmonizing your body and mind, which gives you a sense of inner harmony and wholeness, you're also exploring the living frontier where body, mind, and spirit meet — and attuning yourself to a spiritual dimension of being.

Focusing on your breath

Compared to surfing the Net or catching a movie on HBO, watching your breath may seem like a boring way to spend your spare time. The fact is, the media have conditioned us to be stimulation junkies by flooding our senses with computerized images and synthesized sounds that change at laserlike speed. Recently, I heard the head of an ad agency brag about how his latest TV spot bombarded the viewer with six images per second — far faster than the conscious mind could possibly register them.

By contrast, paying attention to the coming and going of your breath slows your mind down to match the speed and rhythms of your body. Instead of 6 images per second, you breathe an average of 12 to 16 times per minute. And the sensations are far subtler than anything you'll see or hear on TV — more like the sights and sounds of nature, which is, after all, where you and your body came from.

Besides, the great thing about your breath as a focus of meditation is that it's always available, always changing yet always more or less the same. If your breath were totally different each time, it wouldn't provide the stability necessary for you to cultivate concentration; if it never changed in any way, you'd quickly fall asleep and never have an opportunity to develop the curiosity and alertness that are so essential to the practice of mindfulness.

As a preliminary to the practice of following your breath, you may want to spend a few weeks or months just counting your breaths. It's a great way to build concentration — and it provides a preestablished structure that constantly reminds you when you're wandering off. If you were a neophyte

Zen student, you might spend years counting your breaths before you graduated to a more challenging practice. But if you're feeling adventurous or already have some confidence in your concentration, by all means start with following your breath. Trust your intuition to tell you which method is right for you.

Counting your breaths

Begin by finding a comfortable sitting position that you can hold for 10 or 15 minutes. (For a complete discussion of sitting posture in meditation, including diagrams, see Chapter 7.) Then take a few deep breaths and exhale slowly. Without trying to control your breath in any way, allow it to find its own natural depth and rhythm. Always breathe through your nose unless you can't for some reason.

Now, begin counting each inhalation and exhalation until you reach ten; then return to one. In other words, when you inhale, count "one," when you exhale, count "two," when you inhale again, count "three," and so on up to ten. If you lose track, return to one and start again.

Getting to know your breathing

When you first begin paying deliberate attention to your breath, you may be surprised and somewhat frustrated to discover that your body tenses up and your breathing becomes stiff, labored, and unnatural. Suddenly, you can't remember how to breathe anymore, even though you've been doing it just fine ever since your first breath at birth.

Don't worry — you're not doing it wrong. You just need to develop a lighter, gentler touch with your awareness so that you're following but not controlling your breath. It's kind of like learning to ride a bicycle — you keep falling off until one day, miraculously, you just keep going. From then on, it's second nature.

You may find it helpful to begin by exploring your breathing, without necessarily trying to track it from breath to breath. Begin by noticing what happens when you breathe — how your rib cage rises and falls, how your belly moves, how the air passes in and out of your nostrils. You may find that some breaths are longer and deeper, while others are shorter and shallower. Some may go all the way down into your belly, while others barely reach the upper part of your lungs before exiting again. Some may be rough or strong, others smooth or weak.

Spend five or ten minutes exploring your breathing with the fresh curiosity of a child encountering a flower or a butterfly for the first time. What did you discover that you didn't know before? How does each new breath differ from the last? Once you feel comfortable with your breath, you can begin the practice of counting or following your breaths.

Minding your body instead of your breath

Some people seem to find it virtually impossible to count or follow their breaths. Instead, they find it helpful to focus on their body as a whole when they meditate. You can begin by drawing your awareness slowly down through your body from your head to your feet; then switch to holding your whole body in your awareness at once. When your mind wanders off, just come back to your body. Or you can use the Zen approach of focusing on a particular part of the body, like the lower back or lower abdomen. Once you find a focus that works for you, however, stick with it. The point is to develop your mindfulness, not to meander through your body in search of a place to meditate.

To help concentrate, you may find it useful to extend the number in your mind for the full duration of the inhalation or exhalation, instead of thinking the number quickly once and then dropping it. For example, allow "o-o-o-n-n-n-e" to last as long as the inhalation, "t-w-o-o-o-o" to last as long as the exhalation, and so on. You may also find it helpful to subvocalize the numbers, especially at first, saying "one" ever so softly to yourself as you inhale, "two" as you exhale, and so on.

As Mickey Mouse as this exercise may seem at first-read, you may be surprised to discover that you never manage to reach ten without losing count. You don't have to stop your mind chatter in any way. But if you get distracted by your thoughts and lose track of your breath, come back to one and start again.

When you get the knack of counting each in-breath and out-breath — say, after a month or two of regular practice — you can shift to counting only the exhalations. If your mind starts wandering on the inhalations, though, just go back to the first method until you feel ready to move on again. Eventually, you may want to simplify the practice even further by simply noting "in" on the inhalation and "out" on the exhalation.

Following your breaths

Begin by sitting and breathing exactly as you did for counting your breaths. Once you feel settled, allow your attention to focus either on the sensation of your breath coming and going through your nostrils or on the rising and falling of your belly as you breathe. (Although you're welcome to alternate your focus from one session to the next, it's best to stick with a single focus for the entire meditation — and eventually you're better off using the same focus each time you meditate.)

Give your full attention to the coming and going of your breath the way a mother tracks the movements of her young child — lovingly yet persistently, softly yet precisely, with relaxed yet focused awareness. When you realize that your mind has wandered off and you're engrossed in planning or thinking or daydreaming, gently but firmly bring it back to your breath.

At the end of your exhalation (and before you inhale again), there's often a gap or a pause when your breath is no longer perceptible. At this point, you can allow your attention to rest on a predetermined touchpoint, such as your navel or your hands, before returning to your breath when it resumes.

Thoughts and images will definitely continue to skitter and swirl through your mind as you meditate, but don't worry. Just patiently and persistently keep coming back to your breath. Gradually, you may even develop a fascination with all the little sensations — of your belly and ribcage shifting and opening and changing shape as you breathe or of your breath caressing the tip of your nose, tickling your nostrils, and cooling your nasal passages as it enters and leaves. You may also notice that your mind tends to quiet down or your thinking tends to change on either the exhalation or the inhalation. By attuning to a subtler level of experience while you meditate, you can open yourself to a subtler appreciation of each moment of life as it unfolds.

Expanding to sensations

Once you've developed a certain ease in following your breath, you can expand your awareness as you meditate to include the full range of sensations both inside and outside your body — feeling, smelling, hearing, seeing. Imagine that your awareness is like the zoom lens on a camera. Until now, you've been focused exclusively on your breath; now you can back away slightly to include the field of sensations that surrounds your breath.

Keep it simple

The point of meditation is not to discover some cool techniques to occupy your leisure hours; it's to make the simple but momentous shift from doing to being. Don't make the mistake of turning your meditation practice into another urgent item on your list of things to do. Use it, instead, as a welcome oasis from doing, an opportunity to *be,* without strategy or agenda. In other words, keep it simple. Play with a few of the techniques at first to decide which one feels right for you; then stick with the one you've chosen. It really doesn't matter which method you use — they all end up depositing you in the here and now.

Just sitting

As an alternative to mindfulness meditation, you may want to experiment with the Zen practice known as *just sitting,* which usually involves two phases or steps: just breathing and just sitting.

Once you're adept at following your breath, you can practice *becoming your breath.* That's right, I said become your breath — merge yourself completely with the flow of the inhalation and exhalation, until you as a separate observer disappear and only your breath remains. Now you're no longer breathing; instead, your breath is breathing you. Like welcoming whatever arises, this practice,

known as *just breathing,* is supremely simple but requires tremendous concentration.

The next step, *just sitting,* involves expanding to include the whole realm of sensate experience. But instead of being aware or mindful of your experience, you "disappear," and only your experience remains — seeing, smelling, hearing, sensing, thinking. As a Zen friend of mine put it, "When you sit, the walls of the meditation hall come down, and the whole world enters." Ultimately, this practice takes you to the same place as mindfulness; it's simply the Zen alternative.

If you find it difficult to expand your awareness all at once, you can begin by exploring a sensation when it calls attention to itself. For example, you're following your breath when a pain in your back cries out for your attention. Instead of staying focused on your breath as you would have done before, you can turn your attention to the pain and explore it fully until it no longer predominates in your field of experience. Then come back to your breath until you're once again called away.

You can also experiment with expanding your awareness to include one particular kind of sensation, such as bodily feelings or sounds. For example, you can spend an entire meditation just listening to the sounds around you, without focusing on any sounds in particular. In this way, you are able to balance the highly concentrated awareness required to follow your breath with the more receptive, all-inclusive awareness necessary to welcome a broad range of sensations. This blend of focus and receptivity lies at the heart of the practice of mindfulness.

As you get the knack of including sensations in your meditations, you can experiment with expanding your awareness to include the full sensate field. Begin by following your breathing and then just open your lens wide, allowing sensations to arise and pass away in your awareness.

Welcoming whatever arises

Once you become accustomed to including sensations, you can open your awareness gates wide and welcome any and every experience, even thoughts and emotions, without judgment or discrimination. Just like sensations, thoughts and feelings come and go in your awareness like clouds in the sky without pulling you off center.

After all, the sky is never disturbed or constricted, no matter how many clouds pile up; it continues to be as vast and spacious as ever. In the same way, you can sit with a spacious, skylike mind. At first, you may find your attention drawn here and there like a flashlight, exploring one object and then another. But just keep coming back to a spacious, skylike mind. (A note of caution, however: This practice, though supremely simple, is actually quite advanced and requires well-developed powers of concentration to sustain. For more on welcoming whatever arises, see Chapter 12.)

Training Your Puppy

Like a wayward puppy, your mind means well — it just has a will of its own and some pretty obnoxious habits to unlearn. Just as you wouldn't hit a puppy for peeing on the carpet, but would keep carrying it patiently back to its little pile of papers, you need to keep leading your wandering mind patiently back to its focus of concentration, without anger or violence or judgment of any kind. After all, you want your "puppy mind" to like you and treat you as a friend, instead of cowering in your presence.

In fact, your mind deserves even more patience than a puppy because it's developed the tendency to fantasize, worry, and obsess through a lifetime of poor training. As you practice being kind and patient with your mind, you naturally soften and relax into the present moment — which is, after all, the point of meditation. On the other hand, if you force your mind to concentrate like a drill sergeant pushing his troops, you're just going to wind up tense and uncomfortable — and you probably won't be motivated to meditate again.

As I note in other chapters, learning how to meditate is a lot like practicing a musical instrument. First you need to assemble some basic techniques; then you get to practice the same scales over and over. Like following your breath, playing scales can seem incredibly boring — but week by week, you become imperceptibly better, until one day you graduate to playing simple tunes. And the more you practice, the more subtleties you notice, and the more interesting even playing simple scales — or following your breath — becomes.

REMEMBER

Working with your mind at first

Right now, the whole notion of working with your mind may seem totally incomprehensible. After all, thoughts may fill your head like fog, and you can't see even the faintest trace of blue sky beyond them.

The good news is, you don't have to pay any attention to your mind, at least initially; just keep following your breath, and when you become lost in thought, which you will no doubt do again and again, gently come back. The point is not to stop your mind — an impossible task in any case — but to stay focused on your breath no matter what your mind does.

After weeks and months of regular practice, you may begin to notice that your mind settles down more quickly during your meditations and that fewer thoughts disturb your concentration. In any case, the quality of your mind will no doubt vary from day to day and from meditation to meditation.

Here, the point is not to make your mind work differently, but to slowly but surely strengthen and stabilize your concentration. Eventually, you'll begin to notice that your mind doesn't have the same power over you that it once did and that you have moments of deep peace and tranquillity. Trust me — it will actually happen, even to you!

The historical Buddha compared meditating to tuning a lute. If you make the strings too tight, they break, and you can't play the instrument at all. If you make them too loose, you can't get the right sounds. Likewise, you need to listen to your instrument — your body and mind — when you meditate to determine what kind of tuning you need. If you're tense, you may want to begin with some deep relaxation; if you're sleepy or foggy, you may need to sit up straight, pay attention, and emphasize your concentration.

As you gently bring your puppy back again and again, you also get to notice the themes and stories that repeatedly draw your attention away. Perhaps your mind keeps returning to worries about job security, or arguments with your partner or spouse, or sexual fantasies, or popular songs. Whatever the favorite bones your puppy likes to chew, you gradually become familiar with them as you watch them distract you. After weeks and months of regular practice, you develop a deeper understanding of how your mind works — and how it causes suffering and stress. And like hit tunes you love at first but eventually get tired of hearing, the same old stories start to lose their power to disturb you, and you develop greater equanimity and peace of mind. (For more on working with your stories and habitual themes, see Chapter 11.)

Coming back to your breath

Set your watch or clock to signal the beginning of every hour. When the alarm sounds, stop whatever you're doing and follow your breath with full attention for 60 seconds. If you're doing something that can't be stopped, like driving a car in traffic or talking to your boss, follow your breath as attentively as you can while engaging in the activity.

Chapter 7

Preparing for Meditation: Posture, Stretching, and Sitting Still

*P*erhaps you know a few meditation techniques, but you haven't really begun to practice them because you can't sit still for more than a few minutes, let alone five or ten or even fifteen.

Maybe your back or your knees start hurting, and you worry you might be doing yourself irreparable harm. Or your body starts itching in the oddest places, and you can't resist the urge to scratch. Or every sound reaches your ears magnified a thousandfold — in Dolby stereo, no less — and you start imagining burglars or leaky faucets behind every door.

Perhaps you had a teacher (or a mother or father!) who made you sit at your desk until you finished your schoolwork, and now even the thought of having to sit without moving makes you squirm uncomfortably.

Yes, the simple act of sitting still is guaranteed to flush out every ounce of restlessness you never knew you had. And, yes, meditation works best when you can keep your body relatively motionless and your back relatively straight. So what to do?

In this chapter, you explore the *topography* of meditation and find out what sitting still has to teach you. You discover some great techniques for straightening your spine without hurting your back. And you have an opportunity to practice some dynamite yoga poses for lengthening and relaxing the muscles most involved in sitting — so you can sit still longer, and enjoy it more!

Putting a Snake into a Stick of Bamboo — or the Subtle Art of Sitting Still

When talking about the practice of sitting still, one of my first meditation teachers, the Zen master Shunryu Suzuki, used to say that the best way to show a snake its true nature is to put it in a hollow stick of bamboo. Take a moment and give this unusual metaphor some thought. What could he have possibly meant by it?

Well, imagine that you're a snake in bamboo. What does it feel like? Every time you try to slither, which is after all what snakes like to do, you bump against the walls of your straight-as-an-arrow home. If you pay attention, you start to notice how slippery you actually are.

In the same way, sitting in a certain posture and keeping your body relatively still provides a stick of bamboo that mirrors back to you every impulse and distraction. You get to see how fidgety your body can be — and how hyper-active your mind, which is actually the source of your body's restlessness. "Maybe I should scratch that itch or answer that phone or run that errand." For every plan or intention, there's a corresponding impulse in your muscles and skin. But you'll never notice all this activity unless you sit still.

The funny thing is, you can sit in the same position for hours without noticing it when you're happily engrossed in some favorite activity like watching a movie or surfing the Net or working on a hobby. But try to do something you find boring or unpleasant — especially an activity as strange and unfamiliar as turning your attention back on yourself and following your own breath or paying attention to your own sensations — and suddenly every minute can seem like an hour, every ache can seem like an ailment of life-threatening proportions, and every item on your to-do list can take on irresistible urgency.

When you're constantly acting and reacting in response to thoughts and outside stimulation, you don't have a chance to get to know how your mind works. By sitting still like the snake in bamboo, you have a mirror that shows you just how slippery and elusive your mind can be.

Keeping still also gives you a tremendous edge when you're working on developing your concentration. Imagine a heart surgeon or a concert pianist who can't quiet her body while plying her craft. The fewer physical distractions you have, the easier it becomes to follow your breath, practice your mantra — or whatever your meditation happens to be.

Sitting still, doing nothing

When I was a young Zen meditator, I worked as an attendant in a nursing home that hosted a range of different patients, from a young woman recovering from bone cancer to our local Congressman's father, who was dying of emphysema.

Amidst this busy throng, I was fascinated by one person in particular — an old Italian fisherman who had lost both legs in a fishing accident. When his family members came to visit, he would hold court with great dignity, receiving their respects as the family patriarch. Where other patients were content to lie in bed all day in their hospital gowns, he would dress and groom himself and sit with pride — and upright posture — in his wheelchair, silently observing the drama that unfolded around him.

One day, I was running here and there, trying to figure out what I was supposed to be doing. Seeing this, he called out to me, with a mischievous gleam in his eye, "Hey! You got nothing to do?" "Yeah," I said," obviously flustered, "I don't know what I'm supposed to be doing." "You got nothing to do," he said, "then sit down!"

A word of caution, however: These sitting instructions aren't intended to turn your body into a stone, any more than the bamboo is meant to turn the snake into a stick. As long as you're alive, you're going to keep moving. The point is to set your intention to sit still and notice what happens. The Buddha liked to use the metaphor of a lute — if the strings are too loose, you can't play it, and if they're too tight, they'll break! If you're too rigid with yourself, you'll just end up miserable — but if you keep shifting your body this way and that, you'll never get your mind concentrated and quiet enough to reap the benefits of meditation.

How to Sit Up Straight — and Live to Tell About It

If you examine the meditation poses depicted in the world's great spiritual traditions, you'll find that they all have one thing in common — the unshakable stability of a mountain or tree. Look at the kneeling pharaohs in the Egyptian pyramids, for example, or the cross-legged Buddhas in Indian caves or Japanese temples. They sit on a broad base that appears to be deeply rooted in the earth, and they have a grounded presence that says, "I can't be budged. I'm here to stay" (see Figure 7-1).

Figure 7-1:
Sit like a
mountain
(here
shown in
full lotus)
for
grounding
and
stability.

When you sit up straight like a mountain or a tree, your body acts as a link between heaven and earth — and by analogy, connects your physical, embodied existence with the sacred or spiritual dimension of being. Many traditions talk about the importance of bridging the apparent chasm that separates us from God or the Absolute. Jewish and Sufi mystics teach that the soul is a spark of the heavenly fire that yearns to return to its source. Christians depict the soul as a dove ascending, and Indian tantric yogis (see Chapter 3) describe the ecstatic union of *Shakti,* the feminine energy of spiritual evolution that rises through the spine, with *Shiva,* the masculine principle of detached transcendence.

If you find all this spiritual stuff too esoteric or airy-fairy, you might consider that sitting up straight confers some practical benefits as well. By aligning the spine and opening the channels that run through the center of the body, upright sitting encourages an unimpeded circulation of energy, which, in turn, contributes to wakefulness on all levels — physical, mental, and spiritual. Besides, it's a lot easier to sit still for extended periods of time when your vertebrae are stacked like a pile of bricks, one on top of the other. Otherwise, over time, gravity has this irritating habit of pulling your body down toward the ground — and in the process, causing the aches and pains so typical of a body at war with the forces of nature. So, the most comfortable way to sit in the long run is straight, which puts you in harmony with nature.

Of course, you can always lean against the wall — or so you may think. But your body tends to slouch when it leans, even subtly, in any direction; and the point of doing meditation is to rely on your direct experience, rather than to depend on some outside support to "back you up." When you sit like a mountain or a tree, you're making a statement: "I'm deeply rooted in the earth, yet open to the higher powers of the cosmos — independent, yet inextricably connected to all of life."

Dealing with pain

If you sit in the same position for an extended period of time, you're going to experience some physical pain or discomfort, no matter how much stretching you do! An ache in your back here, some knee pain there, a twinge in your shoulder, pins and needles in your foot — the list of complaints is potentially endless. And the longer you sit, the more intense the discomfort may become — and the stronger the temptation to move or fidget to avoid it.

Instead of instantly shifting your position or struggling to ignore your discomfort, practice gently expanding your awareness to include your discomfort, while continuing to attend to your breath or other object of meditation. If the pain is strong, you can explore it directly with the same mindful, compassionate attention you bring to your breath.

Notice also how your mind responds to your discomfort. Does it fabricate some story about your discomfort: "I'm not sitting correctly; there must be something wrong with my back; maybe I'm ruining my knees"? And does it intensify your discomfort by judging it as bad or undesirable, causing you to tense up around it?

By opening your awareness to your pain and how your mind responds to it, you can actually begin to soften and relax in relation to the pain — and you may notice that it diminishes accordingly. Because physical and emotional pain are unavoidable, sitting meditation provides a wonderful laboratory for experimenting with new ways of relating to suffering and discomfort in every area of your life — and ultimately moving beyond them.

By the way, you also have the option of moving (with awareness) when the pain or discomfort becomes too intense. Just play at your own edge between opening and resisting. And remember that certain kinds of pain may merit your immediate attention — especially shooting pain, pain that begins as soon as you start sitting, and sharp (rather than dull) pain in your knees. In such cases, you're better off trying a different sitting position.

What to do from the waist down — and other fantasies

Just as a tree needs to set down deep roots so it won't fall over as it grows, you need to find a comfortable position for the lower half of your body that you can sustain for 5 or 10 or 15 minutes — or even longer, if you wish. After several millennia of experimentation, the great meditators have come up with a handful of traditional postures that seem to work especially well. Different though they may appear from the outside, these postures have one thing in common: the pelvis tilts slightly forward, accentuating the natural curvature of the lower back.

The following poses are arranged more or less in order, from the easiest to the hardest to do, though ease all depends on your particular body and degree of flexibility. For example, some people take to the classical *lotus* position (whose name derives from its resemblance to the flower) like a duck to . . . well, to a lotus pond. Besides, the lotus, though difficult, has some definite advantages (see the sidebar "Why the Buddha sat in lotus position" later in this chapter), and you can work up to it by stretching your hips using the yoga exercises described in the section "Preparing Your Body for Sitting" later in this chapter. Above all, don't worry about which looks the coolest; just experiment until you find the one that works best for you:

- **Sitting in a chair:** Notice that I say sitting, not slouching (see Figure 7-2). The trick to meditating in a chair is positioning your buttocks somewhat higher than your knees, which tilts your pelvis forward and helps keep your back straight. Old-fashioned wooden kitchen chairs work better than the upholstered kind; experiment with a small cushion or foam wedge under your buttocks.

- **Kneeling (with or without a bench):** Popular in ancient Egypt and in traditional Japan where it's called *seiza* — pronounced "say-za" (see Figure 7-3). Kneeling can be — well, hard on your knees, unless you have proper support. Try placing a cushion under your buttocks and between your feet — or use a specially designed seiza bench, preferably one with a soft cushion between you and the wood. Otherwise, your bottom and other tender parts may fall asleep.

- **Easy position:** Not recommended for extended periods of sitting because it's not very stable and doesn't support a straight spine. Simply sit on your cushion with your legs crossed in front of you tailor-fashion. (Believe it or not, tailors once sat this way!) Your knees don't have to touch the floor, but do keep your back as straight as you can.

Figure 7-2:
If you meditate in a chair, you may have to update a few old habits.

Figure 7-3:
Use a cushion or a bench to make sure your tender parts don't fall asleep when you kneel.

You can stabilize the position by placing cushions under your knees; gradually decrease the height of the cushions as your hips become more flexible (which they naturally will over time). When your knees touch the ground, you may be ready for Burmese or lotus position (see later bullets for these positions).

This pose can be a short-term alternative for people who can't manage the other positions in this list, can't kneel because of knee problems, or don't want to sit on a chair for some reason.

✔ **Burmese position:** Used throughout Southeast Asia (see Figure 7-4). This pose involves placing both calves and feet on the floor one in front of the other. Though less stable than the lotus series, it's much easier to negotiate, especially for beginners.

With all the cross-legged poses, first bend your leg at the knee, in line with your thigh, before rotating your thigh to the side. Otherwise, you risk injuring your knee, which is built to flex in only one direction, unlike the ball-and-socket joint of the hip, which can rotate through a full range of motion.

✔ **Quarter lotus:** Exactly like half lotus (see next bullet), except that your foot rests on the calf of your opposite leg, rather than on the thigh (see Figure 7-5).

Figure 7-4:
Burmese position is an easy, comfortable cross-legged alternative that's popular in Southeast Asia.

✔ **Half lotus:** Easier to execute than the famous full lotus (see next bullet), and nearly as stable (see Figure 7-6). With your buttocks on a cushion, place one foot on the opposite thigh and the other foot on the floor beneath the opposite thigh. Be sure that both knees touch the floor and your spine doesn't tilt to one side. To distribute the pressure on your back and legs, remember to alternate legs from sitting to sitting, if you can — in other words, left leg on the thigh, right on the floor, then left on the floor and right on the thigh.

✔ **Full lotus:** Considered the Everest of sitting positions (refer to Figure 7-1). With your buttocks on a cushion, cross your left foot over your right thigh and your right foot over your left thigh. As with its more asymmetrical sibling, half lotus, it's best to alternate legs in order to distribute the pressure evenly.

Full lotus has been practiced throughout the world for many thousands of years. The most stable of all the poses, it should not be attempted unless you happen to be particularly flexible — and even then I would suggest preparing by doing some of the stretches described at the end of this chapter.

Figure 7-5:
As its name implies, quarter lotus is a fraction as hard as its more ambitious counterpart, full lotus.

Figure 7-6:
In half lotus,
try to
alternate
your legs
between
sittings as
much as
you can.

Straightening your spine without rigor mortis

Once you're settled into a comfortable sitting position, with your pelvis tilted slightly forward, you can turn your attention to straightening your back. Of course, "straight" is a misnomer when used to refer to the spine because a healthy back actually has several distinct curves, one at the lumbar region or lower back, another at the thoracic area or midback, and a third at the neck or cervical spine.

Unfortunately, these natural curves are often exaggerated by the demands of computer workstations and other sedentary environments, and you gradually get into the habit of sitting hunched over, with your shoulders rounded, your upper back collapsed, and your neck and head craned forward like a turkey vulture — the way I'm sitting right now!

Why the Buddha sat in lotus position

Unfortunately, we didn't learn to sit cross-legged on the floor when we were kids, the way most Indians and many other traditional Asians did. As a result, you may find it difficult to sit cross-legged at first, and you may feel inclined to resign yourself to the apparent ease and comfort of a chair. But I'd like to encourage you to give cross-legged sitting a try at some point, if your body and comfort level allow. It isn't necessarily as difficult or as painful as it appears — and besides, it has some unique advantages.

For one thing, crossing your legs creates a solid, stable foundation for the rest of your body and tends to tilt your pelvis forward naturally at just the right angle to support your spine. Also, there's something about sitting the way the great meditators of the past used to

sit that lends a certain power and authority to your meditation — as though crossing your legs immerses you in a river of awareness that dates back thousands of years.

Finally, sitting with your buttocks on or close to the earth directly connects you with gravity and the other energies the Earth emanates — and gives a palpable feeling of groundedness and strength to your meditation.

Ultimately, of course, whatever you do with the lower half of your body is fine, as long as you can sit comfortably and keep your back straight with relative ease. But you can work up to the luxury of cross-legged sitting by gradually stretching your hips, until one day both knees touch the floor and *voilà!* — you've arrived.

You may not be able to reverse sitting habits like these in a few sessions of meditation, but you can experiment with *extending* your spine — a more accurate term than straightening — and slowly but surely softening those curves back to their natural, graceful arch. You may find yourself carrying these new sitting habits into your other activities so that in time, you're gently correcting your posture while driving your car or sitting at your desk, for example.

Meditating on your posture

As an alternative to following your breath, especially when you want to calm your mind before turning to the practice of mindfulness (see Chapter 6), you can experiment with the time-honored Zen technique of concentrating on a particular part of your body. Try placing your mind in the palm of your hand, if your hands are folded in Zen *mudra* (refer to

Figure 7-1) — or on your belly, at a point about two inches below your navel (known as the *hara* in Japanese). After you practice this approach for a period of time and your attention stabilizes, you can expand your focus to include your whole body, maintaining the same level of Zen-style concentration.

Try one or all three of the following images to help you discover what a straight or extended spine feels like. Don't bother to look in the mirror or compare yourself to some ideal you've picked up in books (even this one). The important thing is how your body feels from the inside. You want to feel centered, stable, grounded — and aligned with the force of gravity:

✔ **Suspending your head from a string:** Imagine that your entire body is suspended in the air from a string attached to the crown of your head. (The crown is the highest point on the top of your skull, toward the back.) As you feel the string pulling your head up into the air, notice how your spine naturally lengthens, your pelvis tilts forward, your chin tucks, and the back of your neck flattens slightly.

✔ **Stacking your vertebrae one on top of another:** Imagine your vertebrae as bricks that you're stacking one on top of the other, beginning with the first at the base of the spine. Feel your spine growing up toward the sky brick by brick, like a skyscraper.

✔ **Sitting like a mountain or tree:** Imagine your body as a mountain or tree with a broad base that extends deep into the earth and a trunk or peak that reaches toward the sky (see Figure 7-7). Notice how stable, grounded, and self-sufficient you feel.

Figure 7-7:
Here's how you look from the side when you extend your spine.

What to do with your eyes, mouth, and hands

When I started meditating back in the '60s, I couldn't for the life of me figure out what to do with my eyes. They kept crossing and shifting uncontrollably from focused to unfocused, and I became obsessed with doing something right that had always been second nature for me. I mean, I'd never worried about what to do with my eyes before! Eventually, I just forgot about them, and they never bothered me again.

Eyes: Initially, you need to decide whether you want to sit with your eyes closed, wide open, or half open. Then you can just forget about your eyes and let them do what they do. Each alternative has its pros and cons.

Keeping your eyes closed draws your attention away from external distractions and helps you focus on your inner experience. Unfortunately, it also encourages daydreaming and thinking. Keeping your eyes wide open is actually the most difficult position because it expands your awareness to include the full range of outer as well as inner experiences. The good news is that this position makes it easier for you to rise from a sitting position and extend your meditation to your everyday, eyes-open activities. The bad news is that if you haven't developed enough concentration, you can easily be distracted by anything that crosses your field of vision.

I generally recommend that people sit with eyes half open, Zen style, gazing with soft focus at a spot on the floor about four or five feet in front of them — in other words, looking down at a forty-five-degree angle. If you're feeling restless or distracted, you can close your eyes a little more (or completely); if you're feeling sleepy or dull, you can open them wider. And if you find yourself staring, just relax your eyes and soften your focus.

Hands: You can put your hands pretty much anywhere they feel comfortable, as long as you keep them there for the entire sitting period. Seasoned meditators generally put their hands one of two places: in their laps or on their thighs.

In your lap: Try simply clasping your hands. Or you can attempt the more formal Zen mudra (hand position) in which your left palm is placed on top of your right about four or five inches below your navel, with your thumbs lightly touching near your navel, thereby forming an oval with your fingers.

On your thighs: Simply rest your hands there, palms down. Or turn them up and, if you wish, touch your index finger to the thumb of each hand, forming an oval in a traditional yoga mudra. As with all the other options in this chapter, experiment until you find the one that works best for you.

Mouth: Keep it gently closed (but not clenched) as you breathe through your nose, with your tongue lightly touching the roof of your mouth so it doesn't wander all over the place as tongues are wont to do.

Once you know what it feels like to sit upright with your spine extended, you can rock your body from side to side like a pendulum, first broadly and then in gradually decreasing arcs until you come to rest in the center. Next, you can tilt your pelvis forward slightly, accentuating the natural curvature of your lower back, and then lean forward and backward from the waist (keeping your back straight) until you come to center. Finally, tuck your chin and draw your head back gently. Now you're ready to begin your meditation.

At first, you may need to use these techniques and images again and again to help you return to a comfortable, upright sitting position. But eventually you'll find that sitting up straight becomes a far more intuitive and immediate affair — you'll just sit down, rock a little from side to side, gently extend your spine, and start meditating.

Zafus, benches, and other exotic paraphernalia

Depending on which meditation tradition you explore, you're likely to encounter a range of different sitting devices. Some yogis I know like to plop down a tiny rectangular bag filled with rice before they artfully settle onto it and cross their legs in full lotus. Many Zen folks and other Buddhists prefer the plump round cushions known as *zafus* (Japanese for "sitting cushions"), often combined with flat, square cushions filled with cotton batting for extra height, if needed (see Figure 7-8).

Figure 7-8:
Check out this sitting gear: zafu, support cushion, and padded bench.

Zafus have infiltrated the meditation halls of every spiritual lineage and denomination, from Sufis and Buddhists to Christian monastics (see Chapter 3 for more about Sufis). Zafus are generally stuffed with *kapok,* which are silky natural fibers that keep their shape despite repeated sittings. But I've seen hefty zafus filled with buckwheat husks or cotton batting and even thick rectangular ones filled with hard polyurethane foam.

Before buying a zafu, be sure to try out a number of different shapes and sizes, checking them for relative comfort, stability, and height. You want to be able to sit so both knees touch the floor, if possible, and your pelvis tilts slightly forward.

Four tried-and-true meditation positions — plus a few more

If you can't sit comfortably in any of the usual sitting positions, you can take heart from the Buddhist tradition, which offers four equally acceptable alternatives for formal meditation:

✔ Sitting

✔ Standing

✔ Walking

✔ Lying down

Giant statues in India and Southeast Asia show the Buddha himself meditating while lying on his right side with his head cradled in his hand. Yogis and ascetics have long meditated while standing, sometimes on one leg. And walking meditation is still widely practiced throughout the world, from the Zen monasteries of Japan and the forest monasteries of Thailand to the Sufi communities of the Middle East and the Christian hermitages of Europe and North America.

Of course, the Sufis recognize a fifth traditional posture — the spinning dance of the dervishes — and the Taoists teach the martial art t'ai chi as a moving meditation. In the West, some of the followers of Swiss psychologist C. G. Jung have developed a meditative dance form known as *authentic movement,* and some Christians practice walking in contemplation around a spiral labyrinth. Ultimately, any activity can become a meditation if you do it mindfully, as I describe in Chapter 15.

At formal silent retreats, I've seen people meditating in wheelchairs, newcomers perched on high cushions surrounded by bolsters, and old-timers who do nothing but walk or lie down for ten days. And I've seen a photo of the great Indian yogi Swami Muktananda meditating while roosting like a bird in a tree. The point is, there's no one right way to do it — just discover what works for you.

If you're a kneeler, you can try sitting on a zafu or other convenient cushion placed on the floor between your legs, or you can use one of the meditation benches designed exclusively for the purpose. Again, experiment before buying. Chair sitters are better off using the plain straight-backed variety — no exotic paraphernalia here. Just be sure your buttocks are somewhat higher than your knees.

Preparing Your Body for Sitting

If you can sit in meditation for 10 or 15 minutes each day without discomfort, congratulations! You needn't spend any additional time learning how to stretch and strengthen your body — unless, that is, you're so inclined.

But if you're like most people, sooner or later your body will start clamoring for your attention. For example, you may find that regular sitting causes your back to stiffen occasionally. Or you may try to work your way into one of the more challenging cross-legged poses — only to discover that your legs just aren't as flexible as you imagined.

A few well-placed hatha yoga poses can do wonders for your body — and make sitting a whole lot more comfortable too! (If you're interested in finding out more about yoga, try *Yoga For Dummies* by Georg Feuerstein and Larry Payne, published by IDG Books Worldwide, Inc.) Whichever sitting position you choose, you'll enjoy it more if your lower back is flexible and strong enough to support you without complaining. And if you prefer to cross your legs, you'll find that stretching your hips allows you to sit with more stability and far less strain on your knees.

With these needs in mind, the following sections highlight six yoga poses (also known as *asanas*) to help prepare you for sitting. The first three help to stretch and strengthen your lower back; the second three work on opening your hips and making them more flexible. Once you've chosen the poses that seem best for you, be sure to practice them gently and carefully, treating your body with the kindness you would reserve for a close friend. Enjoy the stretch, but back off gently if you feel any pain. (If you don't have carpeting, use a yoga mat or rug between your tender parts and the floor.)

Cat pose with variations

Watch how a cat stretches after a nap, and you'll understand how this pose got its name. Not only does it stretch and strengthen your spine for sitting, it's also a great way to start your day. Try rolling out of bed first thing in the morning, limbering up with Cat pose, doing a few minutes of meditation, and then going about your day (see Figure 7-9).

Figure 7-9: Practice arching your back like a you-know-what.

Here's how you practice the Cat:

1. **Begin on your hands and knees with your spine horizontal and your arms and thighs perpendicular to the floor (like a four-legged animal).**

2. **As you exhale, arch your spine upward slowly like a cat, beginning the stretch at your tailbone.**

    Feel your spine flexing vertebra by vertebra.

3. **At the culmination of the stretch, tuck your chin slightly.**

4. **As you inhale, flex your spine downward, beginning with your tailbone and lifting your head slightly at the end of the stretch.**

5. **Continue to breathe and stretch in this way for 10 to 15 breaths.**

You can also do two variations of the preceding Cat pose, as follows:

- ✔ **Variation 1:** From the four-legged position (Step 1), gently turn your head on an exhalation and look at your left hip, as you simultaneously move your hip toward your head. Inhale and come back to center and repeat to the other side. Continue for 10 to 15 breaths.

- ✔ **Variation 2:** From the four-legged position (Step 1), move your hands slightly forward of perpendicular and draw broad circles with your hips, moving forward as you inhale and backward as you exhale. Continue for 10 to 15 breaths.

Cobra pose

Named for its resemblance to the graceful serpent, this asana provides a great backward stretch for your spine — and an antidote to any tendency to slouch forward. Instead of leading with (and possibly overarching) the lower back, be sure to initiate the stretch in your upper back and gradually extend it down your spine (see Figure 7-10).

Figure 7-10:
As a remedy for slouching, practice lifting your upper back like a snake.

To get the benefits of this stretch, do it just like so:

1. **Lie face down with your forehead on the floor.**

2. **Place your hands under your shoulders with your fingertips facing forward and the outside edge of your hands even with the edge of your shoulders.**

3. **Draw your elbows in so that your arms touch the sides of your torso.**

4. **Keep your feet together and press your legs and thighs into the floor.**

5. **Raise your chest slowly away from the floor, lifting and extending from your upper back, with your head and neck in alignment with your spine.**

   At first, you may find that your chest doesn't rise very far, but don't force yourself in any way. Your back will gradually become more flexible.

6. **Keeping your shoulders relaxed, gently press your chest upward and forward and open your abdomen while pressing your pubic bone into the floor.**

7. **Breathe deeply and smoothly, holding the pose for five to ten full breaths.**

8. **As you exhale, slowly unfold the pose, vertebra by vertebra, until you're once again lying face down with your forehead on the floor.**

9. **Turn your head to one side and relax completely.**

Locust pose

Likewise named for an animal, this asana recalls a grasshopper with its abdomen lifted into the air behind it (see Figure 7-11). Because it stretches and strengthens the lower back, the Locust pose provides crucial support for the practice of sitting up straight, whether in meditation or any other sedentary activity. Begin with the half Locust and graduate to the full Locust when your lower back feels strong enough. (If you have lower-back problems or feel any pain during half Locust, you should abstain from full Locust.) Move slowly and carefully and avoid any movement that causes you pain — except the dull ache of a good stretch.

Figure 7-11:
Imagine lifting your legs like a grasshopper!

Just for the record, here are the steps you follow to practice this pose:

1. **Lie face down with your chin on the floor and your arms at your side, palms up.**

2. **Making a partial fist with both hands, move your arms under your body and position your hands under your pubic bone, thumbs lightly touching.**

3. **At this point, you can do either the half Locust or the full Locust, as follows:**

   For half Locust: Contract your buttock muscles slightly and inhale. As you exhale, lift one leg completely into the air without bending your knee. Hold for five to ten breaths; then lower your leg and do the same with the other leg. Repeat three or four times on each side. When you're done, turn your head to one side and relax.

   For full Locust: Contract your buttock muscles slightly and inhale. As you exhale, lift both legs completely into the air without bending your knees. Hold the pose for five to ten breaths, breathing deeply into your abdomen; then lower your legs, turn your head to one side, and relax.

Lunge pose

Billed as a back stretch, this asana also opens your hips and groin (see Figure 7-12). If you have time for a only few poses, combine this one with the Cat and Butterfly (see later in this section) poses for a mini routine.

Figure 7-12:
Practice stretching your lower back and opening your hips with a gentle lunge.

Follow these steps and enjoy the stretch:

1. **Begin on your hands and knees with your spine horizontal and your arms and thighs perpendicular to the floor (like a four-legged animal).**

2. **Move your left knee forward and place your left lower leg on the floor with your heel close to your right groin.**

3. **Extend your right leg straight behind you with your knee facing downward.**

4. **Sink your pubic bone toward the floor, while lifting your chest gently upward and forward with your weight on your arms and right leg.**

   Make sure that any torque in your bent leg occurs in the hip joint, not the knee. Feel the stretch in your lower back, in the hip joint of your bent leg, and in the groin, hip, and thigh of your straight leg.

5. **Hold the stretch for five to ten breaths; then repeat on the other side.**

Butterfly pose

Especially challenging for runners and other athletes, this pose stretches the inner thigh, groin, and hip. As its shape suggests, it gradually opens your "wings" and helps your knees reach the floor in cross-legged poses (see Figure 7-13).

Figure 7-13:
Rise to the
challenge:
Stretch
your thighs
and groin.

Do the stretch like this and feel yourself soar:

1. **Sit on the floor with your legs extended in front of you.**

   If you have difficulty keeping your back straight, place a cushion under your buttocks so that your pelvis tilts forward slightly.

2. **Bend your knees and bring the soles of your feet together with the outside edges of both feet on the floor.**

3. **Clasping your hands together, grasp both feet, draw your heels in toward your groin, and gently press your knees toward the floor while extending your spine.**

   Feel the stretch in your groin, thighs, hips, and lower back. Resist the temptation to bounce or force your legs. If your knees stick up in the air, don't worry. It's more important to keep your back straight than to touch the floor with your knees.

4. **Hold the stretch for five to ten breaths while breathing deeply into your abdomen.**

5. **As you exhale, release your feet, extend your legs in front of you, and relax.**

REMEMBER

Ten quick steps to prep your body for meditation

This handy list provides a user-friendly summary of the steps described in detail earlier in this chapter:

1. Arrange your legs.

2. Lengthen your spine.

3. Rock your body from side to side like a pendulum.

4. Rock your body from front to back.

5. Tilt your pelvis slightly forward and soften your belly.

6. Tuck your chin gently.

7. Rest your tongue on the roof of your mouth and breathe through your nose, if possible.

8. Rest your hands on your thighs or in your lap.

9. Relax your body from head to toe, letting go as much as possible of any tension or discomfort.

10. Begin your meditation.

Cradle stretch

As the name may suggest, you cradle your leg in your arms as you would a baby, stretching and opening your hips in the process (see Figure 7-14). Be sure to lift your leg slowly and gently — remember, you're stretching, not wrenching.

Follow these instructions with the careful attention of a loving mother:

1. **Sit on the floor with your legs extended in front of you.**

2. **Bend one knee, rotate your thigh to the side, and cradle your lower leg in your arms. Keeping your hands clasped, hold your knee in the crease of one elbow and your foot in the crease of the other.**

3. **Keeping your spine extended and your head erect, gently rock your leg horizontally from side to side, rotating at your hip.**

4. **Continue this rocking motion for five to ten breaths, breathing deeply and smoothly; then gently put your leg down the same way you picked it up and do the same stretch with the other leg.**

Figure 7-14: Gently rock your legs from side to side to open your hips.

Keeping good head and shoulders

In Zen, good posture refers to more than how you position your back and legs; it refers to an attitude toward life in general. Attentive yet relaxed, you face each moment and each situation directly, with a bearing that suggests: "I'm open to whatever arises. I'm present and ready to respond." One of my teachers used to call this "keeping good head and shoulders."

If you have an alarm watch, set it to beep every hour for the rest of the day. (If you don't, just do this exercise at random times.) When your watch beeps, take a moment to pay attention to your body. How am I standing or sitting right now? Am I slouching or slumping? And if so, how would it feel to gently extend my spine and align myself with gravity?

Notice how this subtle shift affects your mood and your outlook on life as you go about your day.

Chapter 8

Where to Sit, What to Wear, and Other Practical Stuff

*W*hen I began meditating in college, I took the subway once a week from my uptown apartment to the little Zen center on the city's East Side. Each time I entered the front door, the smell of incense, the Japanese straw mats, the simple altar, and the dark robes of the members all reminded me that I had entered a special place — a place devoted to the practice of meditation. I could feel my breath deepening and my mind slowing down — and I was frustrated to find that I couldn't translate the quality of meditation I experienced there to the cramped little flat I shared with three friends.

Over the years, I've learned that the physical environment surrounding your meditation — where, when, and how long you sit, what you wear, what kind of energy you invest — can have a powerful impact on the quality of your meditation. Trying to count your breaths in a busy airport or a noisy office can be fun, of course, but you'll go deeper faster in a quiet place that's specifically devoted to meditation.

You may fantasize about going off to an ashram or some other spiritual community where everything is conveniently taken care of and all you have to do is meditate, eat, and sleep. Well, good luck! Instead, you may just have to carve the time and space for meditation out of the raw material of your busy life. That's why I wrote this chapter.

In these pages, you'll find out how to choose just the right spot for your meditation, receive some guidelines for determining when and how long to sit, and pick up a few pointers for setting up an altar that will inspire your efforts. Creating and maintaining your own meditation niche is the next best thing to meditating in a monastery. (For more about meditating with others, turn to Chapter 15.)

What to Wear: Choose Comfortable Over Fashionable

This one may seem like a no-brainer, but you'd be surprised how many people show up for meditation wearing designer jeans and skin-tight tops, which makes it virtually impossible for them to breathe or cross their legs. The key to comfortable sitting is this: Keep clothing loose and roomy and avoid constricting your breathing or your circulation in any way. Sweat clothes generally make great sitting gear. If you're into meditation chic, you can buy a pair of sleek but comfortable draw-string pants in a variety of colors and materials from a mail-order catalog.

Meditating with music

When you're just moving too fast to plop down and be mindful, you can use certain kinds of music to help you tune in to a slower, steadier, less jarring rhythm before you begin meditating. The music you choose depends on your taste — one person's "aaahh" is another one's "ouch." Believe it or not, studies have shown that many teenagers and Generation X-ers actually relax to heavy metal.

By all means, use a favorite CD to soothe your savage beast at the end of a long and stressful day — preferably something that joins you where you are and then gradually lulls you down. When you're breathing a little easier, you can head for your meditation corner.

Or you can make listening to music a meditation in itself. Begin by being mindful of the music the way you'd be mindful of your breathing. Instead of thinking or daydreaming, listen with full attention to the sounds as they unfold in your awareness. When your mind wanders off, return to the music. At times, you may even lose yourself in the sound so that you, as the listener, disappear and only the listening remains. Such moments of deep meditation offer a glimpse of your essential being that can't be understood by the mind, but have a powerful healing effect nevertheless.

Because body temperature and blood pressure tend to drop during meditation, you may get chillier than usual. So be sure to have a sweater or woolen blanket nearby as a wrap.

When to Meditate: Any Time's the Right Time

If you're incredibly busy, pencil in formal periods of meditation whenever you can find the time. But if you have the luxury of choosing or would like to meditate as often as you can, here are some of the best times to sit — and remember that ultimately every moment and every activity can provide an opportunity to be mindful. (For more on mindfulness in everyday life, see Chapter 15.)

- **First thing in the morning:** Traditionally, the hour or two right after you wake up — preferably around sunrise — is considered the best time to meditate. Your mind and body are refreshed and energized by deep sleep, and you haven't yet started to obsess about your usual worries and concerns. As a result, you may find it easier to focus and stay present. By meditating first thing, you also set the tone for the rest of the day and can extend whatever peace of mind you generate to your other activities.

- **Before bed:** Some people take an hour or two to wake up from the dreamy fog of sleep, and others have just enough time to roll out of bed, grab a cup of coffee, and rush out to join the morning commute. If you're groggy when you get up or have to switch to high gear the moment your feet hit the floor, try meditating in the evening before bed. It's a great way to prepare for sleep because it allows your mind to settle down and shift naturally and with ease from waking to slumber. In fact, meditators who sit at bedtime often report that their sleep is more restful, and they need less of it.

  Of course, the downside is that you may feel like you're too tired or stressed out to meditate at the end of the day — and wind up taking a hot bath or watching TV instead. But once you get into the habit, you'll find that evening meditations are an excellent option with some distinct advantages of their own.

- **Right after work:** Though not as reliable as mornings or bedtimes because it's often usurped by errands, early dinners, or family emergencies, the transition between work and home can be a fitting moment to take a few deep breaths and let your body and mind settle — instead of reaching for the paper or flipping on the tube.

✔ **Lunch hours and coffee breaks:** If you have an office of your own and a time set aside for lunch or coffee — a big if, since more and more people eat on the fly these days — plan on bringing your food or scoring your java in advance and spending the rest of the time meditating. You might even set aside a special space in your office — including an altar, if you're so inclined.

✔ **Waiting for your kids and other predictable downtime:** If you're like many parents, you spend hours each week shuttling your kids from one activity or playdate to another — and sitting in the car or running errands while you wait for them to finish. Instead of picking up a magazine or listening to the news, try meditating. (You can take the same approach to waiting for your doctor or dentist.) It may not be the best environment and your posture may not be ideal, but look — it's a stretch of precious idle time. Use it wisely.

Walking meditation

Between periods of formal sitting, meditators throughout the world have long practiced walking with mindful awareness. Besides breaking the monotony of uninterrupted sitting, it's a great meditation in its own right — and a wonderful way to practice extending the mindfulness you learn on your cushion or chair into the ordinary world of movement and activity.

In some Zen monasteries, walking meditation more closely resembles a kind of restrained, conscious running. In parts of Southeast Asia, the movement may be almost imperceptibly slow. Here's a more moderate approach that you can practice not only between periods of sitting meditation, but also anytime you wish to slow down a little and pay attention as you walk. If the weather allows, by all means walk outside. Or you can just walk back and forth in your house.

1. **Begin by walking at your usual pace, following your in-breath and out-breath as you walk.**

2. **Coordinate your breathing with your steps.**

For example, you can take three steps for each inhalation and three steps for each exhalation — which, as you may notice, is considerably slower than most people walk. If you want to change the speed of your walking, just change the number of steps per breath. But maintain the same pace each time you walk. (If your inhalations and exhalations are different lengths, just adapt your walking accordingly.)

3. **In addition to your breathing, be aware of your feet and legs as you lift and move them.**

Notice the contact of your feet with the ground or floor. Gaze ahead of you, with your eyes lowered at a 45 degree angle. Be relaxed, easy, and comfortable as you walk.

4. **Enjoy your steady, mindful walking for as long as you wish.**

If your attention wanders or you start to hurry, gently bring your attention back to your walking.

How Long to Meditate: From Quickies to the Long Haul

Meditation resembles sex in a number of ways, and this is one of them: You may prefer it short and quick or long and slow. But whatever your predilections, you would no doubt agree that some sexual contact with your beloved is better than no sex at all.

Well, apply this dictum to meditation, and you'll get the drift. If you can't schedule a half hour, then meditate for a few minutes. It's much better to sit for five or ten minutes every day than for an hour once a week — though you may want to do both. As with all the guidelines in this book, experiment with the different options until you find the one that suits you best.

 Digital alarm watches provide an accurate and inexpensive way to time your meditations precisely without watching the clock. Also, you might like to signal the beginning and end of your meditation with the sound of a small bell, as is done in many traditional cultures.

✔ **Five minutes:** If you're a beginner, a few minutes can seem like an eternity, so start off slow and increase the length of your sittings as your interest and enjoyment dictate. You may find that by the time you settle your body and start to focus on your breath, your time is up. If the session seems too short, you can always sit a little longer next time. As your practice develops, you'll find that even five minutes can be immeasurably refreshing.

✔ **Ten to 15 minutes:** If you're like most people, you need several minutes at the start of meditation to get settled, a few more to become engaged in the process, and several at the end to reorient — which means that 10 or 15 minutes leaves you a little in the middle to deepen your concentration or expand your awareness. Once you've made it this far, try leveling off at 15 minutes a day for several weeks and watch how your powers of concentration build.

✔ **Twenty minutes to an hour:** The longer you sit, the more time you'll have between preliminaries and endings to settle into a focused and relaxed state of mind. If you have the motivation and can carve out the time, by all means devote 40 minutes or 1 hour to meditation each day. You'll notice the difference — and you'll understand why most meditation teachers recommend sitting this long at a stretch. Perhaps it's the human attention span — look at the proverbial 50-minute hour of psychotherapy or the optimal length for most TV shows. But remember: It's better to keep your practice steady and regular than to splurge one day and abstain for the rest of the week.

Why bother to time your meditations?

You're welcome to experiment with sitting down to meditate when you feel like it and getting up when you're done. But there are some excellent reasons for deciding when and how long before you begin meditating and then sticking to your plan:

✓ **Your mind is seductive:** If you don't make a commitment to stay put for a certain period of time, your mind will find all kinds of compelling reasons for you to get up and do other things. Instead, you can watch your mind go through its gyrations, without being seduced.

✓ **You can forget about the time:** Once you decide how long you're going to sit, you don't have to obsess about the time anymore — and you can relax and concentrate on your practice instead.

✓ **You can develop regularity:** Like building a muscle, you can begin with 5 minutes and gradually work up to 15 or 20 minutes. In the same way, sitting at the same time every day creates a natural circadian rhythm to your meditation, which makes it easier to keep going.

What to Eat and Drink Before You Meditate — and What to Avoid

Big meals can make you drowsy, especially when they're high in carbohydrates, so eat lightly if at all before you sit. Or wait at least one hour after a major repast. You might even consider following the traditional Zen guideline to eat until you're two-thirds full, rather than bursting at the seams. It might not be bad for your waistline, either.

As for drinking (and smoking), here are a few suggestions. I do know seasoned meditators who like to down a cup of cappuccino before they sit, and at least one Zen master who made it a habit of meditating first thing in the morning after drinking too much sake the night before. But as a general rule, It's best to abstain from mind-altering substances (for example, coffee, alcohol, tobacco, marijuana, and other recreational drugs) before meditating.

As your practice grows and you observe the benefits of being present and focused, rather than zoned out or drugged up, you may naturally diminish your intake. In fact, you may discover that meditation makes you more sensitive to your state of mind and provides a natural high that renders these substances unnecessary or obsolete. And if your primary motivation for meditating is to reduce stress or enhance your health, you may consider abstaining entirely from your substance of choice. Believe it or not, indulging only adds to the burden of stress you're already experiencing.

Meditation and TV: From the couch to the cushion

I have to confess that I'm one of those reactionary folks who cheer every time they see the bumper sticker "Kill your TV." Here's why. Not only does television inundate you with disturbing images you would not otherwise have to endure — images of conflict, cruelty, seduction, exploitation, and outright violence that leave a deep and lasting impression — but TV also dulls your mind by habituating it to nonstop stimulation. With your mind accustomed to being flooded with images and sounds, you find it more difficult to enjoy the ordinary moments of everyday life or to register subtler levels of experience — the kind you're trying to access in meditation.

Studies have also shown that tube-time inhibits the natural, age-appropriate development and integration of the various lobes of the brain. Children who grow up on lots of TV are generally less imaginative, more restless, more aggressive, and more easily bored than

those who don't. Did you ever wonder why teenagers hang around shopping malls looking listless and brain-dead? This may be the answer.

Needless to say, you're doing yourself a favor when you substitute an hour on the meditation cushion for an hour on the couch. You're more likely to find what you're looking for — relaxation, happiness, joy, peace of mind. And you'll come away more refreshed and more open to new experiences, both inner and outer.

But like most addictions, a TV fixation can be hard to kick. Start out slowly, say, by giving up a few hours each week and substituting some other activity that you find genuinely nurturing or fulfilling — going for a walk, talking with a friend, spending quality time with your family. Of course, you may not want to give up your favorite sitcom, the Sunday game, or the evening news — but then, who knows?

Where to Meditate: Creating Sacred Space

Perhaps you've seen those Chinese paintings where a bearded sage in a flowing robe sits in deep contemplation at the base of some majestic peak with a waterfall thundering beside him. Maybe you've even had moments when you wished you could become that sage, disappear into the mountains, and meditate in silence and simplicity for the rest of your days. Alas, life doesn't usually support us nowadays in actualizing such fantasies!

Instead of shaving your head and heading for the hills, however, you can follow a few simple guidelines for carving out a special place for the practice of meditation. You'll find that the space you set aside will enrich your life in ways you can't imagine.

Meditating in nature

As you may already have noticed, the natural world has an unparalleled capacity to relax your body and calm your mind. When you're sitting by the ocean listening to the surf or hiking in the mountains among the rocks and the trees, you don't have to practice some formal meditation technique — just open your senses and let nature work its magic. Without any effort on your part, you begin to feel your mind settle down, your worries dissipate, your breathing deepen and slow, your tension melt away, and your heart fill with gratitude and love.

As a species, we evolved in the natural world, and the plants and animals have been teaching us how to meditate for as long as we've had legs to cross. When you meditate in nature, you've arrived where you belong, and the ease and familiarity you feel there invites you to return home to yourself, to your innermost "nature." How fascinating and appropriate that the words are the same! Entering a natural setting can stop your mind in its tracks, causing you to sense the presence of something deeper and more meaningful.

Make it a point to meditate in nature as often as you can, and take note of the state of mind and heart that it evokes. Even if you live in the inner city, you can usually find some park or garden or small patch of woods or water. Then, when you meditate at home again, you can invoke the resonance of your moments in nature to help you deepen your practice.

Why it's best to stay put

Just as it helps to have a regular time to meditate, there are some definite advantages to sitting in the same location day after day, instead of moving from place to place. These include:

- ✔ **Fewer distractions:** As a beginner, you already have plenty of distractions to contend with, both inner and outer. Why add all the nuances of a constantly shifting external environment? Once you get used to seeing those little stains on the carpet and those cracks in the paint, you can free up your attention for the matter at hand: meditation.

- ✔ **Good vibes:** The more often you sit there, the more you infuse your spot and its environs with the energy of your efforts — your good vibes, if you will. Whenever you return, your meditation is buoyed and supported by the energy you've invested, just as you feel especially comfortable and relaxed in your favorite chair.

✔ **Peaceful memories:** Once you've picked your spot, you start associating it with meditation, especially if you keep your altar or your sitting gear there. Just passing it on your way to other activities reminds you to come back to meditate when you next have a chance. And if your meditation involves spiritual aspirations, your spot becomes a sacred site where your deepest insights and reflections take place.

How to pick the right spot

If you share a small apartment with a partner or friend, or your family has usurped every square foot of usable space at your house, by all means choose the only vacant corner and make it your own. If you have more leeway, here are a few guidelines for picking your spot. And remember, even a modest patch of floor that meets these criteria is better than a sumptuous suite that doesn't:

✔ **Off the beaten track:** You know the heavily trafficked highways in your house, so be sure to avoid them. And if you don't want someone inadvertently barging in on you just when you're starting to settle, tell your housemates you're going off to meditate — they'll understand. And if they don't . . . well, that's another issue you may eventually have to face.

✔ **Away from work:** If you work at home or have a desk devoted to personal business, keep it out of sight — and mind — when you're meditating. And if possible, remember to shut off your phone; there's nothing quite as distracting to your mind as wondering who's trying to reach you now!

✔ **Relatively quiet:** Especially if you live in the city, you probably won't be able to eliminate the usual background noises — the drone of traffic, the shouts and laughter of kids on the street, the hum of the refrigerator. But you should if at all possible avoid audible conversations, especially among people you know, and the sounds of TV, radio, popular music, and other familiar distractions. These are the kinds of recognizable noises that can pull your mind away from its appointed task, especially when you're just starting out.

✔ **Not too dark or too light:** Sitting in a bright, sunny spot may be too energizing and distracting, just as sitting in the dark can put you to sleep. Be sure to modulate the lighting with your attention level in mind: If you're sleepy, open the blinds or turn on an extra light; if you're wired, tone down the illumination accordingly.

✔ **Fresh air:** Since we're talking breath here, it's great to have a supply of fresh air where you meditate. Avoid musty basements and windowless closets; besides being bad for your health, they tend to lower your energy (along with your O$_2$ level) and lull you to sleep.

✔ **Close to nature:** If you don't have a tree or a garden outside the window where you meditate, you may want to have a plant or a vase full of flowers or a few stones nearby. Not that you'll be gazing at them while you sit, but natural objects radiate a certain special energy of their own that lends support to your practice. Besides, you can pick up a few pointers by watching how rocks and trees meditate — they've been doing it a lot longer than we have. (See the sidebar "Meditating in nature" earlier in this chapter.)

How to set up an altar — and why you may want to bother

For many people, the word "altar" is fraught with associations. Maybe you have memories of being an altar boy as a kid — or you recall altars you've seen on special occasions like weddings or funerals or memorial services.

For the purposes of this book, I use "altar" to refer to a collection of objects with special meaning and resonance for you that you assemble in one place and use to inspire your meditations. If you're a Christian, for example, your altar may include a crucifix or a dove; if you're a Jew, you may have a holy book or a star of David; or, if you're a Buddhist, you may choose to contemplate a statue of Buddha or a picture of your teacher. And if you have no particular religious inclinations, you may be quite content with a few stones, a candle, and a potted plant.

TIP

Which direction should I face?

If you meditate with your eyes closed, it doesn't really matter which way your body is pointed. But if you keep your eyes open, you're better off avoiding busy, distracting views. For example, Zen monks (in certain traditions, anyway) usually sit facing a wall. Or you can gaze out on a relaxing, natural vista, if you have one, or just face your altar, with its attractive array of meaningful objects. Whatever you see when you meditate, make sure it's simple and contributes to your peace of mind.

Although an altar is not essential to meditation, it can be a creative and constantly evolving expression of your inner life, a reflection of your deepest aspirations, values, and beliefs. Gazing at your altar before you sit can evoke your connection to a spiritual dimension of being — or it can merely remind you of why you're here: to develop concentration, relax, open your heart, heal your body. Here are the main ingredients that appear on most altars (also see Figure 8-1); feel free to improvise and add or subtract as you see fit:

- ✔ Candles
- ✔ Flowers
- ✔ Incense
- ✔ Bells
- ✔ Natural objects
- ✔ Statues (of inspirational figures)
- ✔ Pictures (of nature or inspirational figures)
- ✔ Sacred texts

Figure 8-1:
Use an altar
to inspire
your
meditation.

Some traditions recommend that altars appeal to all the senses — hence, the incense, bells, flowers, and candles, which are mainstays on many home altars. In particular, the fragrance of your favorite incense can quickly become hyperlinked in your brain with meditation, so you relax just a little whenever you smell it.

Like your meditation, it's best to keep your altar simple at first. Use a small, low table or cabinet (if you meditate on the floor) covered with a special piece of cloth. You can enrich and expand it over time, if you wish, or you may prefer to keep a stash of objects and rotate them as the spirit moves you. For example, you can adapt your altar to the seasons, with flowers in spring, seashells in summer, dried leaves in autumn, pine boughs in winter, and so on.

One cautionary note about pictures: You may want to devote your altar to mentors, teachers, and other figures whose presence fills you with unadulterated inspiration — and consign to your desk or bureau those loved ones for whom your feelings may be more ambivalent, like children, parents, spouses, and friends.

Finding the beauty

Even in the most chaotic and unappealing situations, you can attune yourself to a quality or dimension of beauty, if you try. Imagine that your mind is like a CD player, and you're trying to tune in to a particular track. Or take one of those figure-ground puzzles. At first, you can't even perceive the shape in the background. But once you've seen it, you merely need to shift your awareness to see it again.

So, the next time you find yourself in an unpleasant place or circumstance — preferably not one with a strong emotional charge, which might make this exercise too difficult — do the following:

1. Take a moment to look for the beauty.

You may notice a patch of green grass in the distance, or a bouquet of flowers on a table, or the laughter of a child, or an aesthetically pleasing piece of furniture. Or you may just notice a warm feeling in your belly or heart.

2. Take a deep breath, set aside your stress and discomfort, and enjoy the beauty.

Allow yourself to resonate with it for a few moments as you would with a favorite piece of music or a walk in the woods.

3. Shift your focus back to the situation at hand and notice whether your attitude has changed in any way.

Know that you can shift your awareness in this way whenever you feel inclined.

Chapter 9

Effort, Discipline, and Letting Go

· ·

In This Chapter

▶ How to develop great meditation habits without getting uptight

▶ The secret to having more energy, in meditation and in life

▶ The five stages of letting go

· ·

As I mention in previous chapters, meditation has quite a bit in common with sports. First you have to learn the mechanics — how to sit up straight, position your legs, relax your body, and focus on your breath. Then you need to understand the rules of the game — how long it takes, where you should practice, what you should wear. But once you're clear on the details, you need to know how to apply yourself so that you can get the most from what you've learned.

Say that you want to run a marathon and you get some expert coaching on the fundamentals of running. Then you start jogging three or four miles every day. The next step is to learn how to work with your mind and your body so you can go the distance without exhausting yourself completely. You have to master some intangible inner qualities like discipline, effort, and a certain ease or comfort in your execution — qualities that can't really be taught, only described and evoked.

Well, the same is true for meditation. *Discipline* grabs you by the collar and sits you down day after day, even when the going gets tough. *Effort* keeps focusing your mind and bringing it back again and again to your breath or your mantra (or some other object of meditation). And *letting go* allows you to relax and open to whatever you're experiencing, no matter how challenging or difficult. Discovering how to apply these three ingredients to the practice of meditation is just what this chapter is all about.

Discipline Just Means "Again and Again"

If you're like most folks, the word "discipline" may be a bit of a turnoff. Perhaps it reminds you of some bossy teacher who made you stay after school or childhood punishments that were intended to "set you straight."

Or maybe you associate discipline with soldiers marching single file or with prisoners forced to obey their keepers. But the discipline I'm talking about here is quite different.

When I say *discipline,* I mean the kind of self-discipline that prompts top athletes like Jerry Rice or Monica Seles to get up every morning and run several miles and then practice their moves or their shots over and over, long after they've gotten them right. It's the kind of self-discipline that motivates great writers to sit at their computers each day, no matter how they feel, and pound out their copy.

The truth is, you already have self-discipline, though you may not be aware of it. You need self-discipline to get to your job on time or to orchestrate a schedule filled with business commitments, personal interests, and family responsibilities. You need self-discipline to pay your bills or keep up a garden or take care of your kids. You merely need to apply the same self-discipline to the practice of meditation.

Again, self-discipline is nothing more than the capacity to do something again and again. But I find it helpful to break self-discipline down a little further into three parts: *commitment, consistency,* and *self-restraint.*

Making a commitment to yourself — and keeping it

When you commit to marriage or some other monogamous relationship, you make an agreement with yourself and your partner to stay together through thick and thin, no matter what life brings. Without this commitment, you may be tempted to leave when your partner becomes angry or does something you can't stand — or when you find yourself withdrawing or "falling out of love." Of course, you can always decide to end the relationship, but as long as you're committed, you're going to do all you can to maintain it.

The same holds true for meditation. *Commitment* is the foundation for your meditation practice. Without commitment, you won't keep meditating when you're tired, have a headache, don't feel like it, would rather do something else, or run up against some of the roadblocks talked about in Chapter 12.

And what prompts you to make the commitment to meditate in the first place? You have to be motivated (see Chapter 4), which means you have to know how you can benefit from what meditation has to offer (see Chapter 2), and you must have strong personal reasons for continuing. These reasons may include a desire to alleviate personal suffering or stress, an aspiration to achieve greater focus and clarity, and a concern for the welfare of others.

The commitment process usually involves five distinct steps — though it doesn't necessarily have to be so formal:

- ✔ **Becoming motivated:** Ouch, life hurts! I need to find out how to deal with my pain.

- ✔ **Setting your intention:** I know, I'll meditate for one-half hour every day!

- ✔ **Making an agreement with yourself:** From now until the end of the month, I agree to get up at 7 a.m. and count my breaths before I go to work.

- ✔ **Following through:** Whew! I didn't realize how hard it would be to sit still for so long — but I refuse to break my agreement with myself!

- ✔ **Gaining momentum:** Wow! The more I meditate, the easier it gets. I'm really beginning to enjoy it.

Being consistent, day after day

Take sports again. If you train for a day and then slack off for a week, you won't make much progress. In fact, you may end up straining a muscle or hurting your back because you haven't conditioned your body gradually, as most fitness gurus recommend.

When you practice meditation, you're developing certain mental and emotional muscles like concentration, mindfulness (ongoing attention to whatever is arising, moment to moment), and receptive awareness. (See Chapter 1 for more about these "mental and emotional muscles.") Here, too, consistency is the key — you need to keep it up and keep it regular, no

If you don't dig sports, try gardening

Although meditating has a lot in common with practicing and playing a sport, for some folks, meditating may be more akin to gardening. After you plant the seeds, you don't try to force the seedlings out of the ground — do you?! You just water and fertilize, thin and water some more, and eventually the little shoots appear on their own, coaxed into the light by some complex and mysterious mixture of chemistry, genetics, phototropism, and who knows what else.

The point is, you don't have to know — you just have to do your part and get out of the way! If you get carried away and overwater or disturb the ground prematurely, you only interfere with the process.

In the same way, you need to exert just the right amount of consistent effort in your meditation — don't overwater or keep scratching the ground searching for signs of progress, but don't go away for a week and leave your plot unattended, either. Do what you need to do without fixating on the results, and your garden will blossom quite naturally, all by itself.

matter how you're feeling from day to day. In fact, your feelings provide the fodder for your meditation practice, as you expand your awareness from your breath to include the full range of your experience. There's no special way you need to be — just show up and be yourself!

As one old Chinese Zen master used to say, "Sun-faced Buddha, moon-faced Buddha" — by which he meant, happy or sad, energetic or tired, just sit as the being you happen to be.

Be especially wary of two extremes: laziness or *self-indulgence* — "I'd rather be sleeping, resting, watching TV" — and *perfectionism* — "I'm not ready to meditate. I'm not smart or good or focused enough." Remember, we're talking about meditation for beginners here — and besides, the best way to become "good" enough to meditate is to just do it!

Restraining yourself, both on and off the cushion

Broadly speaking, *self-restraint* is the quality of mind that keeps you from acting on every impulse or desire that flits through your brain and that helps you discriminate between behavior that's useful and supportive and behavior that's unsupportive or even harmful. If you're an athlete, you need self-restraint to prevent you from eating junk food or staying out late when you're training for a big competition. If you're a meditator, self-restraint can function on several different levels:

- ✔ **Before meditation:** You may choose to eat well and in moderation or avoid mind-altering substances such as tobacco or caffeine because you want to keep your mind clear and fresh for your meditation.

- ✔ **During meditation:** You can use self-restraint to keep pulling your mind back from its habitual fantasies and preoccupations to the object of your meditation, be it your breath or a mantra or some other focus. Be careful, however, not to confuse self-restraint with repression, avoidance, or judgment. You don't need to criticize yourself for wandering off, nor do you want to push certain "undesirable" thoughts or feelings out of your mind. Instead, just welcome whatever arises, while gently returning your focus to the object of your meditation.

- ✔ **After meditation:** As your practice deepens and strengthens, you build a certain power or energy of mind — in the East they call it *samadhi*. (For more on energy, see the section "The Right Kind of Effort: Not Too Tight or Too Loose.") You can blow off this energy by daydreaming or planning or obsessing — or you can use self-restraint to channel your energy back into your practice of being mindful from moment to moment.

Like self-discipline, self-restraint has a bad rap in our culture. After all, aren't you supposed to say what you think and do what feels right? But what feels right in the moment may not be the same as what feels right in the long run — and self-restraint is the faculty that helps you distinguish between the two. For example, you may be tempted to charge those plane tickets to Hawaii because it feels right, but you may have different feelings altogether when you get your credit card statement. In the same way, it may feel great to spend your meditation indulging in fantasy — until you start wondering in a month or two why you still can't count your breaths from one to ten. Above all, though, remember to be gentle with yourself!

The Right Kind of Effort: Not Too Tight or Too Loose

If discipline is the capacity to keep doing something again and again, then *effort* is the quality of energy and exertion you bring to the activity itself. Although it may take discipline to show up at the gym every day, it takes effort to do those aerobics or lift those weights or shoot those hoops. I'm sure you know what I'm talking about! As with self-discipline, you may find it helpful to break effort into three convenient parts: *energy, earnestness,* and *effortless effort.*

Giving your energy 100 percent

There's a secret "law of energy" that applies just as well to meditation as it does to sports — and to life in general: The more you expend, the more you get back in return. We can be stingy about our energy, parceling it out from one activity to the next as though we have just so much to give and no more. But if you love something and give yourself to it wholeheartedly, you may have noticed that the energy just feeds on itself and keeps growing and growing.

In the NBA finals one year, Michael Jordan was suffering from an intestinal flu so severe that he needed fluid IVs and could barely stand. Yet, carried aloft by his own dedication (what he calls "heart") and fueled by an energy that seemed drawn from a source far vaster than his own exhausted body, he suited up for his team and scored 38 points. Jordan embodies the quality of wholeheartedness.

In meditation, too, the more wholeheartedly you practice, the more you tap into a seemingly limitless energy source. It's as though the flame inside your heart begins channeling the fusion energy that runs the sun. But don't confuse wholeheartedness with struggle; when you meditate, remember to relax and open while you focus your mind. It's this unique balance of active and receptive, yang and yin, that characterizes the practice of meditation. (For more on this balance, see the section, "Making an effortless effort.")

Doing what you love

Choose an activity you especially enjoy. Maybe it's dancing or cooking or painting or making love or simply playing with your kids.

Next time you engage in the activity, give yourself to it wholeheartedly. Don't hold back or conserve your energy in any way. You might experiment with losing yourself completely in the activity, the way children do. Don't keep looking at your watch or wondering how you're doing; just do it without reservation — until you and the activity seem to merge and become one.

How do you know when to stop? Do you suddenly find yourself disengaging? Or do you reach a natural stopping point when you intuitively know it's time? And how do you feel when you're done? Do you feel drained and tired? Or do you feel energized and excited? Think of this exercise next time you sit down to meditate.

Applying yourself "earnestly"

Where self-restraint keeps you from doing what might be harmful or unhealthy and wholeheartedness supplies the spark that ignites your meditation, earnestness keeps bringing your mind back again and again to your focus. No matter what thoughts or feelings arise to seduce you away, you just keep plugging along — following your breaths or chanting your mantra or paying mindful attention in everyday life. Just as it takes consistency to return to your sitting day after day, it takes earnest application to return to the focus of your meditation moment after moment, without struggling or giving up. Earnestness isn't sexy or exciting — it's just essential! (Perhaps this is what Oscar Wilde meant by *The Importance of Being Earnest*.)

Making an effortless effort

When I was a neophyte meditator, one of my teachers, the Zen master Shunryu Suzuki, used to say somewhat mysteriously, "Follow the wave, drive the wave." But I never really knew what he meant until I started to surf. Now I understand!

When I'm out there on the ocean floating on my board, alone with the wind and the sky, I'm excruciatingly aware of how small and insignificant I am in comparison to the awesome power of the water. It would be presumptuous of me to say that I surf the waves — in fact, the waves surf me!

TRADITIONAL WISDOM

Digging your way to freedom

One of the great meditative traditions tells the story of a prisoner who is sentenced to life for a crime he did not commit. At first, he bemoans his fate and indulges in fantasies of revenge and regret. Then he bestirs himself and decides to get free, no matter what happens. So he starts digging a hole in the wall of his cell with a spoon — kind of like Tim Robbins in *The Shawshank Redemption*.

Day after day, week after week, year after year he digs, making slow but steady progress. Then one day, worn out from his labors, he leans against the back door of his cell — and it gives beneath his weight! In an instant, he realizes that all these years, while he was slaving away at his attempts to get free, the door to freedom was open all along — but he might never have realized it had he not worked so hard to escape.

The point of this story is clear: If you practice your meditation with steady and consistent effort, you will eventually experience moments when all effort drops away, the door opens wide, and you're simply present, aware, peaceful, and relaxed.

Although these moments may seem quite ordinary when they occur, they can have a powerful, healing effect on your body and mind because they offer you a brief glimpse of your essential wholeness and completeness, free from the overlays of conditioning and striving.

Yet, the paradox is that the door is always open and the glimpses of being are always available — in a loving glance, a child's laughter, or the silence of the trees — but you may have to exert effort and practice for years before you stumble upon them. And then again, you may not!

I know that I can't possibly attempt to control the water in any way. Yet, I do need to exert a certain effort: I need to concentrate on the swell, paddle at just the right time, and position my body in just the right way to catch the wave at its apex so that it can carry me to the shore. And I need to stay focused as I shift my weight ever so subtly from side to side in order to ride the wave as fully as I possibly can.

Well, meditation is like surfing. If you push too hard and try to control your mind, you'll just end up feeling rigid and tight, and you'll keep wiping out as the result of your effort. But if you hang back and exert no effort at all, you won't have the focus or concentration necessary to hold your position as the waves of thought and emotion wash over you.

Like surfing — or skiing or any sport, for that matter — meditation requires a constantly shifting balance of yang and yin, driving and following, effort and effortlessness. As I mention in Chapter 1, concentration is the yang of meditation — focused, powerful, penetrating — and receptive awareness is the yin — open, expansive, welcoming. Although you may have to exert considerable effort at first just to develop your concentration, try not to become tense or obsessive about it. Let your effort be effortless, like a seasoned surfer's.

Eventually, your concentration will arise quite naturally and take only minimal effort to maintain, and you will be able to relax and open your awareness to whatever arises. Even the notions of yin and yang (awareness and concentration) will ultimately drop away, and you can just *be,* with effortless effort — which is the real point of meditation.

In addition to effortless effort, meditation poses a number of paradoxes that the mind can't quite comprehend but that the body and heart find easy to grasp. To practice meditation, it helps to be:

- **Serious yet lighthearted:** After all, meditation is about lightening up — yet, if you're not serious enough, you won't make any progress.

- **Alert yet relaxed:** Learn to balance these two qualities in your meditation. If you become too relaxed, you risk falling asleep, but if you're too alert (that is, wired), you could become tense.

- **Spontaneous yet restrained:** You can be totally "in the moment" and open to whatever arises in your awareness without becoming impulsive or indulging every fantasy or whim.

- **Engaged yet dispassionate:** While being focused and attentive, you can avoid getting caught up in the compelling and emotionally charged stories your mind spins out.

Cat-and-mouse meditation

To learn how to meditate with effortless effort, combining just the right balance of alertness and relaxation, spend some time watching cats.

Although they seem so settled and self-contained, cats are acutely aware of what's going on around them. If they hear the chirp of a bird or see a mouse scurrying across the floor, they can leap up in a heartbeat and pursue their prey at full speed.

Once their prey has escaped, however, cats don't appear to become attached to the memory of what might have been. Instead, they settle down once again and resume their meditation. You would never associate cats with making an effort — they're simply being themselves wholeheartedly, engrossed in the present moment, open to whatever occurs. Apply this same quality of energy and earnestness to your meditation, and you'll get the knack in no time.

How to Let Go — and What to Let Go Of

In certain parts of Asia, they have an ingenious method for catching monkeys. The hunter cuts a hole in a coconut just big enough for a monkey to reach in with its hand, but not big enough for it to remove its closed fist. Then the hunter puts a ripe banana inside, attaches the coconut to a string, and waits. Upon grabbing the banana, the monkey becomes so attached to keeping the fruit that it refuses to let go, and the hunter can reel the animal in like a fish on a hook.

As I mention in Chapter 6, your mind is like a monkey in more ways than one. Not only does it leap about from thought to thought like a monkey in a tree, but it also has the annoying tendency of holding tightly to certain ideas, opinions, thoughts, memories, and emotions, as though its life (and yours) depends on it — and pushing away others with equal force.

This constant shifting between attachment and aversion causes you stress because you're constantly struggling to control what can't be controlled. Thoughts and feelings come and go whether you like them or not, and the stock market falls and relationships end despite your preferences to the contrary. (For more on how the mind causes suffering and stress, see Chapter 5.)

In Alcoholics Anonymous and other 12-step programs, people recite the following prayer: "Grant me the serenity to accept what I cannot change, the courage to change what I can, and the wisdom to know the difference." In meditation, you develop the power to control or change what you can — not the events or circumstances of your life, but how you relate to them — and the peace of mind to accept what you can't.

Meditation teaches you how to loosen your monkey-grip on your experience and create a kind of inner spaciousness and relaxation by letting go of control and allowing things to be the way they are. This process has several dimensions or stages, which often (though not always) occur in the following order:

✔ **Suspending judgment:** If you're like most people, you're constantly judging your experience as good, bad, or indifferent and reacting accordingly: "Ooh, I like that, I'm going to try to get more of it"; "I hate that, I'm going to avoid it at all costs"; "That doesn't do anything for me, I'm not going to pay any attention to it." When you meditate, you begin to notice the steady stream of judgments and how they dominate your mind and distort your experience. Instead of indulging this habitual pattern, you can practice witnessing your experience impartially, without judgment. When judgments arise, which they undoubtedly will, you can just be aware of them, while avoiding the temptation to judge them as well. Gradually, the habit of judging will loosen its grip on your mind.

✔ **Accepting:** The flip side of suspending judgment involves learning to accept things just the way they are. You don't necessarily have to like what you see, and you're welcome to change it — but first you need to experience it fully and clearly, without the overlays of judgment and denial. For example, you may have lots of anger bubbling up, but you may believe that this particular emotion is bad or even evil, so you refuse to acknowledge it.

In meditation, you have an opportunity to observe the anger just as it is — recurrent angry thoughts, waves of anger in the belly — without trying to change or get rid of it. (For more on meditating with challenging emotions and mind-states, see Chapter 11.) The more you welcome the full range of your experiences in this way, the more space you create inside yourself to contain them — and the more you defuse those old familiar conflicts between different parts of yourself.

✔ **Letting go:** Participants in 12-step programs also sometimes talk about "letting go and letting God." The first stage involves letting go of the illusion that you have unlimited control over your life. In mindfulness meditation, you can practice letting go by dropping all struggles to control your mind — and all ideas you may have about how your meditation is supposed to look — and relaxing into the present moment as it unfolds, both inside and outside. Believe it or not, you already know how to let go — you do it every night when you drift off to sleep.

✔ **Unmasking:** Letting go also has a deeper dimension: The more you loosen the stranglehold of your likes and dislikes, preferences and prejudices, memories and stories, the more you open to the experience of just being, beyond any limited identities or interpretations. These identities are like the layers of an onion or clouds that hide the radiance of the sun. As your meditation deepens, you can learn to accept and then let go of these clouds, without mistaking them for the light they obscure. By disidentifying more and more with what you are not — the masks that hide your true nature — you gradually begin to identify with what you are: pure being. (For more on pure being, see Chapter 1.)

✔ **Surrendering:** As your meditation opens you to an experience of pure being, you may begin to recognize the value of the second stage of the 12-step dictum: "letting God." The truth is, the power or force that's actually controlling your life (and which you essentially are) is far bigger than your small self, and it's eminently trustworthy — some would even say it's sacred or divine. When you begin to loosen your vice-grip on the steering wheel of your life, you don't plunge headlong into the chaotic abyss, as you might fear; instead, you relinquish your apparent control to the one who has always been in control — call it God or Self or pure being. In your meditation, you may actually experience this surrender as a deeper and deeper relaxation into the sacred silence or stillness that surrounds, suffuses, and sustains you.

MEDITATION

Accepting and letting go

Holding on tightly and pushing away hard, lusting and hating, defending and attacking — traditionally known as *attachment* and *aversion* — are the primary causes of suffering and stress. Along with indifference, they form the proverbial three poisons of meditation lore.

Fortunately, you can cultivate the antidotes to these poisons by practicing the two most important gestures or functions of meditation: accepting and letting go. They're inextricably entwined: Until you accept, you can't let go; until you let go, you have no room to accept again. As one Zen master put it, "Let go of it, and it fills your hand." Here's a little exercise that gives you an opportunity to practice both accepting and letting go:

1. **Begin by sitting comfortably and taking a few deep breaths. Now place your attention on the coming and going of your breath.**

2. **After a few minutes, shift your awareness to your thoughts and feelings.**

   Take the attitude that you're going to welcome whatever arises in your experience without judging or rejecting it.

3. **As thoughts and feelings come and go, notice the movement to avoid or push away or not see what you find unpleasant or unacceptable.**

   Accept this movement as you continue to welcome your experience, whatever it may happen to be.

4. **After five or ten minutes, when you have a feel for accepting, shift your attention to the process of letting go.**

   Take the attitude that you're going to let go of whatever arises, no matter how urgent or attractive.

   Notice the movement to hold on or indulge or get involved with thoughts and feelings you find pleasant or compelling. Gently restrain yourself and continue to loosen your grip and let go.

Once you have a feel for both accepting and letting go, you can combine them in the same meditation. Whatever arises, welcome and let go, welcome and let go. This is the twofold rhythm of mindfulness meditation.

IN THE MOMENT

Breathing with your belly

Healthy breathing involves opening and expanding both your belly and your chest. As a culture, we tend to value big chests and small bellies. As a result, we learn early how to "suck it in" and not let our belly (or our feelings) show. (Believe it or not, there are cultures where a relaxed, expanded belly is considered attractive!)

The problem is, we don't allow ourselves to breathe with our bellies. This habit just limits the amount of life-enhancing oxygen we receive and accentuates the stress pattern of tightening our abdominal muscles and diaphragm (the big internal muscle that covers the bottom of the rib cage) and holding our breath.

To counteract this pattern and help you relax, try the following exercise, drawn from hatha yoga:

1. **Notice how you're breathing right now.**

   Which parts of your body expand when you breathe, and which parts do not? How deeply and quickly (or slowly) are you breathing? Where does your breathing feel tight or constricted? How do your belly muscles and diaphragm feel?

2. **Make a conscious effort to expand your belly when you breathe.**

   I use the word "effort" advisedly because your abdominal muscles and diaphragm may be quite tight at first.

3. **Breathe deeply and slowly into your belly.**

   Notice your body's resistance to changing your habitual breathing patterns.

4. **Continue breathing in this way for five minutes and then breathe naturally.**

   Do you notice any differences? Do your abdominal muscles feel more relaxed? Are you breathing more deeply than before? Do you feel more energized or calm?

Practice this exercise regularly — at least once a day. It can be especially useful when you're stressed out or anxious and your belly starts to tighten and your breathing constricts. Just shift to belly breathing and notice what happens.

Chapter 10

Opening Your Heart: Love, Compassion, and Forgiveness

● ●

In This Chapter

▶ The pros and cons of opening your heart

▶ Exploring your "soft spot" and the tender emotions inside

▶ Directing your love to yourself (the hardest part!) and others

▶ Some great techniques for cultivating compassion

▶ Cleaning out your arteries with forgiveness and gratitude

● ●

*P*erhaps you're wondering why I devote a chapter of this book to the heart. After all, isn't it true that meditation involves sitting quietly and focusing the mind, whereas affairs of the heart are best reserved for romantic encounters and intimate family discussions?

Well, the great meditative traditions teach that you can cultivate the energy of the heart in meditation the same way you cultivate awareness (for more on awareness, see Chapter 1). Whether it takes the form of love, joy, peace, compassion, or devotion, you can consciously and deliberately generate and expand this energy to create a field that benefits not only yourself, but also the people around you.

Like sunlight, the radiance of an open heart warms and nourishes everyone it touches. But the heart, like the sun, is often closed in and obscured by clouds, in the form of difficult emotions and mind-states like fear, anger, judgment, and doubt. When you practice meditation, you gradually dispel some of these clouds by quieting and calming your agitated mind (see Chapter 6). You can also work directly with unraveling the negative stories your mind tells you and dealing with challenging emotions, as I explain in Chapter 11. Then again, you can take the approach I describe in this chapter: You can burn the clouds away by amplifying the natural warmth of your heart through practices designed to cultivate love and compassion.

Before I show you how to do this, however, I'd like to take you on a guided tour of the territory. Yes, I know you know where your heart is. But have you ever explored it with focused attention? Do you know what causes it to close — and what keeps it closed? And have you ever considered all the ways you can benefit from opening it? Here are some answers.

How Your Heart Closes — and How You Can Open It Again

Needless to say, you weren't born with your heart closed. As anyone who's ever spent any time with a newborn knows, babies have hearts that radiate love like the sun in the tropics. But as you grow up, the bumps and bruises and hardships of life gradually force you to protect your tenderness and other softer emotions with a layer of toughness and defensiveness — the clouds I talked about earlier. This layer surrounds and encloses the heart, protecting your vulnerability — but also keeping your own love locked inside and the love of other people from entering.

Perhaps you're one of those rare individuals whose heart remains open most of the time. If so, congratulations! Or maybe you wrap yourself in a cloud-cover — or something even denser, like armor — when you head out the door each morning, but lay it aside when you spend time with friends or family members. Perhaps your heart naturally opens and closes in an ebb and flow like the weather. Or you may be among the millions of people who have difficulty letting love in or extending it to others.

Don't lose heart! You can definitely learn how to open your heart again, as I discuss later in this section. But first I'd like to describe the factors that keep closing your heart when it opens — or keep it closed entirely — and the benefits that come with an open heart, in case you hadn't already figured them out.

Some factors that keep closing your heart

Like most human beings, you close your heart, whether automatically or deliberately, because you feel angry, hurt, or threatened by others. Perhaps you're afraid they'll take advantage of your kindness or crush your tender feelings with their insensitivity or restimulate painful memories. Or maybe you're just ticked off about all the times you've been mistreated, and you don't want to let it to happen again. We all have our own unique reasons for closing our hearts. Whatever yours happen to be, they may be preventing you from getting the love you really want.

Here are some of the most common factors that close the heart:

- **Fear:** When you're afraid, for whatever reason — of being attacked, criticized, manipulated, overwhelmed — you close your heart in self-defense. As one popular slogan puts it, love is letting go of fear — and learning how to trust, both yourself and others.

- **Resentment:** When you hold on to old hurts and let bitterness and resentment build in your heart, you shut your heart, not only to the people who hurt you but also to life itself.

- **Unresolved grief:** This natural human emotion can get stuck if you continue to mull over your losses and refuse to let go of the past. When grief fills your heart, you're reluctant to open it because you don't want to feel the pain inside.

- **Jealousy:** Actually a brand of resentment, jealousy can close your heart to the person who has what you wish you had — and to yourself as well for being somehow "inferior."

- **Pain:** Also known as hurt, this feeling, if allowed to build to intolerable levels, may cause you to board up your heart completely and post a sign saying, "Keep out! No trespassing!"

- **Grasping and attachment:** As long as you're emotionally attached to having life go a certain way, you're going to close your heart as soon as other people interfere. In fact, emotions like grief, pain, and even resentment are ultimately rooted in attachment — and the fear of losing what you're attached to.

- **Self-clinging:** If you believe that you're an isolated individual cut off from other people and from your own essential being, you're going to hold on to your own little piece of turf — your own possessions, your own accomplishments, your own happiness — and close your heart, if necessary, to defend it. Also known as *ego* in many of the meditative traditions, self-clinging perpetuates separation and gives rise to the other factors in this list.

Ultimately, of course, only the most enlightened, selfless people can keep their hearts open all of the time. I mean, we're talking Jesus or Mother Teresa here! As for the rest of us, we're going to keep closing our hearts again and again. Only when we've dissolved the barriers that separate us from others — which is what enlightenment is all about — can we keep our hearts open even in the most difficult circumstances.

But, enlightened or not, you can definitely develop the ability to open your heart when you choose to do so. In fact, the regular practice of meditation gradually erodes the experience of separation that causes the heart to stay closed in the first place. (For more on separation, see Chapter 5.) Who knows? One day you may open your heart and never close it again!

Kindness is the key

Although the cultivation of an open heart definitely deserves a chapter of its own, it's traditionally considered the foundation on which meditation practice rests, rather than a separate technique or approach.

In Southeast Asia, for example, meditators are taught how to develop generosity, patience, and lovingkindness before they learn how to meditate. And Tibetan practitioners dedicate the benefit of every meditation to the peace and harmony of all beings, not just themselves. As the Dalai Lama, recipient of the Nobel Peace Prize, says, "My religion is kindness."

You can follow every technique to the *T*, but if your heart's not in it, you won't reap all the wonderful benefits of meditation.

To be open to the present moment, for example, as mindfulness meditation teaches (for more on mindfulness, see Chapter 6), you need to be open with every dimension of your being: body, mind, spirit, and heart. So be sure to bring a measure of love and caring to your meditation — especially toward yourself!

Some good reasons for keeping it open

Imagine that an extraterrestrial lands on Earth and tries to make sense of us human beings from our popular songs. It would probably conclude that we regard love (whatever that might be!) as infinitely more precious than everything else combined. But once the ET figures out how to measure love, it might be surprised to discover how little of the invaluable substance actually flows between us most of the time. Love, the ET would no doubt deduce, is not only precious, it's incredibly hard to find.

For creatures who want to be loved, appreciated, even adored, we certainly go about fulfilling our desire in a curiously unfulfilling way. Instead of manufacturing it ourselves in the little love machine inside our chests, we complain about not getting enough of it, search frantically for someone else to give it to us, and try to make ourselves more lovable by improving our looks or earning more money. But the truth is, the Beatles song has it right: The love you take is equal to the love you make. In other words, the most effective way to get love is to generate it yourself.

By cultivating caring, loving feelings, you can actually provide yourself with the nourishment you seek. At the same time, by radiating those feelings outward to others, you can touch their tender hearts and naturally elicit the same feelings in them, creating a flow of love that keeps circulating between you and building on itself.

If you've never experienced this kind of flow with someone yourself, you've perhaps met people who live this way. Their eyes sparkle with positive regard, their words speak well of everyone, and they elicit love wherever they go. Through the practices described here, you too can begin to generate a flow of loving feelings. It all depends on you.

Here are a few of the innumerable benefits of learning how to love:

✔ **Energy and expansiveness:** If you've ever been in love (maybe you are right now!), you know how vital and alive you can feel when your heart is wide open. Instead of the usual sense of limitation you ordinarily experience, you feel like you have no boundaries, as though you can't really tell where you leave off and the outside world (or your beloved) begins.

✔ **Peace and well-being:** When your heart is filled with love, you feel happy and peaceful for no external reason. In fact, love, happiness, joy, peace, well-being are just different names and versions of the same basic energy — the loving, life-giving energy of the heart.

✔ **Good health:** Yes, love is life-giving and life-enhancing. For one thing, it brings people together to create babies, and in general love contributes to optimal health by providing an immeasurable vital spark that not only nourishes the internal organs but also provides the body (and the person) with a reason to live. Dean Ornish, M.D., author of *Dr. Dean*

The warrior of the heart

For all you tough guys (and gals) who believe that opening the heart is best reserved for sissies and fools, here's some wise counsel from the Tibetan meditation master Chogyam Trungpa. (No stranger to toughness, Trungpa, like the Dalai Lama and thousands of other Tibetans, escaped from his homeland when the Chinese invaded and walked across the Himalayas over a series of precipitous mountain passes to India.)

In his book *Shambhala: The Sacred Path of the Warrior,* he explains that it takes tremendous courage to face your fear and negativity and be willing to keep your heart open — even in the most challenging circumstances.

Although you probably think of warriors as impenetrable, unfeeling, and heavily defended, Trungpa takes the opposite view. The sacred warrior who practices meditation, he suggests, is not afraid to feel tender — or to communicate this tenderness to others.

The point is, you can take care of yourself — even defend yourself from harm, when necessary — without closing your heart. An open heart doesn't make you powerless or ineffectual! Quite the contrary, it allows you to respond to situations wisely and skillfully because you feel others' suffering as well as your own.

Ornish's Program for Reversing Heart Disease, found that love is more important than any other factor in the healing process, including diet and exercise. To heal your heart, he discovered, you need to open your heart. (For more on Dr. Ornish, see Chapter 2.)

✔ **Belonging and interconnectedness:** As another old song puts it, love makes the world go round — and it certainly draws people together and keeps them connected. When you open your heart to others, you naturally feel joined with them in a meaningful way. In the deepest sense, love is the source of all meaning and belonging.

✔ **Spiritual awakening:** As they gradually erode your sense of separateness from others, loving feelings can eventually reveal the essential nature of life, which is, paradoxically, also love. Ultimately, the Sufis teach, we are simply love searching for itself.

Discovering your "soft spot"

One of my teachers, the Tibetan meditation master Sogyal Rinpoche, used to refer to the place inside where you feel tender, loving emotions as your *soft spot.* The soft spot can be found in your heart, beneath all the toughness and defensiveness. To reach it, you have to risk encountering feelings you might otherwise wish to avoid, such as fear, grief, anger, and the others talked about earlier in this chapter. You'll know the soft spot when you get there because it has a tender sweetness to it that's often tinged with a certain sadness or melancholy about the human condition. (In fact, you may find it slightly painful to open your heart at first simply because of this sadness, which is actually one of the seeds of compassion.)

Because you'll need to be familiar with your soft spot in order to practice the meditations provided in the remainder of this chapter, you may want to experiment with the following exercise:

1. **Begin by closing your eyes, taking a few deep breaths, and relaxing your body a little on each exhalation.**

   Remember to be kind to yourself.

2. **Imagine the face of someone who loved you very much as a child and whose love moved you deeply.**

   In the East, they recommend using your mother, but some Westerners tend to have a more problematic relationship with their parents, so you may prefer to use your grandmother or grandfather or some other unconditionally loving figure. (If you never received love like this as a child, you can think of some famous person that you consider to be unconditionally loving, such as Jesus or Buddha or the Divine Mother.)

3. **Remember a particular instance in which this person showed his or her love for you and you really received it and allowed it to nurture you.**

4. **Notice the tender, loving feelings this memory evokes in your heart.**

   The place where you feel them is your soft spot.

5. **Notice if any other feelings accompany the tenderness and gratitude you feel.**

6. **If you find it difficult to reexperience the love, pay attention to what gets in your way.**

   What are some of the feelings standing guard over your soft spot?

7. **Begin to explore the area around your soft spot.**

   What is the state of your heart right now? What are some of the other feelings you find stirring inside, in addition to (or instead of) love? Do you notice any tension or bracing around your heart that keeps it from opening to love?

8. **Be aware of what you find without judgment or self-criticism.**

Love begins with you

You may find it difficult to feel love and extend it to others because you didn't get much of it yourself as a child. Even though you never really learned how to give and receive love freely, people are constantly asking you for what you believe you don't have. You're like a person living in the desert with a dry well; you can't share any water with others because you don't have any yourself. Or you may find that your well has water but constantly runs dry just when you need it most.

The meditations provided in this chapter dig a well deep into your soft spot, where the waters of love never run dry. (In fact, the love I'm talking about doesn't belong to anyone; it just bubbles up from a mysterious and inexhaustible source.) You may need to prime the pump, though. That's why the traditional instructions counsel you to begin each meditation on love and compassion by focusing on yourself. Once you've filled your own well to the brim, you can begin to extend the overflow to include others as well.

Just as you can't really heal others until you've healed yourself to a certain degree, you can't love others until you feel deeply loved yourself. Besides, you deserve love at least as much as anyone else. In the West, we often practice self-denial, while equating self-love with selfishness. Yet, the reverse generally holds true: People who love themselves give love more freely and generously than those who don't.

Appreciating your own goodness

If you have difficulty extending loving feelings to yourself, you may want to take five or ten minutes to reflect on your good qualities or the good things you've done in your life. Go ahead, it won't hurt you!

In the West, we have a cultural taboo against praising ourselves. Instead, we often focus on our shortcomings, which only ends up making us feel contracted and afraid. "Pride goes before a fall," chides the old slogan, suggesting that you'd better watch out because any satisfaction you take in yourself or your accomplishments could destroy you. "Who do you think you are?" intones the childhood voice of an exasperated mother or father, unwittingly teaching shame and self-doubt.

Despite what your parents (or other influential people) may have implied or told you, it's okay to be happy and to feel good about yourself. By focusing on your goodness, you actually generate positive, expansive feelings that nourish you and everyone around you. "Joy," said the Buddha, "is the gateway to nirvana."

As a remedy for the widespread Western disease of self-criticism and self-denial, the meditative traditions offer the practice of self-love. In particular, as you work with opening your heart, you can remember to keep your heart open to yourself even, paradoxically, when your heart is closed.

Four dimensions of love

Like water, love comes in many shapes and sizes. Just as a crystal-clear mountain lake, a still forest pool, a trickling creek, and a roaring river are all composed of water, so tender emotions like kindness, compassion, joy, gratitude, forgiveness, devotion, generosity, and peace or equanimity arise in the heart and ultimately consist of love. Remember, these aren't abstractions — they're natural human qualities that you can learn how to cultivate and communicate to others.

Among all these tender emotions, the Buddhists emphasize the following four as the cornerstones of a happy and fulfilling life:

- ✔ **Lovingkindess:** Arises spontaneously in response to the kindness of others and consists of warm, loving, caring feelings that can be deliberately increased and extended.

- ✔ **Compassion:** Takes love a step further. In addition to caring about others, you also feel their suffering and naturally feel motivated to help relieve it. (The word "compassion" means "to suffer with.")

> ✔ **Sympathetic joy:** Is the flip side of compassion. It consists of happy feelings that arise in response to the happiness and good fortune of others.

> ✔ **Equanimity:** Can be cultivated through the basic meditation practices taught in this book; also known as steadiness of heart. No matter what happens, you expand to include it without allowing it to upset or disturb you.

In the following sections, I focus on love and compassion, with some special attention to gratitude and forgiveness as antidotes to the resentment and fear that so often keep the heart closed.

How to Generate Love for Yourself and Others

As I mentioned earlier, you have a love factory right here in your chest. Now, you're going to discover how to use it! As a child, you probably received lots of advice on how to use your mind. Your teachers taught you how to solve math problems and memorize facts; your parents may have helped you with your homework; perhaps you even read some books on speed-reading or improving your study habits. But did anyone ever sit you down and explain how to love? Sure, you had role models — but did they teach you how to do what they did? In this section, you're going to pick up some skills you never studied at home or in school.

Opening the gates

The following steps are a meditation for connecting with your soft spot and initiating the flow of unconditional love, also known as *lovingkindness*. (To distinguish this kind of love from conditional love, imagine the love of a good mother for her baby. She gives her love freely and unconditionally, without expecting anything in return except her baby's happiness and well-being.) As with all the meditations presented in this chapter, you may want to begin with five or ten minutes of a mindfulness practice like counting or following your breaths (see Chapter 6) in order to deepen and stabilize your concentration. Once you get the knack, though, the cultivation of lovingkindness itself can be an excellent way to develop concentration.

1. **Begin by closing your eyes, taking a few deep breaths, and relaxing your body a little with each exhalation.**

2. **Imagine the face of someone who loved you very much as a child and whose love moved you deeply.**

3. **Remember a time when this person showed his or her love for you and you really took it in.**

4. **Notice the gratitude and love this memory evokes in your heart. Allow these feelings to well up and fill your heart.**

5. **Gently extend these feelings to this loved one.**

   You may even experience a circulation of love between the two of you as you give and receive love freely.

6. **Allow these loving feelings to overflow and gradually suffuse your whole being.**

   Allow yourself to be filled with love.

Directing the flow

Once you've initiated the flow of love, you can channel it, first to yourself and then to the other people in your life. After practicing the preceding meditation for five minutes or longer, continue in the following way:

1. **As you allow lovingkindness to fill your being, you may want to express the wishes and intentions that underlie this love.**

   For example, you might say to yourself, as the Buddhists do, "May I be happy. May I be peaceful. May I be free from suffering." Or you may want to choose something from the Western religious tradition, such as "May I be filled with the grace and love of God." Feel free to use whatever words feel right for you. Just be sure to keep them general, simple, and emotionally evocative. As the recipient, be sure to take in the love as well as extending it.

Allowing life to keep opening your heart

As you go through your day, you no doubt encounter moments when you feel a spontaneous uprush of love or compassion. Maybe you glimpse a homeless old woman pushing a shopping cart or hear a dog howling unhappily or see the face of a starving child or a grieving mother in some faraway place on the evening news, and your heart goes out to this being in compassion. Or perhaps someone does something unexpectedly kind for you or a good friend reminds you that she loves you or you gaze into the eyes of someone you care about deeply, and you feel love and gratitude welling up in your heart.

Instead of rushing on to the next moment or pushing the feeling away uncomfortably, you can take some time to close your eyes, meditate on it, and allow it to deepen. Life has the capacity, all by itself, to keep opening your heart, if you let it. Your job is merely to gently extend those moments until they gradually begin to fill your life.

2. **When you feel complete with yourself for now, imagine someone for whom you feel gratitude and respect. Take some time (at least a few minutes) to direct the flow of love to this person, using similar words to express your intentions.**

   Don't hurry; allow yourself to feel the love as much as you can, rather than merely imagine it.

3. **Take some time to direct this lovingkindness to a loved one or dear friend in a similar way.**

4. **Direct this flow of love to someone for whom you feel neutral — perhaps someone you see from time to time but toward whom you have neither positive nor negative feelings.**

5. **Now, for the hardest part of this exercise: Direct your lovingkindness to someone toward whom you feel mildly negative feelings like irritation or hurt.**

   By extending love to this person, even just a little at first, you begin to develop the capacity to keep your heart open even in challenging circumstances. Eventually, you can extend love to people toward whom you experience stronger emotions like anger, fear, or pain.

Like the other meditations in this book, lovingkindness can benefit from extended practice. Instead of a few minutes for each phase, try spending five or even ten. The more time and attention you give it, the more you'll begin to notice subtle (or not so subtle!) changes in the way you feel from moment to moment.

You may find that your heart continues to radiate a wish for the well-being of others (and yourself) long after you've ended your formal meditation. And you may discover that situations that once provoked you to harsh words or frightened withdrawal now elicit softer feelings like sympathy or compassion. Even if you feel nothing at first, just repeating your wishes and intentions can have a noticeable effect.

In her book *Lovingkindness,* the American Buddhist teacher Sharon Salzberg tells the story of a retreat in which she did nothing but extend loving-kindness to herself from morning to night for seven days. She reports that she felt absolutely nothing and found the whole endeavor excruciatingly boring. The day she left, she dropped a jar, which shattered all over the floor. Instead of a stream of self-recriminations, her immediate response was quite simple: "You're really a klutz, but I love you." "Wow," she thought, "something did happen after all."

How to Transform Suffering with Compassion

Once you've become proficient in opening your heart and extending love to yourself and others, you may want to experiment with *compassion,* which is simply another form of love. (Or you could just start here and leave lovingkindness to later.) When you're moved by the suffering of others and feel a spontaneous desire to help relieve their pain in some way, you're experiencing the emotion known as compassion. Unlike pity, compassion doesn't separate you from others or make you feel superior. Quite the contrary: In the moment of compassion, the walls that ordinarily keep you separate come tumbling down, and you feel others' pain as though it were your own.

You may be reluctant to cultivate compassion because you're afraid of being overwhelmed by the enormous suffering that surrounds you. After all, the world is plagued by violence, poverty, and disease, you might argue, and there's only so much you can do about it. But the truth is, the more you allow yourself to experience compassion, the less overwhelmed you actually feel!

If you just want to use meditation to improve your life, you don't have to bother reading this section (although I'd like to suggest that you can improve your life immeasurably by opening your heart to compassion). But if you want to extend the benefits of your meditation to others — and become a more compassionate human being in the process — then I couldn't recommend a more helpful set of practices. Begin by cultivating compassion. Then, if you wish, you can experiment with using it to transform the suffering of others in your own heart. Though they may be simple, these practices are extremely effective for dissolving the clouds that hide the heart.

Some preliminary exercises for generating compassion

Here are some brief meditations for cultivating compassion. They have been adapted from *The Tibetan Book of Living and Dying* by Sogyal Rinpoche, a Tibetan meditation teacher, who writes, "The power of compassion knows no bounds."

Realizing that others are the same as you

When you're having difficulty with a loved one or friend, look beyond your conflict and the role this person plays in your life, and spend some time reflecting on the fact that this person is a human being just like you. She has

What if you can't open your heart — or difficult emotions arise when you do?

If you don't feel much of anything in your heart as you do the exercises in this chapter, don't worry. Just as you may need to pump for a while before you get water from an underground well, you may find that you need to repeat your wishes and intentions for the well-being of others again and again before you get any noticeable results — and that your feelings fluctuate from day to day. Just keep going, with the confidence that you'll eventually feel love arising in your heart. And if you don't, that's okay, too. No matter what you feel, your good wishes will have immeasurable benefit for everyone, including yourself.

Some people find that these heart-opening practices flush to the surface challenging negative emotions like grief, fear, resentment, or rage. If this happens to you, my advice once again is: Don't worry, you're not doing something wrong!

Quite the contrary, you're bringing to awareness the unresolved and unintegrated emotions that have kept your heart closed. Just extend lovingkindness to yourself and to the emotions themselves, welcoming them into your heart as much as you can. Just as Beauty's love turned the Beast into a prince, you can eventually transform your ugliest parts through the power of lovingkindness. (For more on working with challenging emotions, see Chapter 11.)

the same desire for happiness and well-being, the same fear of suffering, the same need for love. Notice how this meditation changes your feelings for her and affects your difficulties.

Putting yourself in another's place

When you encounter someone who's suffering and you don't know how to help, take some time to imagine yourself in this person's position. What would it be like for you if you were experiencing the same problems? How would you feel? What would you need? How would you like others to respond? Notice if you have a clearer sense now of how to help this person.

Imagining a loved one in place of another

Instead of putting yourself in the place of someone who's suffering, you may find it even easier to generate compassion if you imagine that someone you love deeply is experiencing the same difficulties. How would you feel? What would you do to help them? Now, transfer these feelings to the person who's actually suffering, and notice how it changes your appreciation of the situation. (Not only will this meditation cause no harm to your loved one, assures Sogyal Rinpoche, she may actually benefit from having compassion directed her way.)

Dedicating the merits

Once you know what compassion feels like, you can practice dedicating the value of all your positive actions to the well-being of others. In particular, you may want to follow the traditional practice of dedicating whatever virtue or merit may accrue from your meditations to all beings everywhere. You can do this simply by expressing the intention in words of your own choosing, accompanied by a heartfelt wish that all beings be happy and free of suffering.

Transforming suffering with the power of the heart

As you may discover when you do the following practice, the heart is a powerful organ indeed. Of course, I'm not referring to the physical heart, but to an *energetic center* located in the middle of the chest, right near the anatomical heart. Yet, the two have an intimate connection, as Dean Ornish's work confirms: To heal your heart, you need to open your heart. (For more on Dean Ornish's Opening the Heart Program, see Chapter 2. For more on energy centers, see Chapter 12.)

By doing this meditation regularly, you can actually develop the capacity to transform your own suffering and the suffering of others into peace, joy, and love. The amazing thing is, the process doesn't weaken or overwhelm you, as you might fear. Quite the contrary, it helps you develop confidence in the strength and resilience of your own heart and in your ability to touch the lives of others.

If you don't believe me, give this meditation a try. Once you get the knack, practice it regularly for several weeks, and notice what happens. Whether or not the people in your life suffer less (and they may), I can guarantee that you'll eventually end up feeling more peaceful and loving yourself.

1. **Begin by sitting in a comfortable position, taking a few deep breaths, and meditating in your usual way for a few minutes.**

   For complete meditation instructions, see Chapter 6.

2. **Close your eyes and imagine the most loving and compassionate individuals you've ever known or heard about gathered together above your head.**

   If appropriate, include religious or spiritual figures like Jesus, Mohammed, Mother Mary, the Dalai Lama, or your favorite saint or sage.

3. **Imagine that they all merge into one being, who glows and radiates the warmth and light of love and compassion.**

4. **Imagine that this being descends into your heart, where it takes the form of a sphere of infinitely radiant, infinitely compassionate light that merges with your own soft spot.**

In the following phases, you practice taking in negativity, transforming it in the sphere inside your heart, and sending out positive energy to yourself and others:

Phase 1: Transforming the atmosphere

1. **Take a moment to notice the state of your mind right now.**

2. **On an inhalation, breathe in any negativity, agitation, darkness, or depression you find there and take it into the sphere of light in your heart, where you imagine it being transformed into clarity, calm, peace, and joy.**

3. **On the exhalation, breathe these positive qualities into your mind and feel them filling and purifying it.**

4. **Continue to breathe in the dark and breathe out the light for several minutes.**

   If it helps, you might imagine the negative as a hot, dark smoke and the positive as a cool, white light.

Phase 2: Transforming yourself

1. **Imagine yourself in front of you and become aware of your own stress, suffering, and dissatisfaction.**

   You may find, for example, that you're angry at your boss or afraid of an upcoming challenge or still hurt or bitter about some mistreatment you received as a child.

2. **Allow yourself to feel compassion for yourself and your own suffering.**

3. **As you inhale, breathe in to the sphere of light in your heart whatever suffering you find and breathe out a soothing, caring, compassionate energy that envelops and fills the "you" in front of you.**

   If you find it helpful to use a particular image for this energy, such as fresh flowers or a cool breeze, go right ahead. Or you can use the image of white light suggested in the previous phase.

4. **Continue taking in and giving forth in this way for five minutes or longer.**

Phase 3: Transforming situations

1. **Recall a recent situation in which you acted badly or inappropriately.**

Perhaps you blame yourself or feel guilty or remorseful, or maybe you've been resisting these feelings. Recollect the situation as vividly as possible.

2. **Notice how your actions affected the other people involved.**

3. **Take full responsibility for your actions.**

   Notice that I said *responsibility,* not blame. You blew it, and you whole-heartedly acknowledge that you blew it, without beating yourself up about it, but also without denying or justifying what you did.

4. **Breathe in the responsibility as well as any blame, pain, or other negative emotions involved and breathe out forgiveness, understanding, reconciliation, and harmony.**

5. **Continue in this way for several minutes.**

   If another situation comes to mind, set it aside and do this practice with it at another time.

Phase 4: Transforming others

1. **Imagine a friend or loved one who happens to be suffering right now.**

2. **Breathe in the person's pain and suffering with compassion and breathe out love, peace, joy, and healing.**

3. **After several minutes, begin to widen the circle of your compassion to include first other people you care about, then those toward whom you feel neutral, and then those you dislike or find difficult.**

   (For more on the order of this progression, see the section "How to Generate Love for Yourself and Others" earlier in this chapter.) Breathe in their suffering and pain and breathe out peace, love, and joy, using any images you find helpful.

4. **Extend your compassion in this way, first to all the people in the world and then to all beings everywhere.**

   Though you won't be able to visualize them, you can sense their presence as you breathe in and breathe out.

5. **End the meditation by dedicating any virtue you may have accumulated through this practice to the benefit of all beings.**

You can do these phases out of order or separately, if you choose, but it's important to begin the practice each time with yourself.

How to Cut through Your Resistance with Gratitude and Forgiveness

Opening the heart and keeping it open poses a challenge even to the most loving among us. So don't be surprised if you have plenty of resistance to doing the exercises presented in this chapter. When you attempt to open your heart, you may unearth layers of resentment toward people who mistreated or harmed you in some way in the past. Or you may simply feel resentful toward life for all the curveballs it's thrown you, all the unfulfilled expectations and broken dreams. If so, join the club!

To soften this resentment, which may form a kind of crust over your heart, you might like to develop the qualities of forgiveness and gratitude. The first allows you to dissolve and let go of all the old wrongs (including those that you believe you yourself committed); the second cultivates an appreciation of all the good things you've received (and continue to receive) in this life but may never have fully acknowledged.

Forgiveness: The universal solvent

If resentment — which is just another word for old anger that has built up over the months and years — is the gunk that clogs the free flow of love in and out of your heart, then forgiveness is the universal solvent that washes it away. You may harbor resentment for one person in particular or for a room full of people, harking all the way back to early childhood. Whatever your situation, you can dissolve the resentment if you choose — but you have to be willing! To make it easier, you may want to begin by including the people you resent in your lovingkindness meditation. (See the section "How to Generate Love for Yourself and Others" earlier in this chapter.) And guess what? Here again, you may discover that the person you most need to love and forgive is yourself.

Here's a meditation to help you dissolve resentment, hurt, and guilt and open your heart again to yourself and others:

1. **As usual, begin by sitting comfortably, taking a few deep breaths, relaxing your body, and closing your eyes.**

2. **Allow images and memories of words, actions, and even thoughts for which you've never forgiven yourself to float through your mind.**

   Perhaps you hurt someone you loved and drove them away or took something that didn't belong to you or said no to an opportunity and later regretted it.

3. **Reflect on how much suffering you've caused and how much you may have suffered yourself. Allow yourself to feel any pain or remorse.**

4. **Gently and wholeheartedly extend forgiveness to yourself, using words like the following:**

   "I forgive you for all the mistakes you've made and all the suffering you've caused. I forgive you for all the pain you've caused others, whether intentionally or unintentionally. I know that you've learned and grown; now it's time to move on. I forgive you! May you be happy and joyful. I take you back into my heart." (Here and elsewhere, feel free to use your own words, if you prefer.)

5. **Open your heart to yourself and allow yourself to fill with love.**

   Feel the clouds around your heart dispersing.

6. **Imagine a person you love toward whom you feel some resentment.**

   Reflect on how they may have hurt you. Reflect also on how many times you have hurt others in a similar way.

7. **Gently allow the clouds around your heart to continue dispersing as you wholeheartedly extend forgiveness to this person, using words like the following:**

   "I forgive you for the ways that you've caused me pain, whether intentionally or unintentionally. I know that I too have hurt others and let them down. With my whole heart, I forgive you. May you be happy and joyful. I take you back into my heart." Feel your heart opening once again to this person.

8. **Imagine someone whose forgiveness you need.**

   Perhaps you hurt or mistreated them in some way.

9. **Gently ask their forgiveness in words like the following:**

   "Please forgive me for what I did or said to cause you pain, whether intentionally or unintentionally. I ask your forgiveness. Please take me back into your heart."

10. **Imagine this person's heart opening to you and the love flowing freely back and forth between you once again.**

11. **Imagine someone toward whom you feel great resentment — someone, perhaps, whom you've excluded from your heart because of how they once hurt you.**

12. **Gently allow the clouds around your heart to disperse and wholeheartedly extend forgiveness to this person, as described earlier.**

13. **Reflect on all the many people toward whom you've closed your heart because of the pain they seemingly caused you.**

    Feel all the layers of resentment and pain that have built up around your heart over the years.

14. **Reflect on all the many ways that you've acted as they did.**

15. **Imagine all these people in front of you, and with your whole heart forgive them all and ask their forgiveness in words like the following**:

    "I forgive you for whatever you may have done to cause me pain, whether intentionally or unintentionally. I forgive you. Please forgive me. May we open our hearts to one another and live together in peace and harmony." Again, feel your heart opening wide and allow love to flow freely between you.

16. **Take a few moments to breathe deeply and rest your attention in your heart before getting up and going about your day.**

Instead of doing the full forgiveness meditation presented here, you can just extend forgiveness to particular people as the situation requires. But every time you practice forgiveness, be sure to include some for yourself.

Gratitude: The source of joy

When you look at other people, what do you notice? Do you register all the many ways they withhold from you or ignore you or deliberately hurt you? Do you see how life fails to live up to your expectations and how you fail to live up to your own potential? Or do you notice all the many, often invisible, ways that life supports and sustains you — and people love and help you?

Depending on whether you're an optimist or a pessimist, your glass can seem half empty or half full. Well, believe it or not, you actually have the power to choose which perspective you take. In the following meditations, you have a chance to remind yourself how full your cup actually is!

Remembering the good

Here's an exercise that's designed to evoke appreciation even in the most stubbornly negative person:

1. **Begin by settling comfortably and taking a few deep breaths.**

2. **Spend a few minutes reviewing all the good things that happened to you in the past 24 hours.**

   You may recall a moment when someone treated you with love or kindness — maybe it was a friend or family member or just a person in a store or on the street. Perhaps you're reminded of some simple pleasure, like eating a good meal or seeing the sunlight in the trees or the smile on a baby's face.

3. **Reflect in the same detail on all the good things you did during the same 24-hour period.**

4. **Allow yourself to feel appreciation and gratitude for these special moments.**

5. **Reflect in the same way on the previous week.**

   Continue to breathe while you recall all the good things that happened. If negative memories come up, set them aside for now.

6. **If you have enough time, gradually extend the meditation to the past month, the past year — the past two years, the past five.**

   Recall as much as possible all the pleasant, happy, joyful moments, as well as all the good things you did and all the ways you were gifted or supported by others.

7. **Allow feelings of gratitude and appreciation to well up in your heart.**

If you have plenty of time, you can extend the meditation to include your whole life. Of course, you won't be able to remember all the good things, but be sure to cover all the headline events, including the ways that your parents nurtured and supported you and made it possible for you to grow into the person you are today. If you have resentment toward one or both of your parents, do the forgiveness meditation in the previous section.

Seventy-two labors

When I was a Zen monk, we used to chant a meal dedication that expressed our gratitude for the "seventy-two (that is, innumerable) labors" that brought us our food. By reflecting on all the efforts that make it possible for you to live the way you do, you can cut through any tendency you may have to feel bitter, resentful, or unappreciative.

Here's a brief exercise to help you appreciate how dependent you are on the energy and hard work of others:

1. **Begin by settling comfortably and taking a few deep breaths.**

2. **Bring to mind some modern convenience that you find indispensable.**

   It may be your car, your computer, or your telephone.

3. **Reflect for a few moments on how important this object is to you and what your life would be like without it.**

   Sure, you could always get another one, but right now you depend on this particular object — it's the only one you have.

4. **Think of all the people and hard work that contributed to creating this object, from raw material to finished product.**

   If it's your car, for example, you can think first of the miners in various parts of the world, possibly working in difficult circumstances, who extracted the iron and chromium and other ores that make up the metal. Then you can imagine the steel and iron workers who mixed the alloys and forged the parts. You can also imagine the oil workers who drilled the oil and the plastic workers who synthesized and then cast the plastic for the steering wheel, dashboard, and other plastic components. Next, you can imagine the engineers who designed your car and the autoworkers who put it together, part by part — and so on.

5. **Take a few moments to appreciate these people.**

   Sure, they got paid for what they did, but they also contributed their precious life energy. Without their love, sweat, and dedication, you would not have a car to drive. You may feel moved to thank them for their gifts.

As you can imagine, you could spend quite a few minutes reflecting on the "innumerable labors" that brought you this car — or this computer or telephone. The point, of course, is to reflect with gratitude and appreciation on your interdependence — on all the many ways that you depend on the energy and dedication and good intentions of others to make it through your day. Once you've spent some time reflecting in this way, you may find that you see even simple things through fresh eyes.

Softening your belly

Stephen Levine, an American meditation teacher who has written extensively on healing and dying, counsels that the state of your belly reflects the state of your heart. By consciously softening your belly again and again, you can let go and open to the tender feelings in your heart. (The following meditation is adapted from his book *Guided Meditations, Explorations and Healings*.)

1. **Begin by sitting comfortably and taking a few deep breaths.**

2. **Allow your awareness to gradually settle into your body.**

   Begin by becoming aware of the sensations in your head and slowly allow your awareness to descend through your neck and shoulders until you reach your torso and arms.

3. **When you reach your belly, gently soften this area of your body.**

   Consciously let go of any tension or holding.

4. **Allow your breath to enter and leave your belly.**

   When you inhale, your belly rises. When you exhale, your belly falls.

5. **With each breath, continue to soften your belly.**

   Let go of any anger, fear, pain, or unresolved grief you may be holding in your belly. You may want to help the process along by silently repeating a word or phrase like "soften" or "let go."

6. **As you continue to soften your belly, notice how your heart responds.**

7. **After five minutes or longer of this soft-belly meditation, open your eyes and go about your day.**

   Every now and then, check in with your belly. If you notice that you're tensing it again, gently breathe and soften.

Part III
Troubleshooting and Fine-Tuning

The 5th Wave   By Rich Tennant

"I usually mix my meditations. Today I'm doing healing, insight, and bad hair-day meditations."

In this part . . .

Learning how to meditate is like learning to drive a car. You can tool around the parking lot to your heart's content, but just wait till you hit rush hour.

In this part, you receive expert guidance in negotiating the twists and turns of meditating in heavy internal traffic — like when intense emotions or repetitive thinking threaten to box you in. Or when detours and distractions seem to throw you off course and you keep falling asleep at the wheel. You also find out how to use your meditation offroad to explore spiritual terrain. And you have a chance to piece together all your newfound skills into a routine you can follow day after day.

Chapter 11

Meditating with Challenging Emotions and Habitual Patterns

*M*editation tends to make you calmer, more spacious, and more relaxed — at least most of the time. When you follow your breath, repeat a mantra, or practice some other basic technique every day, your mind begins to settle down naturally, while thoughts and feelings spontaneously bubble up and release like the fizz in a bottle of soda. The process is so relaxing that the folks in Transcendental Meditation call it *unstressing*.

When you meditate regularly for a period of time, however, you may find that certain emotions or states of mind keep coming back to distract or disturb you. Instead of dispersing, the same sexual fantasies, sad or fearful thoughts, or painful memories may keep playing in your awareness like a CD stuck in the same old groove. Or you may be meditating on lovingkindness (see Chapter 10), but keep coming up against unresolved resentment or rage. Rather than watching the mist rising from the lake, you've begun your descent into the muddy and sometimes turbulent waters of your inner experience. (Refer to Chapter 5 for a more detailed exploration of these waters.)

At first, you may be surprised, dismayed, or even frightened by what you encounter, and you may conclude that you're doing something wrong. But have no fear! The truth is, your meditation has actually begun to deepen, and you're ready to expand your range of meditation techniques to help you navigate this new terrain.

At this point, you may find it helpful to extend your practice of mindfulness (see Chapter 6) from your breathing and your bodily sensations to your thoughts and emotions. As you gently focus the light of your awareness on this dimension of your experience, you can begin to sort out what's actually going on inside you. In the process, you can get to know yourself better — even make friends with yourself. If you keep it up, you can eventually start to penetrate and even unravel some old habitual patterns of thinking, feeling, and behaving — patterns that have been causing you suffering and stress and keeping you stuck for a long, long time. (For more on how the mind causes suffering and stress, see Chapter 5.)

How to Make Friends with Your Experience

If you're like most of the people I know (including me!), you tend to be exceptionally hard on yourself. In fact, you probably treat yourself in ways you wouldn't consider treating any of your loved ones or friends. When you make a mistake, you may call yourself names or heap harsh judgments and criticisms on yourself, including a laundry list of all the other mistakes you've made over the years. When you feel some tender or vulnerable emotion, you may dismiss it as weak or wimpy and attempt to push past it, rather then give yourself time to feel it fully.

Just the other day, for example, when I couldn't find my keys, I was startled to hear this irritable, impatient voice inside my head chiding me for being so stupid and forgetful! Sound familiar? Most of us hold some image of how we're supposed to act, think, and feel, and we're constantly struggling to get our experience and behavior to conform to it — and blaming ourselves when we don't.

In meditation, you have an opportunity to reverse this trend and explore your experience just the way it is, without trying to judge it or change it. (For more on reserving judgment and accepting what is, see Chapter 9.) To replace the stress, conflict, and turbulence inside you with peace and harmony, you need to make friends with yourself — which means treating yourself with the same kindness, care, and curiosity that you would give to a close friend. You can begin by bringing a gentle, nonjudgmental awareness to your thoughts and feelings.

Embracing your thoughts and feelings

Once you're familiar with following your breath and expanding your aware-ness to include sensations (see Chapter 6), you can expand your awareness even further to include thoughts, images, memories, and feelings. As with sensations, begin by following your breath and then allow yourself to explore a thought or feeling when it becomes so strong that it draws your attention to it. When it no longer predominates in your field of awareness, gently return to your breath.

Of course, if you've been meditating for a while, you may have noticed that you're constantly being carried away by the torrent of thoughts and feelings that flood through your mind. One moment you're counting or following your breaths or practicing your mantra, the next moment you're mulling over a conversation you had yesterday or planning tomorrow's dinner. It's as though you had inadvertently boarded a boat and suddenly found yourself several miles downstream. When this happens, you simply need to notice that you've wandered and immediately return to where you began.

Now, however, instead of viewing this dimension of your experience as a distraction, you're going to include it in your meditation with mindful awareness. When you find your attention wandering off into a thought or feeling, be aware of what you're experiencing until it loses its intensity; then gently return to your primary focus.

Naming your experience

As you expand your meditation to include thoughts and feelings, you may find it helpful to practice *naming,* or noting, your experience. Begin with mindful awareness of your breath and then start silently naming the in-breath and out-breath. When you get really quiet and focused, you may even want to include subtleties such as "long breath," "short breath," "deep breath," "shallow breath," and so on.

Keep the naming simple and subdued, like a gentle, nonjudgmental voice in the back of your mind. As Buddhist meditation teacher Jack Kornfield says in his book *A Path with Heart,* give "ninety-five percent of your energy to sensing each experience, and five percent to a soft name in the background."

Once you become adept at naming your breath, you can extend the practice to any strong sensations, thoughts, or feelings that draw your attention away from your breath. For example, as you follow and name your breath, you may find your focus interrupted by a prominent emotion. Name this experience softly and repeatedly for as long as it persists — "sadness, sadness, sadness" or "anger, anger, anger" — then gently return your attention to your breath. Take the same approach with thoughts, images, and mind-states: "planning, planning," "worrying, worrying," or "seeing, seeing."

Use the simplest words you can find, and focus on one thing at a time. This practice helps you gain a little perspective or distance from your constantly changing inner experience, instead of becoming lost in the torrent.

By naming particular thoughts and emotions, you're also acknowledging that they exist. As I mentioned earlier, we often attempt to suppress or deny experiences we deem undesirable or unacceptable, such as anger, fear, judgment, or hurt. But the more you try to hide from your experience, the more it can end up governing your behavior, as Freud so wisely pointed out more than a century ago.

Naming allows you to shine the penetrating light of awareness into the recesses of your heart and mind and invite your thoughts and feelings to emerge from their hiding place, into the light of day. You may not like what you encounter at first — but then you can name your self-judgments and self-criticisms as well. Ultimately, you may notice that you're not surprised anymore by what you discover about yourself — and the more you make friends with your own apparent shortcomings and frailties, the more you can open your heart to the imperfections of others as well.

Welcoming whatever arises

When you become accustomed to including sensations, thoughts, and feelings in your meditation, you can open your awareness gates wide and welcome whatever arises, without judgment or resistance. Imagine that your mind is like the sky, and inner and outer experiences come and go like clouds.

At first, you may find your attention drawn here and there, exploring one object and then another. You don't have to control your attention in any way; just allow it to wander where it will, from thoughts to sensations to feelings and back again.

Eventually, you may have periods in your meditation when your mind feels spacious and expanded and doesn't seem to be disturbed by thoughts, feelings, or outside distractions. Whatever you experience, just keep opening your awareness and welcoming whatever comes. (For more on the different levels of experience you may encounter, see Chapter 5.) A note of caution, however: This practice, though supremely simple, is actually quite advanced and requires well-developed powers of concentration to sustain. It's also difficult to teach — rather like riding a bicycle. First, you have to *discover* what it feels like to hold your balance; then you just keep returning to the balance point whenever you start to fall off.

How to Meditate with Challenging Emotions

As a psychotherapist, a meditator, and a meditation teacher, I've discovered a thing or two over the years about how people relate to the mysterious and sometimes formidable world of human emotions. For one thing, many people believe they have a Pandora's box of ugly, disgusting emotions like rage, jealousy, hatred, and terror hidden inside them, and they're afraid that if they open it up, these demonic energies will overwhelm them and those they love. For another thing, they tend to think that these "negative" feelings are bottomless and irresolvable, and they're better off avoiding them, no matter how painful it may be to hold them in.

Unfortunately, you pay a steep price indeed if you spend your life resisting and denying your feelings. Unacknowledged negative feelings can impede the flow of more positive feelings like love and joy. As a result, you may end up feeling lonely because you lack close emotional contact with others, and you may be unable to give and receive love when you have an opportunity to do so. In addition, negative feelings that build up inside you tend to cause stress, suppress the immune system, and contribute to stress-related ailments like ulcers, cancer, and heart disease. They also hold valuable life energy that you might otherwise channel in constructive or creative ways. Besides, emotions that are persistently suppressed and denied have an annoying habit of bursting forth inappropriately, when you least expect them, prompting you to do and say things you may later regret.

Of course, some people go to another extreme and seem to be so completely awash in powerful emotional reactions that they can't make simple decisions or carry on a rational conversation. But these people aren't really experiencing their emotions, they're indulging them and allowing them to run their lives.

Meditation offers you an alternative way of relating with your emotions. Instead of suppressing, indulging, or exploding, you can directly experience your emotions as they are — as an interplay of thoughts, images, and sensations. Once you've become skillful at following your breath and expanding your awareness to include the flow of thoughts and feelings — which may take months or even years — you can focus your attention on particular emotions that you find challenging or problematic and develop *penetrating insight* into the nature of the experience.

Instead of being bottomless or endless, as some people fear, you may find that even the most powerful emotions come in waves that have a limited duration when you experience them fully. As one of my teachers used to say, "What you resist persists" — and what you welcome has a tendency to let go and release. (See the sidebar "Facing your demons" later in this chapter.)

Here are some guidelines for exploring a few of the most common emotions. Although feelings come in many shapes and sizes, I've found that they're all more or less variants or combinations of a few basic ones: anger, fear, sadness, joy, excitement, and desire. (In my view, love is deeper than emotion; it's a fundamental expression of being itself.) Just as an artist's rich array of colors can ultimately be broken down into blue, yellow, and red, the difficult or challenging emotions like jealousy, guilt, boredom, and depression are combinations (or reactions) to four basic feelings: anger, fear, sadness, and desire. (If you find a certain feeling problematic, work on it as you would one of these four. For more on desire, see Chapter 12.)

Meditating with anger

After practicing meditation regularly for several years in my twenties, I prided myself on being consistently calm and even-tempered and never getting angry. Then one day, my girlfriend at the time confessed that she'd had an affair with another man! Without hesitating, I picked up a cup from the table and threw it against the wall. I remember being startled by the sudden intensity of my emotions. One moment I seemed perfectly peaceful, and the next moment I was flying into a rage. My anger may have been appropriate to the circumstances, but I certainly hadn't expressed it skillfully. Humbled, I headed back to the meditation cushion for some deeper investigation — after breaking up with my girlfriend, of course.

Facing your demons

The Tibetans tell a wonderful story about the great meditation master Milarepa, who lived about 900 years ago. Milarepa sought out remote caves high in the Himalayas where he practiced meditation. Once he found himself in a cave inhabited by a company of demons that distracted him from his practice. (Demons apparently frequented caves in those days — looking for some action, no doubt!)

First, he tried to subdue them, but they wouldn't budge. Then he decided to honor them and extend friendliness and compassion to them, and half of them left. The rest he welcomed wholeheartedly and invited to return whenever they wished. At this invitation, all but one particularly ferocious demon vanished like a rainbow. With no concern for his own body and with utmost love and compassion, Milarepa went up to the demon and placed his head in its mouth as an offering. The demon disappeared without a trace and never returned.

Consider the story of Milarepa the next time you're struggling with your own inner demons — emotions and states of mind you find challenging or unpleasant. Imagine what might happen if you welcomed them instead of trying to drive them away!

Many people, especially women, have a taboo against getting angry because they weren't allowed to express their anger, even as children. So they expend enormous amounts of energy trying to skirt around the feeling. Other people seem as though they're perpetually seething with current anger and old resentments, although they may not realize it themselves.

When you meditate with your anger, you might begin by noticing where and how you experience it in your body. Where do you find yourself tensing and contracting? What happens to your breathing? Where do you notice a buildup of energy? How does it affect softer emotions? As you continue to be aware of your anger, do you notice it shifting or changing in any way? How long does it last? Does it have a beginning and an end?

Next, you can turn your attention to your mind. What kinds of thoughts and images accompany the angry feelings? Do you find yourself blaming other people and defending yourself? If you investigate further and peel back the initial layer of anger, what do you find underneath? In my experience, anger generally arises in response to one of two deeper emotions: hurt or fear. When you're hurt, as I was by my girlfriend's betrayal, you may lash out in anger against the one you believed hurt you. And when you're afraid, you may protect yourself with the sword and armor of anger rather than ac-knowledge your fear, even to yourself. Beneath the hurt and fear, anger generally masks an even deeper layer of attachment to having things be a certain way. When circumstances change or don't go according to plan, you feel hurt or afraid and then angry in response.

With anger, as with all emotions, set aside any judgment or resistance you might have and face the anger directly. You may find that it becomes more intense before it releases, but stay with it. Beneath the anger may lie deep wellsprings of power, which you may eventually discover how to evoke without getting angry.

Meditating with fear and anxiety

Many people are reluctant to admit they're afraid, even to themselves. Somehow, they believe that if they acknowledge their fear, they give it power to run their lives. In other words, deep down, they're afraid of their fear! Men especially will often go to great lengths to hide their fear or anxiety behind a facade of confidence or anger or rationality. At the other extreme, of course, some people seem to be afraid of just about everything.

The truth is, if you're human and not bionic or extraterrestrial, you're going to be afraid or anxious, at least occasionally. In addition to the raw rush of adrenaline you feel when your physical survival seems to be at stake, you experience the fear that inevitably arises when you face the unknown or the uncertain in life — which can be quite often these days. Ultimately, you're afraid because you believe that you're a separate, isolated entity surrounded by forces beyond your control. The more the walls that separate you from others crumble through the practice of meditation, the more your fear and anxiety naturally diminish. (For more on separation and isolation, see Chapter 5.)

As with anger, you can use your meditation to explore and ultimately make friends with your fear. After all, it's just an emotion like other emotions, composed of physical sensations, thoughts, and beliefs. When working with fear, it's especially important to be kind and gentle with yourself.

Begin by asking the same questions you asked about anger: Where and how do you experience it in your body? Where do you find yourself tensing and contracting? What happens to your breathing? Or to your heart? Next, notice the thoughts and images that accompany the fear. Often fear arises from anticipating the future and imagining that you'll somehow be unable to cope. When you see these catastrophic expectations for what they are and return to the present moment — the sensations in your body, the coming and going of your breath — you may find that the fear shifts and begins to disperse. Then when it returns, you can simply call its name — "fear, fear, fear" — like an old, familiar friend.

You may also want to amplify the sensations a little and allow yourself to shake or tremble, if you feel so inclined. You can even imagine the fear overwhelming you and doing its worst (knowing, of course, that you will survive) — an especially helpful approach if you're afraid of your fear, as so many people are. Facing your fear directly without trying to get rid of it or escape from it requires tremendous courage; yet these practices also have the capacity to bring you into the present moment and open your heart to your own vulnerability.

Meditating with sadness, grief, and depression

Most people find sadness easier to feel and express than anger or fear. Unfortunately, they don't give it the time and attention it deserves because they were told as children to stop crying before they were ready. Since life inevitably presents us with a series of disappointments and losses, unexpressed sadness and grief can build up inside and ultimately lead to depression. (Many of the people I see in therapy suffer from mild depression, which may also result from repressed anger or "learned helplessness." For more on learned helplessness, see Chapter 5.)

To make friends with your sadness, you need to hold it gently and lovingly and give it plenty of space to express itself. As with anger and fear, begin by exploring the sensations. Perhaps you notice a heaviness in your heart or a constriction in your diaphragm or a clogged sensation in your eyes and forehead, as though you are about to cry but can't. You may want to amplify these sensations and see what happens.

Then pay attention to the thoughts, images, and memories that fuel the sadness. Perhaps you keep reliving the loss of a loved one or the moment when a close friend said something unkind to you. If you're depressed, you may keep recycling the same negative, self-defeating beliefs and judgments, such as "I'm not good enough" or "I don't have what it takes to succeed."

As you open your awareness to include the full range of experiences associated with the sadness, you may shed some heartfelt tears — and in the process feel yourself lightening up and your sadness lifting a little. (To find out how to work with core beliefs, consult the following two sections of this chapter.) Ultimately, as long as you are open to your own suffering and the suffering of others, you will experience a certain amount of tender sadness in your heart.

How to Unravel Habitual Patterns — with Awareness

As you explore your emotions (as described in the previous section), you may gradually discover that they're not as overpowering or as endless as you feared. With mindful awareness and naming, most emotions will flow through your body and gradually release. For example, as you gently investigate your anger or fear, it may intensify at first, but then break and disperse like a wave on the beach.

But certain persistent emotions and physical contractions, along with the thoughts and images that accompany and fuel them, seem to keep returning, no matter how many times you notice and name them. These are the *stories* and habitual patterns that run deep in the body-mind like the roots from which recurring thoughts and feelings spring. (For more on these stories, see Chapter 5.) In your meditations, you may keep replaying a story from your past (including all the accompanying emotions and mind-states) in which you suffer some abuse or injustice. Perhaps you see yourself as a failure and fantasize obsessively about an imaginary future in which you're somehow happier and more successful. Or you may worry repeatedly about your job or relationship because you believe you can't trust people or the world's not a safe place.

In his book *A Path with Heart,* Buddhist meditation teacher Jack Kornfield calls these habitual patterns *insistent visitors* and suggests that they keep returning in your meditation (and your life!) because they're stuck or unfinished in some way. When you give them the loving attention and deeper investigation they require (applying the penetrating insight I discuss at length in Chapter 5), you may at first discover that they're more complex and deeply rooted than you may have imagined. But with persistent exploration, they gradually unravel and reveal the hidden energy and wisdom they contain. In fact, the more you undo your patterns, the more you release the physical and energetic contractions that lie at their heart, and the freer, more spacious, more expansive — and, yes, healthier! — you become.

Here's a brief synopsis of the primary techniques for unraveling habitual patterns. Experiment with them on your own, and if you find them helpful, feel free to incorporate them into your meditation. If you get stuck or would like to delve deeper but don't know how, you may want to find yourself a meditation teacher or psychotherapist familiar with this approach. (For more on finding a therapist, see the section "How (and When) to Seek Help with Your Patterns" later in this chapter. For more on finding a teacher, see Chapter 13. And for a more detailed treatment of many of these techniques, check out *A Path with Heart*.)

Naming your "tunes"

As a rather humorous way to start, advises Kornfield, you can name and number your "top ten tunes." (You can stop at five, if you prefer.) Then when a particular tune recurs, you can simply notice and name it without getting embroiled once again in the same painful pattern. Merely another version of naming your experience (described earlier), this approach can be helpful but only takes you so far.

Expanding your awareness

The part of the pattern that reveals itself to you in your meditation may be just the tip of the proverbial iceberg. Perhaps you keep feeling tense in your lower belly and you don't know why. If you expand your awareness, you may discover that beneath the surface lies fear about the future, and under the fear lies a layer of hurt. When you include thoughts and ideas as well, you may find that deep down you believe you're inadequate. So you're afraid you can't cope, and you feel hurt when people criticize you because it just corroborates your own negative self-image. By welcoming the full range of thoughts, images, and feelings, you create an inner spaciousness in which the pattern can gradually unfold and release. (Trust me — this approach actually works, though you won't get results instantaneously!)

Feeling your feelings

Patterns often persist until the underlying feelings are thoroughly felt. That's right, I said *felt* — not merely acknowledged or named! Many people keep their feelings at arm's length or confuse them with thoughts or ideas. I could talk in the abstract about grief or fear, but it took years of meditation (and some skillful therapy; see the section "How (and When) to Seek Help with Your Patterns") before I knew how they actually felt in my body. Other people (as I mention earlier in the section "How to Meditate with Challenging Emotions") get completely entangled in their feelings. As you expand your awareness, ask yourself, "What feelings haven't I felt yet?" Remember, feeling your feelings doesn't make them bigger or worse — at least not in the long run. It actually allows them to move through and release!

Noticing your resistance and attachment

As I mentioned earlier, what you resist persists — to which I might add that what you're attached to persists as well. If a particular story or challenging emotion keeps replaying in your mind, you might explore your relationship to it. For example, you might ask: How do I feel about this particular pattern or story? Do I have a vested interest in holding on to it? If so, what do I get out of it? Or what am I afraid might happen if I let it go? Am I judging it as undesirable and struggling to get rid of it? If so, what don't I like about it? When you can relax and gently open to accept the pattern with awareness (as described in the previous sections), you may find that the pattern, which felt so tight and entrenched, relaxes as well.

Finding the wisdom

Sometimes recurring stories or patterns have a message to impart, and they won't stop nagging until you listen. If I keep having the same uncomfortable or difficult feeling during meditation and it doesn't shift or change with awareness, I may "give it a voice" and ask it to speak to me as though it were a close friend. "What are you trying to tell me?" I may ask. "What am I needing to hear?" Sometimes I discover that a tender, vulnerable part of myself needs caring, nurturing attention. At other times, I hear the voice of responsibility reminding me to tend to some important commitment. (For a helpful way of listening to these voices and parts, see the sidebar "Focusing: Western meditation for getting unstuck" later in this chapter.)

Replacing negative patterns with positive energy

Many meditative traditions suggest invoking outside help in the lifelong process of purifying and eliminating habitual patterns. No, I'm not talking about psychotherapy or Prozac here — I'm referring to spiritual beings or energies that purportedly exist for the sole purpose of inspiring and encouraging your spiritual evolution. Western religions have their angels and saints, Hinduism and Buddhism have their deities and protectors, shamanism has its spirit helpers and animal powers.

Now, you may not buy all this spiritual stuff, but I'd suggest giving this exercise a try just the same. In place of spiritual allies, you may want to imagine people who have given you unconditional support in the past — or you could just stick to the image of a luminous sphere. The point is, this exercise by itself can be a powerful ally in the process of dealing with painful or difficult emotions or experiences. As with all meditations, the more you practice it, the more effective it becomes.

1. **Begin by sitting down and meditating in your usual way for several minutes.**

   If you don't have a usual way, you can find one in Chapter 6 — or just sit quietly and wait for further instructions.

2. **Imagine a luminous sphere of white light suspended about a foot above your head and slightly in front of you.**

   Like a sun, this sphere embodies and radiates all the positive, healing, harmonious qualities you most want to manifest in your life right now. (You may want to be specific at first — strength, clarity, peace, love;

eventually, you can just flash on the light.)

3. **Imagine yourself soaking up all these qualities with the healing light as though you were sunbathing.**

4. **Imagine this light radiating in all directions to the farthest corners of the universe and drawing the energy of all the benevolent forces that support your growth and evolution back into the sphere.**

5. **Visualize this positive, healing energy shining from the sphere, like the light of a thousand suns streaming down through your body and mind, eliminating all negativity and tension, darkness and depression, worry and anxiety and replacing them with radiance, vitality, peace, and all the other positive qualities you seek.**

6. **Continue to imagine this powerful, healing light flooding every cell and molecule of your being, dissolving any contractions and stuck places you may be aware of and leaving you clean, clear, and calm.**

7. **Visualize this luminous sphere gradually descending into your heart, where it continues to radiate this powerful light.**

8. **Imagine yourself as a luminous being with a sphere of light in your heart that constantly radiates clarity, harmony, and purity — first to every cell and particle of your own being and then, through you, to every other being in every direction.**

You can carry the feelings and images this exercise evokes throughout the rest of your day.

Getting to the heart of the matter

Like the great Tibetan meditator Milarepa (see the sidebar "Facing your demons" earlier in this chapter), sometimes you need to stick your head into the demon's mouth before it disappears for good. In other words, you may need to explore the *energetic contraction* that lies at the heart of your pattern. (When I use the term *energetic* here, I'm referring to the Eastern model of the human organism as a system of energetic pathways and centers that can get blocked or contracted. These blockages give rise to painful emotions and mind-states and may ultimately cause disease. For more on energy pathways and centers, see Chapter 12.)

To do this, you can gently direct your awareness into the very center of the contraction and describe in detail what you find there. When you unearth the memory, feeling, or belief that holds the pattern together, you may find that the contraction releases, your awareness expands, and your meditation begins to flow more smoothly. (***Note:*** When you're dealing with exceptionally painful, deep-seated contractions, you may want to consult a qualified professional. See the section in this chapter "How (and When) to Seek Help with Your Patterns.")

Infusing the stuck place with being

After you've meditated for a while and received some glimpses of your own inherent wholeness and completeness (which I call *being* in Chapter 1), you may want to try the following shortcut. Set aside the thoughts and ideas that accompany your pattern and simply be aware of the physical and energetic contraction. Now shift your attention to your wholeness and completeness, which you may experience as a calm, relaxed energy in your body, a deeply loving feeling in your heart, a sense of expansiveness or space, or some other feeling unique to you. Imagine your wholeness and completeness gradually spreading, penetrating and infusing the contraction with pure being. Continue this exercise as the contraction releases and dissolves into being. (For an even more powerful version of this technique, refer to the sidebar "Replacing negative patterns with positive energy.")

Working with patterns before you get stuck

Once you get the knack of observing your reactive patterns and repetitive stories and concerns and unraveling them in meditation, you can begin to work with them as they arise in everyday life. For example, you may notice in your meditation that you tend to rehearse a drama in which other people are constantly depriving you of what you rightfully deserve and you end up

Working with habitual patterns: A case in point

Here's an example of how to work with habitual patterns based on my own experience. Not long ago, I noticed a particular tightness in my lower abdomen, not only when I meditated but also between sessions. When the tightness persisted for several days, I decided to investigate it further. Gently, I directed my awareness and my breath to the area.

As I expanded my awareness, I noticed that I also felt tight in my throat and jaw. When I inquired into the feeling, I gradually became aware that I was afraid of something, though I wasn't sure at first of what. Not only that, I was resisting the feeling by tightening my jaw. Somehow I didn't like the feeling and wanted to get rid of it.

Without trying to change the feeling in any way, I meditated and breathed with it for a

while. Soon, it began to loosen a little, but not to unravel completely. Then I gently asked for more information, and I realized that I was afraid of an upcoming presentation. Several memories of being made to feel inadequate as a child came vividly to mind, and I experienced waves of sadness and some tears, followed by compassion for myself.

Now, as I directed my awareness to the center of the contraction in my belly, it quickly released, and feelings of ease and well-being filled the area instead. Feeling more relaxed and expanded, I returned to my usual meditation. Several days later, when I made the presentation, I noticed that I felt more relaxed and self-confident than usual.

feeling hurt and resentful. When you notice this story and the beliefs that accompany it (for example, "I never get what I want" or "Nobody cares about me") showing up in your relationships or at work, you can use the skills you've acquired to step back a little and resist the temptation to get sucked in as usual.

The more consistently you unravel your patterns in meditation, the more quickly you can catch them as they arise — and the freer and less reactive you gradually become. Eventually, you can even begin to shift your identity from the patterns to the spacious awareness in which the patterns arise and pass away.

How to Set Patterns Aside — for Now!

If you find that your habitual patterns are too deeply entrenched to unravel (at least for now!), you can still get some temporary relief by applying one or more of the following techniques. Remember, you don't necessarily have to wrestle a pattern to the mat for the count of ten; sometimes you just have to get it to shift or budge a little so that you can get on with your meditation.

Letting go — or letting be

Believe it or not, you may be able to drop the pattern and move on. Be careful, though — if you're actually trying to push it away, it may come back to haunt you. Instead of struggle and aversion, this approach requires a willingness to accept things the way they are. (For more on the stages of letting go, see Chapter 9.) Sometimes you can just stop, be aware of the contraction, and gradually relax your body until the contraction releases. (For detailed instructions on how to relax deeply, see Chapter 6.) Or you can shift your awareness to being itself (however you may happen to experience being), and just let the pattern be without trying to change it.

Shifting attention

As the Bible says, "There's a time for every purpose under heaven" — including working with your habitual patterns. If you're preoccupied with more pressing concerns, you need to be able to set your patterns aside and shine your attention where you need it most. You can come back to your difficulties later, when you have the time and energy.

Moving the energy

Sometimes you may find it helpful to direct the energy bound up in a particular pattern into another activity. Go for a run or dance to loud music or wash the dishes. You may not be unraveling the pattern, but you're stealing its thunder, so to speak. (To continue the metaphor, you can even use the rain to water your crops.) Perhaps you've seen one of those westerns where the hero goes out and chops some wood instead of picking up his gun and shooting his neighbors. Well, he's "moving the energy," whether he knows it or not. You can also move the energy internally — for example, by turning your fear about an upcoming event into excitement and curiosity.

Acting it out in imagination

When an emotion or impulse just seems too intense to handle, you can act it out in one of two ways. First, you can try enacting it in your meditation by imagining yourself exaggerating it and then allowing it to unfold completely with mindful attention. This approach differs from mere fantasy, which tends to have an obsessive, unconscious quality. Instead, by paying attention as you give this emotion or pattern free rein, you get to realize that it's not as overpowering as you may have believed. At the same time, you have an opportunity to observe its limitations and the damage or pain it could inflict. For example, you could imagine yourself enacting your rage or your desire mindfully and noticing what happens. Does it completely overwhelm you? How does it affect the other people involved? Does it really bring you the fulfillment you seek?

Acting it out in real life — mindfully

As an alternative, especially when the pattern seems irresistible, you can act it out in life, as you usually do, but this time with mindfulness. Notice how you feel in your body as you follow the enactment through to completion. For example, you may be bravely trying to resist your desire for a hot fudge sundae, but rapidly losing your willpower. Instead, you might go for it while noticing every bite and every sensation, both during and after. In fact, you could even try eating as much as you want. I guarantee that you'll transform your relationship to hot fudge sundaes in the process. (For more on mindfulness in everyday life, see Chapter 17.)

Focusing: Western meditation for getting unstuck

Here's a meditation technique called *focusing* developed by Eugene Gendlin, a psychology professor at the University of Chicago, to help folks like you and me figure out where we're stuck and effect the necessary changes, both inner and outer. (Although this technique uses the same term, it differs from the focused attention described elsewhere in this book.)

By focusing on your felt sense about a problem — the place in your body where you hold it and know it — you can discover valuable information about who you are and what you really want and need. (For more detailed instructions, I recommend Gendlin's book *Focusing*.)

1. **Begin by taking a few moments to settle comfortably and relax.**

2. **Check in with that place inside where you feel things and ask, "How am I doing? What doesn't feel quite right? What do I need to pay attention to right now?"**

You're not looking for an intense emotion but something subtler and more elusive: a

felt sense. (For example, a felt sense is the place inside that you consult when someone asks you, "What is your sense of that person or situation?" It's not a feeling, exactly, and definitely not a thought, but more like a bodily knowing.)

3. **Take whatever you get, set it aside, and ask the same questions again until you have a list of three or four things you might focus on right now.**

4. **Choose one, but don't go inside it. Instead, allow some space around it.**

Set aside any thoughts and analyses you may have and just be with your felt sense of this one thing, in its entirety.

5. **Ask yourself, "What is the crux of this problem?"**

Don't jump to any conclusions or try to understand it. Just allow this crux to emerge in the silence. You may find that what you get is different from what your mind expected. You'll know it in your body.

6. **Sit with the crux of this felt sense for a minute or more and allow a word, image, or feeling to emerge from it.**

   Don't try to understand it. Just be aware of the crux with gentle curiosity, waiting for a deeper knowing to reveal itself.

7. **Compare this word, image, or feeling with the felt sense in your body, asking "Is this right? Does this really fit?"**

   If it is, you'll notice a felt shift: a deep breath or sigh of relief or slight relaxing inside. If not, ask the felt sense, "Then what does feel right?" and wait for an answer. Remember, you're asking your body, not your mind, for information.

8. **When you receive an answer that feels right, sit with it in silence for a few moments and allow your body to respond.**

   The felt shift may continue to unfold, or you may experience a release of energy or some other noticeable reverberation in your body.

Here's an example of focusing. Say that you've been obsessing about a conversation you had yesterday with a friend, playing it over and over again in your mind without resolution. So, you decide to set your thoughts aside and pay attention to your inner felt sense of the conversation. When you turn inward, you find that the felt sense is localized in your heart and the crux of it turns out to be something about your friend's tone of voice.

As you sit with the felt sense, you realize that the crux of the problem is not her tone of voice exactly, but it's something that was triggered in you. What is it? Well, it's a feeling of jealousy . . . no, that's not quite right; it's a sense of not quite measuring up, of not being as good as she is — or even more accurately, of not doing what you really love, the way she does. That's it, you're aware that you're not doing what you really want to do with your life, and your friend's words triggered that sense inside you.

With this realization, you notice a felt shift or release inside, possibly accompanied by tears of recognition and sadness. You've just completed a round of focusing, and you can use the same technique for any problem or felt sense.

How (And When) to Seek Help with Your Patterns

Perhaps you're so full of negative thoughts and feelings that you find it virtually impossible to concentrate, even in meditation. The voices (or images) in your head keep spewing forth worries, regrets, judgments, and criticism with such volume and velocity that you can barely hear yourself think. Or maybe you can focus on your breath or recite your mantra with some success, but when a particularly compelling story or pattern gets triggered, you're swept away by the intensity.

My first suggestion is to keep meditating regularly and see what happens. How do you feel after a few weeks or months of steady practice? Are you making any headway? Do you feel more calm and peaceful? Does your concentration deepen?

If certain patterns persist, however — especially if they interfere with your capacity to do your work or maintain loving, satisfying relationships — you might consider psychotherapy. Now, I know that some people still feel a little embarrassed or ashamed if they admit they need help with their problems. But look at it this way: People have been consulting medicine men and women, shamans, rabbis, priests, and local elders for as long as human beings have had problems — maybe longer.

The thing is, psychotherapy (our modern, secular version of wise counsel) comes in many shapes and sizes — as many, in fact, as the professionals who practice it. Without devaluing any particular brand of psychotherapy (after all, I'm talking about my own profession here), I'd like to offer a few guidelines for choosing a therapist who can help free you from the limitations of your habitual patterns. Admittedly, I base these recommendations on my own particular interests and preferences — and on more than 15 years as a therapist and 25 years as a meditator and meditation teacher.

Talk is important — but you need to do more

Even classical Freudian therapy, which consists entirely of talk, aims for the moment when the insights touch a deeper place and trigger an inner felt shift or emotional release. (Remember the crucial point in the movie *Good Will Hunting* when Robin Williams tells Matt Damon, "It wasn't your fault"?) The problem is, talk-only therapy gets there more slowly — and sometimes not at all. Unless you happen to have a Robin Williams nearby, find a therapist who combines talk with one or more techniques that take you deeper faster — for example, hypnotherapy, guided imagery, active imagination, sand play, body-centered therapy, breathwork, focusing, or EMDR (eye movement desensitization and reprocessing).

Shop around

If you want the names of appropriate therapists, turn first to friends, family members, or others who share similar interests or values. Don't be shy — you may be surprised to discover how many people you know have seen a shrink in recent years. Then call these therapists and spend some time talking with them over the phone. Remember, you have a right to ask them anything you want to know. You might even schedule a session or two with each one before making your decision. After all, you're better off spending a couple of hundred bucks now on trial runs than discovering in six months or a year that you made a mistake.

Choose the person, not the credentials

Even though she comes highly recommended and her wall is covered with degrees and certificates, check this person out. (Needless to say, "this person" could just as well be a man.) Does she listen to you carefully and hear what you say? Does she seem emotionally attuned as well as insightful? Do you feel comfortable in her presence? Do you trust her with your most tender places and difficult issues? In the final analysis, you need to trust your feelings and your intuition on this one.

Decide whether spirituality matters to you

If you have a particular spiritual orientation — or are in the process of developing one — you may want to search out a therapist who comes similarly equipped. If you don't have a large enough selection to choose from, at least find a shrink who honors spirituality, rather than debunking it. Not only will he be open to talking with you about meditation and transpersonal (that is, beyond the personal) experiences, he may be able to help you combine meditation with therapy to work on your issues more effectively. (For more on transpersonal experiences, see Chapter 12.)

Checking in with your inner child

When you're feeling agitated or upset, you may want to check in with the little child inside you, the part of you that feels things deeply. Here's a meditation to help reassure and nurture your inner child.

1. **Begin by noticing what you're feeling and where you're feeling it.**

2. **Take some time to breathe and relax into the feelings.**

3. **Imagine that there's a little boy or girl inside you having these feelings.**

   This child is the young, undeveloped part of you. You may have an image or just a gut sense or inner knowing.

4. **Ask yourself these questions: "How old is this child? What is her (or his) name? What kind of attention does she want from me right now?"**

She may want to be reassured or held, or she may just want to play.

5. **If possible, imagine giving her what she wants.**

6. **Continue to commune with her for as long as you like, giving and receiving words or physical contact, as appropriate.**

7. **When you're done, notice how you feel.**

   You may be more relaxed or confident — or at least less upset or afraid.

8. **Be sure to give your inner child a hug (if she feels comfortable receiving one), tell her that you love her, and reassure her that you'll check in with her again from time to time — and please do!**

Chapter 12

Troubleshooting the Roadblocks and Side Effects

• •

In This Chapter

▶ Using the obstacles to your meditation as grist for your mill

▶ Dealing with altered states and unusual experiences without getting distracted

▶ Exploring your seven energy centers and what they have to teach you

• •

*L*ike any journey, meditation can have its share of breathtaking vistas and roadside attractions that inspire you and pique your curiosity — and it can also present obstacles, detours, and breakdowns that keep you from moving forward. As I mention in Chapter 1, I like to think of this book as a detailed travel guide, and the present chapter provides a troubleshooting manual to use when you encounter engine trouble, a flat tire, or an unexpected delay.

Of course, you may just breeze along and get where you're headed with nary a glitch in your itinerary. If you're doing just fine in your meditation, you're welcome to skip this chapter for now. But if you want a preview of the obstacles you may face — or have already started to face! — then read on. You can pick up some helpful tips for dealing with the most common roadblocks when they get in your way, and you'll find descriptions of scenic way-stations that could turn into detours if you get confused and don't know how to negotiate them carefully.

How to Navigate the Roadblocks on Your Meditative Journey

Although meditation can be as complex as you want it to be, the basic practice (as I mention in Chapter 1) is actually quite simple: Just sit down, be quiet, turn your attention inward, and focus your mind. Nobody ever said it would be easy, however — not all the time, anyway!

In addition to the difficult emotions and habitual patterns I describe in Chapter 11, every persistent meditator inevitably encounters at least a few of the many classical roadblocks or obstacles. (Don't be put off by the word "obstacle." These challenges may slow you down, but they don't need to stop you.) You're not doing something wrong when you get sleepy or restless or bored or keep putting off your meditation or wonder whether it's worth the effort. In fact, you're merely confronting more of the habitual patterns that cause you problems in every area of your life. Meditation offers a laboratory in which to investigate these patterns with mindful attention so you can apply your results in your work or your friendships or your family life. (The "obstacles," in other words, provide grist for the mill of self-awareness and behavioral change.)

As I encourage throughout this book, be sure to treat yourself and the roadblocks that arise on your journey with the same kindness, care, and curiosity that you would give to a close friend. Remember, the point is not to push through them to some loftier place of clarity and repose. Rather, the obstacles themselves provide exceptional raw material for your lab work as you discover how to open to whatever arises in your experience with gentle, nonjudgmental awareness. Instead of obstacles, you might prefer to think of them as messengers bearing the gifts of increased energy, wisdom, and self-acceptance. As I describe in Chapter 11, it can be helpful to begin by naming your experience before proceeding to further exploration.

Sleepiness

Most of us sleepwalk through much of our lives, paying only minimal attention to what's happening around us. Have you ever driven home and wondered, when you arrived, how you got there? Since the point of meditation is to wake up and be mindful, it's no wonder that all meditators contend with dullness and dreaminess at least occasionally.

Probably the most common roadblock, sleepiness comes in a number of shapes and sizes. Begin by exploring your experience: Where do you feel the sleepiness in your body? What happens to your mind? Are you physically tired or just mentally dull? You may be yawning because you haven't slept well in days — in which case, stop meditating and take a nap.

More often, though, your mind will become foggy when you're resisting feeling some unpleasant or undesirable emotion like fear or sadness. You might ask yourself, "What am I avoiding right now? What lies just beneath the surface of this sleepiness?" (You could even extend this inquiry to the other moments of your life when you dull out or glaze over.)

Once you've been meditating for a while, you may find that you get sleepy when your mind settles down and no longer has lots of stimulation to keep it occupied. At this point, you may need to rouse your energy by opening your eyes wide and sitting up straight. If your sleepiness persists, you can get up and walk around or splash cold water on your face to help you stay awake.

Restlessness

When you have difficulty paying attention in your meditation because your mind is agitated, worried, or anxious and you're eager to get on with other activities, you can begin by naming the restlessness and noticing how you experience it in your body. Perhaps you're tensing in your belly or head or have an uneasy feeling in your arms and legs. Maybe you notice that you're perched uncomfortably on the edge of your cushion, as though you were ready to jump off at any moment and grab a bite to eat or make a phone call.

Notice also what your mind is doing. Does it skip uncontrollably from topic to topic or worry obsessively about some upcoming event or responsibility? As much as possible, observe your restlessness without getting caught by the agitation — or seduced by the impulse to get up and go. You may also want to practice counting your breaths or some other concentration technique to help quiet your mind until you can resume your regular practice (or perhaps that is your regular practice). Like sleepiness, restlessness can also be a response to painful or unpleasant feelings you don't want to experience.

Boredom

Like most people, you may believe you get bored because the object of your attention lacks value or interest. But you might want to examine your boredom more closely. The truth is, boredom arises because you're not paying close enough attention or you have some judgment or preference that keeps you from showing up wholeheartedly for the present moment. In fact, most of us have become accustomed to constant stimulation and have difficulty sitting still when we're focusing on something simple like . . . well, like following our breath.

Boredom, like restlessness, can prevent you from experiencing the subtler beauties of life — and meditation can provide a wonderful opportunity to explore your boredom. Begin by naming it: "boredom, boredom." How do you experience it in your body? What stories does the mind spin? Instead of reacting to your boredom, just let yourself be mindfully bored. You may become so fascinated by your own boredom that you're no longer bored!

Fear

Sometimes you sit down to meditate and notice that your mind is filled with fearful thoughts and feelings that weren't apparent before. Where did they come from? You may have been anxious or afraid about something but didn't realize it until you began to meditate. Or your mindful attention may have flushed old fears to the surface to be explored and released. Perhaps you're afraid of your meditation itself — afraid that you won't be able to do it right or deal with your stress or afraid of what challenging memories or feelings might come up while you meditate.

If so, you're not alone! Fear is one of the most pervasive and basic of human emotions — no wonder it rears its head in meditation. You can use your practice as an excellent opportunity to work with your fear by following the instructions offered in Chapter 11.

When fear is no longer an obstacle

In her book *When Things Fall Apart,* the American born Buddhist teacher Pema Chodron tells the story of a young Westerner who went to India in the 1960s. He desperately wanted to overcome his negative emotions, especially fear, which he believed to be an obstacle to his progress.

The teacher he met there kept telling him to stop struggling, but the young man took this instruction as just another technique for getting rid of his fear.

Finally his teacher sent him to a hut in the foothills to meditate. Late one night, while he was sitting, he heard a noise and turned to see a huge snake with hood lifted, swaying in the corner. The young man was terrified. He sat facing the snake, unable to move or fall asleep. He couldn't use any meditation techniques to avoid his feelings — he could only sit with his breath and his fear and the snake in the corner.

Toward morning, as the last candle flickered out, the young man experienced a flood of tenderness and compassion for all the animals and people in the world. He could feel their suffering and their longing, and he could see that he had been using his meditation to separate, not only from others but also from himself.

In the darkness, he began to cry. Yes, he was angry and proud and frightened — but he was also unique and wise and immeasurably precious. With deep gratitude, he got up, walked toward the snake, and bowed. Then he fell asleep on the floor. When he woke up, the snake had disappeared — and so had his desperate need to struggle with his fear.

Doubt

This roadblock can be an especially challenging one because it calls the whole journey into question. "Do I have what it takes to meditate? My mind never settles down — maybe I should try yoga or t'ai chi. What's the point of following my breath? How can this practice possibly bring relaxation and peace of mind?" Of course, it's important to ask questions and get satisfactory answers — but once you've decided to give meditation a try, you need to treat your doubts as grist for your mill, instead of constantly taking them seriously.

Doubt can also result from pushing yourself too hard and holding high expectations; in meditation you need to set your expectations aside (as I mention in Chapter 6) and just do it, with the faith that the benefits will naturally accrue over time. To develop such faith, you may want to read other books like this one that extol the virtues of meditation.

Doubt stirs up your mind and makes concentration difficult. Begin by naming your doubt and noticing the sensations it evokes and the stories it spins. With mindful awareness, doubt gradually settles down and recedes to the background. Eventually, all your little doubts may even coalesce into a great doubt that motivates you to inquire deeply into the nature of existence and come up with some answers for yourself.

Procrastination

Like doubt, procrastination can bring your meditation to a screeching halt. After all, if you keep putting it off, you won't be able to reap the benefits. If you tend to procrastinate in other areas of your life, you now have an opportunity to look beyond your usual excuses to the deeper feelings and concerns that fuel this pattern. Take some time to ask yourself honestly — but also gently and without judgment — what gets in the way of your following through on your intentions.

As described in the previous sections, you may be afraid or bored or have doubts about the value of meditation. Perhaps a self-sabotaging part of you doesn't want you to make the positive changes that meditation offers, and so it keeps undermining your efforts. Or you may be too restless and distracted to find the time for the very activity that could help you deal with your restlessness and distractibility. Once you get your meditation back on track, you can explore these patterns further. (You may also want to refresh your motivation or develop self-discipline — in which case, turn to Chapter 4 or Chapter 9.)

Hypervigilance

The next time you see a loving new mother, notice how she attends to her baby. Does she constantly monitor his face for signs of illness or discomfort? No, if she has a healthy relationship with her child, she gently gazes into his eyes with warm and caring attention, but without anxiety or concern.

You might find it helpful to bring the same gentle, mindful attention to your meditation. If you tend to get obsessive or perfectionistic or laserlike in your focus, you may just end up getting more stressed out than when you began. Instead, relax your attention like a loving mother, noticing your experience without becoming concerned or tense. You may also want to inquire into the deeper fear that may be motivating your hypervigilance.

Hypervigilance may also take the form of constantly monitoring your progress, constantly asking "How am I doing now?" The problem is, true progress in meditation involves simply being present without extra concerns like wondering how you're doing. Again, you can relax your awareness and just let yourself do what you do.

Self-judgment

Like fear, self-judgment is a nearly universal human experience, at least in the West. You may focus your judgment on your meditation — you're not doing it right, you don't know how to concentrate — or on your being as a whole — you're inadequate, unlovable, not quite good enough. The judging mind may even disguise itself as an objective observer or a spiritual coach, constantly comparing your progress to some internalized ideal. "If you were like the Buddha, you would be totally calm and undisturbed," it might say. Or, "If you were a good Christian (or Moslem or Jew), you would experience no anger or fear." Unfortunately, as one of my teachers used to say, "comparison kills" — meaning that it tends to dampen the unique vitality and expression that belong to you alone and can't be compared with anything else.

By naming or noticing your self-judgments, you can gain some distance from them, rather than take their word as gospel, as so many of us do. What does your voice of judgment sound like? What stories does it foist upon you as truth? Does it remind you of someone — say, a parent or boss? Are you trying to push away parts of your experience because they're undesirable in some way? Notice how judgment feels in your body. When you get caught up in judgment, you may find yourself tightening and tensing in response.

As you become familiar with your judgments, you can begin to welcome them as old friends, not only in meditation but in everyday life as well — without buying their story.

Attachment and desire

Just as fear and judgment attempt to avoid or resist certain experiences, attachment holds on tight to what you have — while desire keeps trying to find something better. When you're attached — to your career or your relationship or your material possessions — you may resist letting go when circumstances change. Who wouldn't? But attachment can be a set-up for pain, since life has this curious tendency to do what it pleases, despite your preferences to the contrary. With desire, the dissatisfaction of not having what you want and having what you don't want runs like a painful undercurrent just beneath the surface of conscious awareness.

I'm not recommending complete nonattachment and desirelessness here — after all, only the Buddha could pull that one off! Nor am I equating desire with pleasure — in fact, the experience of desire can be extremely unpleasant, like a tormenting itch that never goes away, no matter how much you scratch. True pleasure, by contrast, fulfills a deep and natural human need. But I am suggesting that you can discover how to create some space around your desires and attachments so that you're not overwhelmed by the unpredictable ups and downs of life. (For more on attachment, see Chapter 5.)

Attachment and desire can show up in your meditation in a number of forms. Perhaps you covet the moments of relative calm and become upset when your mind gets agitated or preoccupied. Or you may have a particular fondness for certain thoughts — fantasies of financial success, for example, or images of last month's vacation — and find that you're reluctant to let go of them and return to your breath or your mantra. Maybe you're constantly lusting and longing for some imagined fulfillment that's just out of reach.

As with the other roadblocks, you can explore your attachment and desire, first by gently naming them as they arise and then by noticing the thoughts and sensations that comprise them.

Pride

Here's a classic meditation scenario. You've been sitting regularly for a few weeks, and one day your mind calms down like the surface of a still forest pool. The next thing you know you're having the following thoughts: "Wow, I'm hardly thinking at all, and I've counted my breaths from one to ten now for at least five minutes. Cool! I'm really getting the hang of this meditation stuff. Pretty soon I'll be an expert. Maybe I'll even become enlightened. . . ." Not only have you been bitten by the bug of pride, which latches on to your accomplishments and uses them to bolster your sagging self-image, but you've also gotten sidetracked in your meditation. Pride can also take the form of bragging to your family and friends about how often you meditate or merely feeling special and superior to others.

As I explain in the section "Attachment," you might want to investigate the thoughts and feelings that make up your pride. Underneath it, you may find some fear or insecurity or a desire to be loved and appreciated. Or you can remind yourself that meditation has nothing to do with achievement and everything to do with being present in the moment for whatever is arising. As soon as you get puffed up about how well you're meditating, you're gone — so gently bring yourself back to your breath.

Hiding out

If you're trying to avoid confronting certain problems or challenges in your life, you may turn to meditation as a convenient escape and end up logging hours on your cushion that might be better spent paying your bills or preparing for a career change or sharing your feelings with your partner. The *New Yorker* magazine ran a cartoon a few years back that speaks to this issue: A Zen monk sits peacefully on his cushion, while behind a screen in the background lies a huge, chaotic pile of stuff.

Meditation can help you calm your mind, open your heart, and face the fears and other feelings that may stand in your way — but ultimately you need to take down the screen and apply what you've learned to the real world. (In other words, meditation, like work, sex, and watching TV, can become addictive if you abuse it.) Now, you're not becoming addicted if you spend a half hour or an hour each day meditating — or even head off for a retreat every now and then. But if you find yourself hiding out from the challenges of life, pay attention — the themes that keep recurring in your meditation may not be distractions at all, but pressing concerns that require your response.

Bypassing

Just as you can hide out from life's problems, you can also use meditation as a convenient way to avoid facing deeper psychological and emotional issues. Particularly if you develop strong concentration, you can focus on your breath or some other object of meditation while actively suppressing unpleasant or "unspiritual" feelings. I know people who, after many years of meditation in monasteries or ashrams, finally discover that they're literally sitting on a lifetime of unresolved grief, resentment, or pain. If you follow the guidelines provided in Chapter 11 for working with your emotions, you might not have to contend with this particular roadblock.

How to Enjoy the Side Effects — without Getting Sidetracked

In addition to the roadblocks, you may also encounter a number of unusual and compelling experiences on your journey — what I like to call the side effects or *roadside attractions*. Earlier in this chapter and in Chapter 11, I describe ordinary emotions, patterns, and mind-states that may prove challenging as your meditation deepens. Here I'm talking about what consciousness researchers call *altered states* — nonordinary experiences of body, mind, and heart that, though essentially harmless, may be startling, confusing, or frightening for the neophyte meditator.

Some people meditate for years and never experience anything out of the ordinary. As a Zen monk, for example, I kept hoping for some dramatic breakthrough but got only the occasional insight to punctuate thousands of hours of meditation. Others sit down and within a few sessions begin to have glimpses of what researchers call the *transpersonal dimension* of experience. A friend of mind has always seen angels and other transcendent beings, both on and off her meditation cushion.

Meditation traditions differ too in how they regard such extraordinary experiences. Some teach that the point is simply to be here now — and anything else that occurs is merely a potential distraction. Another *New Yorker* cartoon puts it succinctly: A grizzled old monk sitting in meditation turns to his young companion and says, apparently in response to a question, "This is it. There *is* nothing else." If a moment of true awakening occurs, according to these traditions, it merely takes the form of a shift in perspective, without fireworks or flashy signs. By contrast, other traditions view extraordinary experiences as meaningful or possibly even necessary landmarks on the path to freedom and awakening. (For more on spiritual experiences, see Chapter 13.)

In mindfulness meditation, the method I describe in this book (see Chapter 6), you simply approach the extraordinary in the same way you greet the ordinary — with gentle, mindful attention. Since the point is to welcome whatever arises — and in the process to awaken to who you already are — any experiences you encounter along the way are just roadside attractions. Enjoy them and keep going. If they become distracting or painful, you may want to seek a qualified teacher.

To help you deal with these experiences without getting sidetracked or overwhelmed, Buddhist teacher Jack Kornfield, in his book *A Path with Heart*, suggests that you keep in mind the following three guidelines:

> ✔ **Side effects are just that.** Don't get attached to them or take them as an indication of either spiritual accomplishment or spiritual failure. Just keep going.
>
> ✔ **Apply the brakes if you must.** If the side effects get too intense, stop meditating for a while and engage in more "grounding" activities that connect you with your body and the earth, like working in the garden, getting a massage, or walking in nature. (To help you ground, try the meditation in the sidebar "What to do when you're feeling ungrounded" later in this chapter.)
>
> ✔ **Appreciate altered states as part of the larger dance of meditation.** Don't get caught resisting or struggling with them. Just try to welcome them as you do every experience.

The following subsections highlight a few of the extraordinary experiences you may encounter in your meditation, divided for your convenience into four separate categories. (For more detailed descriptions of these experiences, I highly recommend *A Path with Heart*.)

Rapture and bliss

Once your concentration deepens (but sometimes before), you may begin to have nonordinary physical experiences known as *rapture*. (As I mention earlier, many people never experience rapture at all.) Perhaps the most common form of rapture involves the pleasurable movement of subtle (or not so subtle) energy through the body. As it moves, this energy encounters areas of tightness and contraction that open and release in response. The energetic releases can take the form of vibrations, trembling, or sudden or repetitive spontaneous movements known in the yoga tradition as *kriyas*. For example, you might feel spasms going up your spine or involuntary movements of your arms or head.

Although the energy of rapture is generally experienced as pleasurable, you might be understandably surprised and a bit disturbed to find your body moving in ways you can't seem to control. Jack Kornfield, for example, reports that his arms began to flap like a bird's while he was meditating intensively in a monastery in Thailand. After several days, he followed his teacher's advice to observe the movement without trying to stop or control it, and it gradually subsided on its own.

Just remember that you're not going insane or doing something wrong if you experience rapture; in fact, rapture generally signifies a deepening of concentration. As much as possible, keep meditating as you bring mindful awareness to your experience and allow the energy to do its healing work of releasing your stuck places. If the energy gets too intense, just stop meditating and do something ordinary and physical, as Kornfield recommends.

But rapture refers to more than just energy; it comes in other forms and flavors too. For example, you may have chills or hot flashes for no apparent reason. Or you may experience your body as extraordinarily heavy and dense or as transparent and filled with light. Or you may have prickling or tingling sensations followed by waves of pleasure and delight. Rapture can take as many forms as the people who experience it.

As for *bliss,* it's the powerful rapture that accompanies a spiritual insight or unitive experience. Mystics from the Judeo-Christian tradition, for instance, often report experiencing bliss when they achieve the pinnacle of their journey: oneness with God.

Visions and other sensory experiences

If you don't experience rapture, don't be disappointed — you may get your altered states in the visual channel. My friend who sees angels also has visions of traveling to other realms in her meditation where she meets enlightened beings that teach and empower her. These experiences don't disturb her; quite the contrary, she enjoys and even invites them.

Though you may not have such elaborate visions, you still may see colored lights or images of what appear to be past lives or vivid memories or glimpses of other realities. Again, you needn't be disturbed — just take them as evidence of deepening concentration and don't get distracted from the focus of your meditation. (Of course, if you find them meaningful, by all means appreciate what they have to offer. But the point of meditation as I teach it in this book is to awaken to the present moment, not to spend your meditation time exploring the endless world of altered states.)

In addition to visual phenomena, you may also have auditory or olfactory experiences, including inner voices or music or powerful, resonant sounds or unusual smells. Or you may find that your meditation heightens your perceptual sensitivity so that you see, hear, smell, feel, or taste things more acutely. (Depending on your particular tastes and what you happen to be sensing, you may find this increased sensitivity pleasant or unpleasant.)

Emotional rollercoaster

As your mind settles down and you welcome your experience, you create inner space for unfelt (and possibly unconscious) emotions to bubble up and release. (For more on the process of spontaneous release, see Chapter 11.) One of my early Zen friends spent her first few years of meditation crying quietly on her cushion. Often, she reported that her feelings didn't have much content or story line — they just occurred as waves of energy in her body. Other people I know meditate regularly for years with little emotion, then suddenly like an airplane hit a patch of turbulence and experience days or even weeks of anger or grief.

If you find the emotions difficult to handle, you can consult the guidelines I provide in Chapter 11 — or you may want to seek the advice of a qualified meditation teacher. (For advice on finding a teacher, see Chapter 13.) Otherwise, you can continue to sit with mindful awareness as you allow the emotions to ripple through your body, mind, and heart. Sometimes these feelings — which, incidentally, can include ecstasy and joy as well as sadness and pain — come from deep unconscious layers that hark back to early childhood or infancy. At other times, the feelings may seem like they have nothing to do with you at all. Whatever your experience, you can practice welcoming it with mindful awareness without trying to change it or push it away.

Energetic openings

When you meditate regularly for weeks or months, you generate energy that begins to accumulate in your body. Eventually, this energy may take the relatively subtle form of rapture (as described in the previous section) — or it may express itself as *kundalini*, the powerful life force that (according to the Indian tantric tradition) animates all things and lies coiled at the base of the spine like a serpent. (For more on Indian tantra, see Chapter 3.)

Meditation can awaken kundalini and send it up the central energetic channel (which is aligned with but distinct from the spine) — and so can certain other activities and events like childbirth, sex, prayer, powerful emotions, and physical trauma. As the kundalini rises — which may occur slowly and gradually or suddenly and unexpectedly — it encounters the seven major energy centers (also known as *chakras*) that lie situated along the central channel from the base of the spine to the crown of the head. (For a detailed map of the chakras, see Figure 12-1. *Note:* The chakras are shown in order from the bottom up, with the first chakra located at the base of the spine and the seventh at the top of the head.)

Described by those who can see them as spinning wheels or vortexes of energy, the chakras transform energy from one frequency to another (for example, from spiritual to emotional) and act as intermediaries between an individual's inner life and the external world. Apparently, they work best when they're open and relatively balanced. When they're closed or imbalanced — a common occurrence — you may experience certain problems, ailments, or issues that correspond with particular chakras.

In particular, people who meditate frequently may have a tendency to open their upper chakras (above the heart) relatively easily, while keeping their lower chakras relatively closed. For example, many people find it easier to have spiritual experiences or feel unconditional love for all beings than to deal with core personal issues like trust, safety, intimacy, and self-assertion. As a result, these lower centers may require special attention and tender, gentle investigation before they open.

What to do when you're feeling ungrounded

Sometimes people who meditate find that their *upper chakras* (that is, the energy centers from the heart to the crown) open more quickly than their lower chakras, bringing a rush of energy and insight to their head and shoulders while the lower half of their body remains relatively stagnant or numb. In particular, those who get sidetracked by some of the flashy side effects of meditation may start to feel ungrounded and lose touch with their basic needs for food, sleep, and physical exercise.

Here's a simple exercise that can help you ground down into the earth when you start feeling like you're going to lift out of your body into some more ethereal realm:

1. **Begin by sitting quietly, closing your eyes, and taking a few slow, deep breaths.**

   If possible, sit on the ground, with your back relatively straight (see Chapter 7 for more on sitting positions).

2. **Focus your awareness on your lower abdomen, at a point about two inches below your navel and an inch and a half inside your body.**

   Martial artists call this area the *t'an t'ien* and believe it's a focal point for life energy, or *chi*. Explore this area with mindful attention, noticing how it feels.

3. **Direct your breath into this area, expanding it when you inhale and contracting it when you exhale.**

Consciously and deliberately breathe into your t'an t'ien for five minutes or more, allowing your awareness and your energy to concentrate there. Notice how your center of gravity shifts from the upper part of your body to your t'an t'ien.

4. **Continuing to breathe with your t'an t'ien, imagine that you're a tree with roots that go deep into the earth.**

   Both feel and visualize these roots originating in the t'an t'ien and growing down through the base of your spine into the ground, spreading through the soil as far down as you can imagine.

5. **Feel and visualize these roots drawing energy up from the earth into your t'an t'ien on the inhalation, and feel the energy spreading down through the roots on the exhalation.**

   Continue to feel and visualize this circulation of energy — up on the inhale, down on the exhale, for five or ten minutes.

6. **Once your t'an t'ien feels charged and strong, you can get up and go about your day.**

   Every now and then, you can stop for a moment or two and imagine your roots once again.

Figure 12-1:
Here's a map of the chakras (energy centers), with the traditional symbols for each one.

Certain meditation techniques aim to awaken the kundalini and guide it through the chakras until it reaches the crown of the head, where it ultimately bursts forth in a moment of powerful illumination. Others work on opening and energizing particular chakras. (For example, see Chapter 10 for meditations that open the heart.) The primary technique I propose in this book, known as mindfulness meditation, doesn't focus on the chakras at all. But people who practice mindfulness may experience the opening of particular energy centers as a side effect of their meditative journey.

To help you recognize these openings if and when they do occur, I'm going to describe each of the chakras in some detail. (Incidentally, the Indian tantric tradition, which includes both Hinduism and Buddhism, is not the only one that talks about chakras: Jewish kabbalists, Sufi dervishes, and Taoist sages all have their own unique energy systems and centers.) In addition to the experiences described in the bullets that follow, you may feel tightness or constriction in the area when a chakra is relatively closed and a noticeable increase of energy when it opens.

✔ **First chakra:** Located at the base of the spine and connected with issues of survival and safety. When it's relatively closed, you may feel insecure and ungrounded, possibly even terrified and mistrustful of your capacity to survive. As it opens, you may feel energy flowing down through your body into the earth, accompanied by images and feelings associated with safety and survival as well as an overall sense of stability and trust. *Positive expression:* "I'm safe and at home in the world and in my body."

✔ **Second chakra:** Located in the lower abdomen about two inches below the navel; connected with issues of sexuality, creativity, and emotional attachment. When it's relatively closed, you may feel ashamed of your body, sexually inhibited, and emotionally disconnected from others. As it opens, you may experience a rush of sexual feelings or imagery, including possible images of past abuse or dysfunction, as well as a sense of potency, playfulness, and flow with others. *Positive expression:* "I'm a creative, sexual, emotional being."

✔ **Third chakra:** Located at the solar plexus just below the diaphragm and connected with issues of interpersonal power and authenticity. When this chakra is relatively closed, you may find it difficult to trust (either yourself or others), to set interpersonal boundaries, or to express or even acknowledge your own anger or vulnerability. As it opens, you may experience a release of anger or shame and a deepening and expansion of your breath, accompanied by feelings of personal power and vitality. *Positive expression:* "I trust myself and others."

✔ **Fourth chakra (often called the "heart chakra"):** Located in the center of the chest near the heart and connected with issues of love and self-esteem. When this chakra is closed, you may feel self-hatred, resentment, and alienation from others, and you may find it difficult to give and receive love freely. As it opens, you may experience a release of old grief or pain, accompanied by love or joy or poignancy and a sense of boundless expansiveness. (For more on opening the heart chakra, see Chapter 10.) *Positive expression:* "I'm loving and worthy of being loved."

✔ **Fifth chakra (also known as the "throat chakra"):** Located in the center of the throat; connected with issues of honest, direct, and responsible self-expression. When it's relatively closed, you may find it difficult to share your feelings, thoughts, or concerns without diluting or distorting them to make them more acceptable to others. As this chakra opens, you may experience a sudden upsurge of things you've always wanted to say, accompanied by increased confidence in your own voice and creativity. *Positive expression:* "I have a right to express my truth."

✔ **Sixth chakra:** Located between and slightly above the eyebrows; connected with intellectual clarity, intuition, and personal vision. When this chakra is relatively closed, you may have difficulty thinking clearly or planning for the future, and you may have strong personal opinions, prejudices, or negative beliefs about yourself. As this chakra opens, you may have sudden insights or intuitions that expand your intellectual or spiritual horizons, possibly accompanied by inner visions or even psychic abilities. *Positive expression:* "I see things clearly."

✔ **Seventh chakra (also known as the "crown chakra"):** Located at the very top of the head; connected with issues of freedom and spiritual transcendence. When this chakra is relatively closed (as it is in most people), you may feel cut off from the sacred or spiritual dimension of life. As it opens, you may feel a subtle pressure or pain at first, followed by a release of energy through the crown of the head and an influx of what people have described as grace, peace, blessing, or illumination. At the same time, you may feel your identity dissolving and merging with the vast expanse of being itself. Needless to say, the opening of this chakra is a precious event much sought after in certain spiritual traditions. *Positive expression:* "I am."

Checking out your chakras

Because the energy centers, or chakras, figure so prominently in certain meditative traditions and may naturally open in response to regular meditation, you may want to take a brief tour through your own chakras, just to get a lay of the land. Begin by sitting quietly, relaxing your body, and taking a few deep breaths.

✔ **First chakra:** Bring your awareness to your perineum, which is the point halfway between your anus and your genitals. (If you don't know what I'm talking about, just focus on the area deep down in your pelvis, at the very base of your abdomen.) As you rest your awareness there, imagine gently caressing the area with your breath. How does the area feel to you? Do you notice any tightness, vibration, or agitation? Does it feel like this energy center is open and energized or closed and constricted? Take your time, and don't try to figure it out — just be aware of the sensations.

✔ **Second chakra:** Bring your awareness to a point about two inches below your belly-button and an inch or two inside your abdomen. As described in the previous bullet, breathe into the area and check out how it feels.

✔ **Third chakra:** Bring your awareness to your solar plexus, the area in your upper abdomen right beneath your sternum, or breastbone. As described earlier, breathe and feel.

✔ **Fourth chakra:** Bring your awareness to the center of your chest inside, near your heart. Again, breathe and feel.

✔ **Fifth chakra:** Bring your awareness to the center of your throat, near your Adam's apple. Breathe and feel.

✔ **Sixth chakra:** Bring your awareness to your "third eye," the point on your forehead between and just above your eyebrows. Breathe and feel.

✔ **Seventh chakra:** Bring your awareness to the crown of your head. Breathe and feel.

As you locate each chakra in turn and settle your awareness there, you can do the following exercise. (Alternatively, you might just choose to focus on one or two chakras that seem to be calling out for your attention because they feel tight or uncomfortable or especially energized.)

Here's the exercise:

1. **Begin by sitting quietly, closing your eyes, and taking a few slow, deep breaths, relaxing a little with each exhalation.**

2. **As you rest your awareness gently on the chakra, set aside all thoughts and allow an image (or images) to arise.**

   The image may take the form of a memory, an object, or a geometric shape or color. Take whatever comes and sit with it for a few moments.

3. **Ask yourself: "If this chakra had a voice, what would it say?"**

   Allow it to speak its mind to you fully, and take the time to listen.

4. **Finally, you may want to ask yourself: "If this chakra were an animal, what would it be?"**

   Allow an image or felt sense of an animal to appear and unfold in your awareness.

If you don't get a response to every one of these questions, don't worry. Many people are stronger in one channel (for example, auditory) than in another (for example, visual). With continued practice, you'll gradually tune in to your chakras and what they have to share with you. Each time you do the exercise, you'll get different information, depending on the current state of your energy centers.

IN THE MOMENT

Preparing for sleep

Most of us go to bed at night filled with the worries, concerns, and excitements we've accumulated during the day. Instead, try preparing for sleep using one of the following exercises:

✔ As you undress, imagine removing all your cares and responsibilities, one by one. Imagine feeling yourself growing lighter, more relaxed, and more spacious, until your mind is completely empty and filled with a pleasant, rosy glow. Imagine this glow descending to your heart, and rest your awareness in the center of your heart as you drift off to sleep.

✔ Before going to sleep, review your day in some detail. Take some time to appreciate your positive accomplishments and experiences. When you come to something you regret, consider the lesson you learned. Feel gratitude in your heart to all the people who contributed to your life today in various ways, as you drift off to sleep.

✔ Lie on your back and feel the contact of your body against the bed. Beginning with your feet and working slowly up through your legs, hips, torso, arms, neck, and head, gradually relax your body from bottom to top. When you're done, feel your body as one luminous sphere of relaxation as you drift off to sleep.

Chapter 13

Cultivating Spirituality

*T*hroughout this book, I refer repeatedly to *spirituality,* though I often disguise it in metaphors or abstractions. After all, how else could I express the inexpressible? In Chapter 1, I talk about climbing the mountain of meditation and briefly describe what you might encounter if you ever get to the top. Elsewhere, I use words like "pure being" or "true nature" or "innate perfection." Well, if these rather puzzling allusions to a *spiritual dimension of being* piqued your interest, here's where you find out how to use meditation to explore spirituality to your heart's content.

No, I won't be giving you detailed instructions on how to get enlightened or meet God directly. You might have to check out other books and teachers for that. But I do offer a brief glimpse of what the spiritual path has to offer so that you know which direction to take on your journey.

If you've ever wandered through the spirituality or religion section of your local bookstore, you know how many books have been written purporting to show you the right way to go. But you may still be wondering what all this spirituality stuff means anyway. Or you may want a little guidance in sorting out one approach from another. Here's where you find a few answers — based on my admittedly limited understanding, of course.

Note: The chapter you're about to read is filled with spiritual terminology that may prove offensive to the secular reader. If you find yourself squirming in your seat when you hear words like "spirit" or "grace" or "higher reality," you may prefer to skip this chapter altogether. Then again, you *could* open yourself to a whole new dimension of experience. Oops, there's one of those words again!

What Does Spirituality Mean Anyway?

If you meditate regularly, you're going to have spiritual experiences — guaranteed. By following your breath or reciting a mantra or merely sitting quietly and listening with full attention to the sound of the wind through the trees, you're cutting through your usual preoccupations and attuning yourself to the present moment. That's where glimpses of the spiritual dimension of being generally occur — in the present. (In fact, as the title of the 1970s bestseller *Be Here Now* suggests, being present with awareness is an inherently spiritual activity. See the sidebar "Where the vertical meets the horizontal" later in this chapter.) To paraphrase an old saying, spiritual experiences are accidents — but you make yourself accident-prone when you meditate.

Here are a few of the experiences you may encounter:

- ✔ An insight into your interconnectedness with other beings and things
- ✔ An upsurge of boundless, unconditional love that spreads throughout your body
- ✔ A pleasurable stream of grace or blessings or illumination from above
- ✔ A direct perception of the empty, insubstantial, or impermanent nature of everything
- ✔ A current of energy up the spine through the energy centers that leaves you feeling more expanded or in touch with spirit (for more on the energy centers, see Chapter 12)
- ✔ An experience of subtle inner sounds, colors, or shapes that have spiritual significance
- ✔ An experience of your body dissolving into light or expanding its boundaries and dissolving into space
- ✔ A shift in identity from being the body-mind to being the space or awareness in which the body-mind exists
- ✔ A deep and certain knowing (beyond the mind) of a sacred presence that exists both within and beyond the world of space and time
- ✔ Visions of angels or other spiritual beings
- ✔ A direct awareness of the presence of the Divine
- ✔ The inner experience of being loved by (or even one with) God

How do you know you've had a spiritual experience? Or to put it another way, what makes an experience spiritual? Well, you might get up from your meditation and actually say, "Wow, that was a spiritual experience." Or the experience may somehow fit with your spiritual beliefs and provide further proof or amplification of what you already know. Or perhaps you simply feel inspired or expanded or more loving or open to yourself or others as a

result. (As I mention in Chapter 6, the word *spiritual* comes from the Latin for "breath" or "life force." Related words include "spirited," "inspiring," and "respiration.")

The definitions of *spirituality* and *spiritual experience* really depend on the person you ask. Some people view spirituality as the vital spark that animates and enlivens their religious involvement. Others take their spirituality straight, without religious dogma or ritual. But whatever their orientation, all the definitions point to a glimpse of something deeper or higher or more real or more meaningful than our ordinary, workaday lives.

In his classic book *The Varieties of Religious Experience,* written at the turn of the twentieth century, the American scholar William James notes that spiritual experiences generally have four characteristics:

- **Ineffability:** They can't be adequately expressed in words but must be experienced directly.
- **Insight:** They generally involve the discovery of deep, important truths that can't be understood by the rational mind.
- **Impermanence:** They last for a limited period of time but may recur, and their meaning may continue to reveal itself, even though the experiences themselves have faded into memory.
- **Passivity:** You can prepare for spiritual experiences, but once they occur, you receive them passively, and they unfold in your awareness with a power of their own.

Where does the "spiritual dimension" exist? Some people experience it inside themselves, as the heart or center or deepest part of their being, beneath the body or the personality. Others experience it outside, above, or all around them, through spiritual beings on other planes of reality (like angels or spirits or bodhisattvas) or simply as the current or spirit that infuses all life. You may get your spiritual experiences when you watch a sunset or walk along the beach, for example, or when you play with your kids or spend solitary time communing with yourself. Ultimately, it seems, the spiritual dimension exists both inside and outside of us, in our deepest heart of hearts and in every being and thing, beyond the ordinary limitations of space and time.

The "perennial philosophy": Where all religions converge

Just so you don't think this spirituality stuff belongs to one particular tradition or another, I'd like to point out that certain philosophers have surveyed the world's great religions, from Christianity to Zoroastrianism, and discovered that a common spiritual river runs through them all. This

Where the vertical meets the horizontal

Here's a helpful framework for understanding the relationship between the ordinary and the spiritual — and how meditation brings them together.

Your everyday life occurs on the horizontal plane of space and time, cause and effect. (Some traditions call this plane the *relative* level of reality.) You're constantly moving from here to there, past to future, planning for tomorrow and evaluating yesterday, doing and achieving and hurrying — and maybe occasionally stopping to relax or watch TV. It's on the horizontal plane that you evolve outwardly: You grow up, learn life's lessons, create relationships and family, pursue your career, achieve some measure of maturity and wisdom — all extremely important accomplishments.

At the same time, there exists a vertical plane that has nothing to do with space and time. (In contrast to the relative, this plane is called the *absolute* level.) It's the timeless or eternal realm that all the great religious traditions describe — the top of the mountain that I mention in Chapter 1. They call it vertical because

it intersects and pervades the horizontal in every moment. And if you know how to attune yourself to it, you can allow it to inform you, inspire you, and suffuse your being with grace, spirit, wisdom, compassion — the words depend on the nature of your experience and the tradition you follow (if any).

Meditation brings you out of your time-bound planning and thinking into the present moment precisely where the spiritual dimension meets your ordinary life. You know those bumper stickers that say: Grace happens? Well, it's more likely to happen when you're open to it.

As you sit and coordinate your body , breath, and mind through the practice of following your breath or reciting a mantra, you create an inner harmony or alignment that invites the influx of the vertical plane. (In fact, the vertical and horizontal planes are always intersecting – you just don't notice.) And when you keep comming back to the present moment in your ordinary life between meditations, you're more likely to see the spirit in every being and thing you encounter.

river is called the *perennial philosophy,* and it consists of three interconnected currents or principles. (I know this discussion is getting a little serious, but bear with me — I'll lighten it up as much as I can.)

> ✔ **A greater reality exists that underlies the ordinary world of things and lives and minds.** Whether they claim that it transcends or infuses or is essentially identical with the ordinary world, the great traditions agree that this divine or spiritual reality exists. Some call it *God* or the *Holy Spirit,* the one (or ones) who created the universe and continues to orchestrate your life from above. Others call it the *ground of being,* the impersonal essence that supports and sustains you. Still others call it *emptiness* or *essential nature* or *Self* or *Tao.* Whatever they call it, this spiritual dimension is a sacred mystery that gives meaning and purpose and truth to human life.

✔ **In each person there exists something similar to, or even identical with, this greater reality.** Here again, the traditions may disagree on the form this something might take. Christians call it *soul,* Jews refer to the *divine spark within,* Hindus call it *atman,* and Buddhists use words like *Buddha nature* or *big mind.* But all agree that this something connects us with the greater (or higher or deeper) reality that underlies ordinary life.

✔ **The ultimate goal of human life is to realize this greater reality.** The Sufi mystic may seek to unite with it, the Buddhist monk may strive to awaken to it, the Christian contemplative may yearn to have glimpses of it — and the rest of us may be quite content to feel connected with it (or merely pay homage to it at church or temple or synagogue every now and then). However you approach it, the great spiritual traditions agree that every human being harbors a deep longing (however buried or disguised) to realize this greater reality.

As I mention in Chapter 1, you can take many paths up the mountain of being. But all the paths agree that the mountain exists, that you're somehow called to climb it (perhaps just because "it's there," as Sir Edmund Hillary said of Everest), and that what you discover at the top exists (in some form, at least) inside you all along.

From faith to fruition: The levels of spiritual involvement

You can relate to all this spiritual stuff in a variety of ways. You can ignore it entirely — but I doubt that you would have gotten this far into the chapter if you had no interest in the subject at all. You can believe in it in one form or another. (Perhaps you have faith in the existence of angels or adhere to the doctrine of a particular religion or read books about shamans or saints or sages and believe in the reality they describe.) Or you can aspire to experience the spiritual dimension for yourself.

For convenience, I like to break spiritual involvement down into six levels. They aren't mutually exclusive — you can engage in one or two or all of them, if you like. They're not hierarchical; in other words, one isn't necessarily better or higher or more advanced than another. And they're certainly not hard and fast; they're just my way of making sense of something that's ultimately unfathomable. Here are the six levels:

✔ **Believing in spirit:** I use the word "spirit" here to refer to the greater reality I talked about earlier that underlies the ordinary world of people and things. Believing in spirit is an important first step because it opens you to the possibility of getting closer to it in some way.

✔ **Awakening to spirit:** When you have a glimpse of the spiritual dimension (one of the spiritual experiences listed earlier in this chapter), you no longer merely believe — now you know. But such experiences may fade and become little more than memories, unless they're sustained or rekindled through regular spiritual practice.

✔ **Being in touch with spirit:** Sometimes the awakening leaves you substantially transformed. When you look at people and things, you no longer see them in the same old way. Instead, they're infused with new meaning and depth, and you're in touch with the spiritual dimension wherever you go and whatever you do.

✔ **Being infused with spirit:** Not only do you sense the presence of spirit in every being and thing, now you know with certainty that spirit infuses every fiber of your own being as well — or, in other words, that you and spirit are essentially the same. You clearly experience spirit as the greater reality or substance of your life that connects you with everything.

✔ **Being one with spirit:** When separation falls away and you merge with the greater reality, you achieve the state of *oneness* that mystics and Zen masters describe. But until you thoroughly integrate this realization into every aspect of your life, you may still enter and leave the oneness without being fully established or rooted in it.

✔ **No separation between spirit and ordinary life:** Now you know without doubt that ordinary, everyday reality, the sacred spiritual dimension, and your own essential nature are one and the same. No matter where you go or what you do, you meet the divine in everyone and everything, without the slightest trace of separation.

Dissolving or expanding the self: The point of spiritual practice

The great spiritual traditions also agree that the primary reason we suffer — and the primary problem we need to resolve — is the experience of being a separate, isolated individual, cut off from God or source or our own essential nature. When you meditate, you're bridging the apparent chasm that separates you and connecting with your breath, with your body and senses, with your heart, with the present moment, and ultimately with a greater reality. (It's this connection that promotes healing, as Dr. Dean Ornish and other researchers have found. For more on Ornish's ground-breaking work on reversing heart disease, see Chapter 2.)

As I mention in the previous section, you can believe in spirit, awaken to it, stay in touch with it, and become infused by it — all very important and invaluable stages on the spiritual journey. (In fact, just about everyone I know, including myself, lies somewhere along this continuum.) But the ultimate aim of spiritual practice is to help you overcome all apparent separation and become one with spirit completely.

Contemplating a spiritual text

Here's a meditation that's as old as the written word — or even older, since people were memorizing spiritual texts long before they could write.

1. **Begin by sitting quietly, closing your eyes, and taking a few slow, deep breaths, relaxing a little on each exhalation.**

2. **Take a favorite passage from spiritual literature and read a few sentences or paragraphs — just enough to impart some spiritual truth but not enough to engage your analytical mind.**

   If you're not sure where to turn for material, you may want to begin with a general anthology like Stephen Mitchell's *The Enlightened Heart* or the recent bestseller *Spiritual Literacy* by Frederic and Mary Ann Brussat.

3. **Notice how the passage affects you.**

   Does it make you feel more spacious or relaxed? Does it inspire you or bring tears of gratitude or appreciation to your eyes? Does it remind you of some spiritual experience or insight you once had?

4. **Let the passage continue to act on you.**

   You can read it again and dwell on it, if you like, or just allow certain words or phrases to resonate in your heart and mind. But don't think about it or analyze it in your usual way — just be with the resonance or moisture of truth that it conveys.

5. **Consider that the words are merely a box that holds a precious treasure.**

   By contemplating the words, you discover the treasure — but don't get fixated on the words.

6. **When you feel complete, you can begin meditating in your usual way.**

   Or just get up and go about your day.

7. **As a word or phrase from the passage comes to mind during the day, pause for a moment and allow it to act on you.**

The more you read spiritual teachings in this way, the more you can assimilate them and gradually make them your own.

Dissolving the self

What keeps you separate? Well, some traditions call it *ego* or *self,* others call it *personality* or *pride* or *self-image* or *self-clinging.* Essentially, it's the beliefs and stories I describe in Chapter 5, the inner turbulence and self-centered preoccupations and patterns that keep you from seeing things clearly. Of course, these preoccupations and patterns run deep and can take a lifetime (or lifetimes!) of dedicated practice to undo, but you can begin to unravel them using some of the meditative practices described in Chapter 11. (At a deeper level of understanding, you're actually never separate from spirit even for an instant — you just think you are. But therein lies the riddle we all need to solve. As the great Indian sage Ramana Maharshi used to say, "The only thing that separates you from the Self is the belief that you're separate.")

As you unravel these patterns, you gradually dissolve the limited self you thought yourself to be and realize your identity with the greater reality. Again, this journey can take a long, long time (even lifetimes, if you believe in reincarnation), and it may be fraught with difficulties, fears, and uncertainties, as you will discover if you read the biography of any great saint or sage. In addition, you need to develop a healthy measure of self-love and self-acceptance to navigate the journey at all. (You also need the guidance of an experienced teacher. For more on teachers, see the section "How to Find a Teacher — and Why You May Want to Bother" at the end of this chapter. For more on self-love, see Chapter 10.)

Expanding the self

In addition to dissolving the self, you can also understand the spiritual journey as an expansion of identity from the narrow to the vast, until you're finally identified with the *luminous, eternal vastness* itself (a.k.a. spirit or God). The ancient Indian sages used the model of the five bodies, which are subtler and subtler levels of identification beginning with the physical body and moving to identification with the ground of being or greater reality itself.

Here's a similar model (based on the five bodies and loosely adapted from the writings of philosopher Ken Wilber) that you may find helpful in understanding your own spiritual experiences and unfolding. (Apologies, Ken, for turning some of your thinking on its head!) Remember that each time you expand your identity to a new level, you incorporate the level that came before, rather than leaving it behind.

✔ **Physical body:** Some people seem to think of nothing else but eating, drinking, working, sleeping, and sexing — they're largely identified with their physical needs and instincts. Children, too, identify mostly with this level, though they also have one foot in the spiritual realm, especially during the first three or four years.

✔ **Persona:** As you grow up and interact more with others, you develop a personality — a set of habits and tendencies and preferences — along with a self-image based largely on how others see you. Gradually, you begin to expand your identity to include this social persona, and you may become preoccupied with how you look or come across or the other accouterments of a self-image, such as material possessions.

✔ **Mature ego:** If you spend enough time exploring your inner life and sorting through your deeper feelings, values, and visions, you may eventually develop a mature ego — a healthy, well-rounded sense of who you are, what you want, and how you can contribute to others. People who identify themselves with their mature egos seem grounded and self-confident and tend to be self-actualizers — that is, those who express their full potential as human beings in their relationships and career. According to traditional Western psychology, the mature ego represents the culmination of human development.

✔ **Energy body:** The spiritual traditions pick up where secular Western psychology leaves off. Beyond the body-mind lies the energy body (the aura that surrounds the physical body), which expands and contracts depending on your mood, your energy level, and countless other factors. (Whether you notice it or not, you're constantly reacting to the energy bodies of the people you meet.)

The classic exercise for experiencing your energy body goes as follows: Rub your palms and fingers together vigorously for a few minutes, then hold them an inch or two apart and notice the energy field between them. Bring them closer together and farther apart, feeling the energy get denser and thinner and pulsate as your hands move. To explore this dimension further, check out the sidebar "Playing with your energy body" later in this chapter.

People who expand their identities to include their energy body realize that they're more than just their body-mind, which opens them to a spiritual dimension of being.

✔ **Transpersonal dimension:** This broad category encompasses the full range of nonordinary experiences, from clairvoyance and other forms of extrasensory perception (ESP) to rapture and bliss to visions of angels, gods and goddesses, and other otherwordly beings to direct communion with your higher self — or even with a personal manifestation of God. (For more on rapture and bliss, see Chapter 12.) When you expand your identity to include these subtler levels of being, you know without doubt that who you are is far vaster than you once believed, and you begin to access a higher source of wisdom and compassion as well. (Near-death experiences often fit this category, as do the experiences described in bestsellers like *Conversations with God* and *The Celestine Prophecy.*)

✔ **Glimpses of being:** When you experience being directly in all its innate perfection and completeness, you realize that you've never been separate from who you really are even for an instant. The Zen masters call such a direct experience of being *kensho* — literally, seeing your true nature — but you may need a number of kenshos before you know who you are without doubt and stop shifting back to a more limited identification.

✔ **Ground of being:** Only the great mystics and sages get this far. Now, you're one with spirit or the ground of being without separation — in the words of the Indian scriptures, "You are That." Sure, you continue to eat, drink, sleep, and blow your nose, but you never forget even for an instant who you really are — and your being radiates wisdom and compassion to others.

Now that we've covered the territory, you can close your books and prepare for a quiz. No, seriously, folks — people actually do have experiences like the ones I describe, and I thought you might like to know what you're getting yourself into if you decide to use your meditation for spiritual purposes. (Again, I strongly urge you to find a teacher if you do.) The approach of dissolving the self and the approach of expanding the self ultimately take you to the same place: the deep inner knowing that you and God or the ground of being are identical — "not two," as some teachers put it. Although most spiritual traditions tend to emphasize one approach over the other, they generally offer both as alternatives, depending on your inclinations.

In the same way, the world's spiritual traditions differ in the paths they emphasize. The Judeo-Christian tradition, for example, tends to focus on the *path of devotion,* whereas Buddhism for the most part stresses the *path of insight.* But those who practice devotion often have profound insights into the nature of existence, and those who pursue insight may also use devotional practices to assist them in their quest. Besides, some traditions, like Hinduism and Sufism, emphasize both. (The third principal path, *selfless service,* which involves dedicating every action to spiritual rather than personal ends, can be used to deepen the experience of either devotion or insight. For example, Mother Teresa served the poorest of the poor as an expression of her devotion to Jesus, while the bodhisattvas of the Buddhist tradition serve others to help free them from the limitations of ignorance.)

Playing with your energy body

Did you ever have the sense that you were bigger than your physical body? Or that the space you occupy expands and contracts depending on circumstances? (No, I'm not talking about dieting here.) Did you ever have the feeling that you had no boundaries and you went on forever? Well, you're experiencing the expansion and contraction of your energy body, the aura of energy that surrounds your physical body.

Here's a little exercise for playing with your energy body:

1. **Begin by sitting quietly, closing your eyes, and taking a few slow, deep breaths, relaxing a little on each exhalation.**

2. **Spend a few minutes imagining going for a walk in nature or spending time with someone you love.**

   Notice how big you feel.

   Then notice how your size (but not your waistline) changes when you imagine getting stuck in traffic or paying your bills or getting into an argument.

3. **Next, check out your energy body without imagining anything.**

   How far do you think it extends beyond your physical body? Six inches? Several feet? Does it extend farther in front than behind? Farther above your body than below into the ground? Is it thicker than the air, or thinner? Thicker in some places than in others?

4. **Pick a room where you feel comfortable, stand or sit near the center, and check out the boundaries of the room in every direction.**

5. **Fill the room with your energy — fill it with you!**

   Imagine it, sense it, visualize it, sing it, whatever helps you fill the space as much as you can.

6. **Draw your energy back in until it forms a sphere around you, about two or three feet away.**

   Notice how the energy becomes denser.

7. **Play with expanding and contracting your energy in this way several times, then relax and notice how you feel.**

By regularly experimenting with your energy body, you can acquire a direct understanding of the spiritual truth that you're more than your physical body. (This exercise is adapted from a series of exercises in the book *The Lover Within* by Julie Henderson.)

The Path of Devotion: In Search of Union

If you believe in the existence of a personal God or have had experiences of a presence greater than yourself that inspired feelings of awe and reverence, you may be drawn to the path of devotion. It's the primary spiritual path in the Judeo-Christian tradition and Islam and forms one of the main currents of Hinduism.

Although devotees may feel deeply connected to God and believe that a spark of divinity shines in their hearts, they often experience themselves to be painfully separate from God. As the anonymous author of the mystical Christian text *The Cloud of Unknowing* puts it, "The person who has a deep experience of himself existing far apart from God feels the most acute sorrow. Any other grief seems trivial in comparison." Through contemplation, mantra recitation (see the section "Mantra: Invoking the divine in every moment" later in this chapter), chanting, selfless service, and other devotional practices, devotees seek to get closer to God by focusing all of their love and attention on God — and ultimately, if they're mystically inclined, to merge with God completely in a state of ecstatic union.

As a bridge between the self and the Divine (especially when the Divine doesn't have a personal face, as in certain schools of Hinduism and Buddhism), devotion may also be directed to the spiritual guide. In the West, for example, the great Sufi poet Rumi spoke in rapturous terms of his love and reverence for Shams of Tabriz, his "friend" and teacher; and certain Christian mystics wrote love letters in which they directed the same devotion to one another as they directed to God. In the East, some Hindu teachers require the devotion of their students as an essential step toward spiritual maturity, and Tibetan Buddhists practice guru yoga, in which they revere the teacher as the embodiment of their own essential nature. (See the section "Guru yoga: Tibetan devotional meditation" later in this chapter.)

Although the path of devotion follows the general guidelines for spirituality discussed earlier in this chapter, it also has its own unique aspects or phases of development. (Again, this stuff may seem pretty lofty — but if you're a budding mystic, you definitely want to have an overview of the path.) These phases include the following:

✔ **Developing virtue:** In all the great devotional traditions, devotees are required to prepare themselves for union with God by living a life of purity and restraint.

✔ **Cultivating a higher octave of love:** The devotee may begin by feeling personal love for God or teacher, but eventually this love evolves into an unconditional, transpersonal love that knows no bounds and does not depend on the love object to evoke. (For more on unconditional love, see Chapter 10.)

✔ **Overcoming duality:** Beginning with a painful sense of separation, the devotee gradually gets closer and closer and ultimately merges with God, until no trace of separation remains. As the Hindu sage Swami Vivekananda put it, "love, the lover, and the beloved are one."

✔ **Transcending the personal God:** Ultimately, the devotee must transcend even God, if God is experienced as having a particular name or form. At this stage, the lover and the beloved dissolve into God as the absolute ground of being, the nameless, formless greater reality whose essence is love.

✔ **Everything is God:** The distinctions get pretty subtle at these higher levels, but here goes: When the devotee no longer needs to contemplate or meditate in order to experience oneness with God but sees God everywhere in every moment, waking or sleeping, he or she has reached the pinnacle of the devotional path. Now that the separate self and all self-centered striving have fallen away, every activity reflects a complete alignment with the divine purpose: "Not my will but Thy will be done."

To give you a flavor of the devotional path, here are three practices you might like to try. The first two have their counterparts in all the world's great spiritual traditions, and the third provides an example of devotional practice in the Buddhist tradition.

Mantra: Invoking the divine in every moment

Throughout history, meditators and mystics in the great devotional traditions have recommended the constant recitation of a *mantra* (a sacred word or phrase usually transmitted directly from a teacher) to bring the devotee closer to the Divine. (For more on mantra, see Chapter 3.) At first, you can practice repeating it aloud; then, when you become proficient, you can repeat it silently to yourself; and ultimately you can graduate to purely mental recitation (which is considered the most powerful).

Some practitioners of mantra also manipulate a rosary (or *mala* in Sanskrit) to help them keep track, ticking off one bead for each recitation. (You can buy a basic mala in any meditation supply store or metaphysical bookstore.) Or you can coordinate the sound with the coming and going of your breath.

Although you might begin by limiting your mantra recitation to a few minutes or hours of meditation each day, the traditional goal is constant practice. That is, you want to get to the point where you're repeating the sound or phrase nonstop in order to keep your attention focused on the Divine and away from habitual patterns of thought. Ultimately, your mind will become one-pointed, and you'll think always and only of God — which is the first step on the path to union. (If you watched the movie *Gandhi,* you may remember that he died with the mantra "Ram" [one of the Hindu names for God] on his lips.)

Needless to say, you'll be lucky if you can remember your mantra for a few minutes at first. But if you've received a mantra from a teacher (or know a mantra you find particularly meaningful or resonant) and you feel strong devotion, who can say how far you can go in your practice? (For inspiration on your path, you might like to read the spiritual classic *The Way of a Pilgrim,* the anonymous story of a devout Russian Orthodox peasant who chants the Jesus prayer day and night.)

The practice of the presence of God

Here's a time-honored practice that has counterparts in all the world's great spiritual traditions. Once you catch a glimpse of the sacred, you can practice seeing it everywhere you look, in everyone and everything. One ancient Zen master used to say "Buddha! Buddha!" to every being he encountered. When the contemporary Tibetan teacher Kalu Rinpoche visited an aquarium in San Francisco, he went around tapping the glass to get the fishes' attention so he could bless them and wish them happiness and well-being.

The *practice* is just that simple: Remember to see the sacred or divine in every being and thing. Brother Lawrence of the Resurrection, a seventeenth-century Catholic brother, called it the "practice of the presence of God." You may believe that everything is God, or infused by God, or created by God, or has the spark of divinity inside. Whatever your belief, the practice reminds you to look not at the surface or at what you like or don't like or want or need, but at the sacred, spiritual dimension that is perpetually present. For those who do this practice, God, like beauty, is in the eyes of the beholder. (For example, instead of responding to the stressed-out expression on people's faces, you may want to look beyond to the love in their hearts or the gleam in their eyes or the purity of their essential nature, however hidden.)

Of course, the practice may be simple, but it's certainly not easy. You might like to begin by doing it for ten minutes and see how it goes. If you enjoy it, you can naturally extend it as you feel inspired. (To help you remember, you may want to repeat a phrase like "This too is divine," not constantly like a mantra, but intermittently, as a reminder.)

Guru yoga: Tibetan devotional practice

For the Tibetan Buddhist practitioner, the root teacher, or *guru,* embodies the wisdom and compassion of all the enlightened beings throughout space and time. By invoking the guru and "fervently praying with uncontrived devotion," in the words of the great contemporary master Dudjom Rinpoche (quoted in *The Tibetan Book of Living and Dying* by Sogyal Rinpoche), "after a while the direct blessing of the wisdom mind of the master will be transmitted, empowering you with a unique realization, beyond words, born deep within your mind."

The point of guru yoga, in other words, is to become one with the greater reality (call it God or spirit or Buddha nature) by first merging with the mind and heart of an enlightened master. (In the Tibetan tradition, the wisdom mind of the guru, which is said to resemble the vastness of the sky, is ultimately identical with being itself.)

Fortunately, you don't have to be a Tibetan Buddhist to benefit from this practice. Here's a brief version that anyone can do (adapted from Sogyal Rinpoche's *The Tibetan Book of Living and Dying*):

1. **Sit quietly, close your eyes, and take a few slow, deep breaths, relaxing a little with each exhalation.**

   If you already know how to meditate, you can do so in your usual way for a few minutes.

2. **Imagine in front of you and above your head an enlightened being or saint for whom you feel particular love or reverence — perhaps Jesus or Buddha or Moses or Mother Teresa.**

   If you don't gravitate toward saints and sages, just imagine a being of infinite wisdom and compassion. And if you don't find it easy to visualize, just sense this being alive in your heart.

3. **Intensify the experience by deepening your feelings of inspiration and devotion.**

   This being actually exists right here and now, and it embodies the blessings of all the enlightened saints and sages.

4. **Relax your body, feel the presence of this being in your heart, and call on it to help you realize your own essential nature.**

5. **Allow your mind and heart to merge with the mind and heart of this enlightened being as you ask to be filled with clarity and compassion.**

6. **Continue to merge your mind and heart with those of the enlightened being as you recite a devotional mantra, if you have one.**

   (See the section "Mantra: Invoking the divine in every moment" earlier in this chapter.) If you don't have one, just sit with reverence and devotion.

7. Gradually feel your mind and heart becoming one with the guru's — that is, vast, clear, and luminous like the sky.

8. Imagine that thousands of rays of pure white light stream from the guru and penetrate every cell of your body, healing, purifying, and empowering you completely with the skylike mind of enlightenment.

9. Allow the guru to dissolve into light and become one with you so that you and the guru are inseparable.

10. Rest for several minutes in the vast, luminous, skylike nature of mind.

Know without doubt that your mind and the mind of the guru are one.

REMEMBER

Chanting and bowing

Besides meditation and contemplation, the devotional path usually involves active practices like chanting, singing, and bowing. As you may have noticed if you've ever sung along with a gospel choir or chanted Indian devotional hymns, you can lift your spirits, open your heart, and intensify your devotion by raising your voice in praise of the Divine.

If you're devotionally inclined (or devotionally impaired!), try mixing your meditation with a little chanting or singing every now and then. Choose songs that have resonance or meaning for you. (For example, I know plenty of Hindus and Buddhists who love to sing "Amazing Grace.")

Traditional wisdom suggests that chanting sacred words and phrases also has the power to open, stimulate, and harmonize your energy centers. (For more on energy centers, see Chapter 12.) In this way, chanting helps "tune up" your body and prepare it for meditation and other spiritual practices.

As for bowing: What better way to practice surrendering your self-centered preoccupations and habitual patterns than by falling down on your knees on a regular basis? One famous Zen master wore a perpetual callus on his forehead from bowing repeatedly to soften his stubbornness. My first Zen teacher used to say, "Buddhism is a religion of bowing."

Of course, bowing figures prominently in the Judeo-Christian tradition and Islam as well; like meditation, it's a universally recognized practice for overcoming separation and approaching the spiritual dimension of being.

But bowing doesn't mean giving up your autonomy to some outside power or force. When you bow — to God, Jesus, Buddha, or the picture of a teacher or saint — you're ultimately bowing to your own essential nature.

In fact, I like to think of bowing as an expression of the essential oneness of inside and outside, the one bowed to and the one bowing. Or, as they say in India, "The divine in me bows to the divine in you."

The Path of Insight: Discovering Who You Are

If you find yourself seeking answers to core spiritual questions like "Who am I?" or "What is reality?" but don't have a particular interest in God or devotion, you may be drawn to the path of insight. Every religious tradition has its versions or counterparts — Christianity has the *via negativa* (negative way) of the desert fathers, Judaism has the mystical practices of Kabbalah, Hinduism has its nondual teachings (like Advaita Vedanta), and Buddhism focuses almost exclusively on the cultivation of insight. (Even Buddhist devotional practices like guru yoga ultimately aim for greater insight or wisdom.)

Unlike devotion, which concentrates the mind on a representation of the Divine, the path of insight uses direct investigation and awareness of present experience to see beyond surface appearances to the deeper reality that underlies them. When you keep questioning and looking deeply into what is apparently real, you inevitably happen upon the ultimately real — the formless, indestructible essence of all appearances. (It's kind of like peeling the layers of an onion).

Now, the point of this approach is not to deny the relative reality of ordinary people and things (including you and me). Rather, the path of insight generally teaches that reality has two levels: the *relative* and the *absolute*. (See also the sidebar "Where the vertical meets the horizontal" earlier in this chapter.)

On the relative level, sure, it's important to make a living, pay the bills, spend time with family or friends — if you pretend that the *relative* is not real, you're going to have some problems. (Traffic court and bankruptcy proceedings spring immediately to mind!) As the Sufis say, "Trust in God, but make sure to tie your camel to the post."

At the same time, though, there's an absolute level — a divine presence or sacred dimension that underlies this world and gives it meaning. When you encounter this level, you see the deeper reality of things, just as the mystic sees God everywhere she looks. Whether directly or more gradually, the path of insight in its various incarnations leads you to an experience or knowing of this absolute level of reality. (In the East, they call this knowing *enlightenment* or *liberation*. In the West, they call it *gnosis* — the Latin word from which "knowing" derives.)

Most of the core practices highlighted in this book show you how to investigate your present experience so that you can eventually develop insight. To give you a glimpse of the absolute level, here are three exercises designed to cut through your usual way of perceiving things to reveal a deeper reality. Generally, they work best after you've been practicing some basic meditation technique like following your breath or reciting a mantra.

Expanding your boundaries

Picking up where the energy body meditation leaves off (see the sidebar "Playing with your energy body" earlier in this chapter, this technique shows you that you don't end with your skin — or with the farthest edges of the Milky Way, for that matter.

1. **Begin by sitting quietly, closing your eyes, and taking a few slow, deep breaths, relaxing a little on each exhalation.**

2. **Sense the solidity and density of your body as you usually perceive it.**

3. **As you inhale, imagine that your head is filling with a soft, clear mist; and as you exhale, imagine that all solidity and density drain from your head, leaving it pleasantly empty, spacious, and open to sensation and life-energy.**

   Don't worry, you won't disappear!

4. **Breathe the mist into your neck and throat and breathe out any tension or density, leaving the area spacious and open.**

5. **Continue to apply this meditation to your chest, lungs, and heart; your arms and hands; your abdomen and internal organs; your pelvis, buttocks, and genitals; and your thighs, lower legs, and feet.**

6. **Feel your whole body completely empty, spacious, and open to the current of life energy.**

   Rest in this feeling for a few moments without thought or analysis. Enjoy the buzz!

7. **If certain areas still feel dense or solid, breathe into them until they empty and open.**

   You may notice that the boundaries of your body are now diffuse — you're not sure where you leave off and the outside world begins.

8. **Expand the boundaries of your body and your awareness until you include the whole room and everything it contains.**

9. **Expand to include the whole building, then the whole block, the whole town or city, the state.**

   Take a few minutes with each expansion.

10. **Expand even further to encompass the Earth, then the solar system, the Milky Way, the universe, and beyond the farthest boundaries of the known universe.**

    Again, spend a few minutes at each level. You're vast beyond measure — you contain everything. Allow any thoughts, feelings, or sensations to arise within this vast expanse.

11. **After spending several minutes in the vastness, you can begin to pay attention to how you feel.**

    If you find it difficult to locate any feelings, that's fine — just enjoy the expansion for a few more minutes! Then check in with your body: Are you feeling more calm and relaxed than when you began? Has your breathing changed in any way?

12. **Gradually come back to your body before getting up and going about your day.**

    Notice whether your self-image or your experience of people and things has changed in any way.

You can practice the first part of this exercise (emptying and opening) by itself, if you like; it has the power to calm your mind and relax and harmonize your body. With regular practice, you'll be able to create a spacious, open, radiant feeling in your body with one sweep of your awareness.

Looking into the nature of mind

In Zen, they tell the story of the first Chinese patriarch Bodhidharma, who supposedly sat for nine years in meditation facing a wall without moving. The Zen folks credit this legendary character with all kinds of superhuman feats. For example, he reportedly cut off his eyelids so he could meditate without sleeping, and the first tea plants sprang up where his eyelids landed. (After all, tea's a kinder, gentler way to stay awake.)

Anyway, an earnest monk named Hui-ko came to Bodhidharma and humbly asked the patriarch to help pacify his troubled mind. After refusing to talk to Hui-ko for a long time, Bodhidharma finally told him to find his mind and bring it to Bodhidharma to pacify. For months, the young monk searched for his mind in meditation, but finally he returned to Bodhidharma and reported that he couldn't find it anywhere. "Then I've pacified your mind for you," Bodhidharma replied — and Hui-ko was immediately enlightened. (You know how these Zen stories go!)

As this anecdote suggests, the Buddhists have devised some powerful techniques for exploring the mind and realizing its essential nature (which happens to be the greater reality I talked about earlier in this chapter). And you don't have to study with a Zen master to get a taste of this essential nature for yourself. Here's an exercise I've adapted from the Tibetan tradition:

1. **Begin by sitting quietly, closing your eyes, and taking a few slow, deep breaths, relaxing a little with each exhalation.**

2. **Meditate in your usual way for a few minutes to relax and focus your mind, then allow it to rest in its "natural state," as the Tibetans put it, without doing anything special.**

If you can follow this exercise with your eyes open and gazing straight ahead at the space in front of you, great — that's how the Tibetans do it. But if you get distracted, you can close your eyes.

3. **Ask yourself a series of questions, and respond by using your mind to look directly at mind.**

Don't think about your mind or analyze your mind or become preoccupied with the contents of your mind, such as thoughts or feelings. Instead, just look at your mind the way you would look at a bird or a tree. You see it and then you rest your mind there. Take a few minutes to respond to each question.

4. **Begin by noticing a particular thought as it arises and endures in your mind.**

   - For example, you can take a memory or a plan or a fantasy.

   - Does this thought have a particular shape or form? How big is it?

   - Does it have a particular color or colors?

   - Does it have a beginning, a middle, and an end?

   - Where is the thought located? Is it inside or outside your body?

   - From where did this thought arise? Where does it go when you're no longer thinking it? How does it last when you continue to think it?

   - Does the thought have substance, or is it just empty and open and filled with space? Does it leave a trace in your mind, like footprints on the beach, or does it leave no trace, like writing on water?

5. **Turn your attention to your mind itself and ask the following questions.**

   - Remember, I'm talking about the mind here, not the brain. If you believe your mind resides in your brain, well then, find it and bring it to me!

   - Does your mind itself have a shape or form? How big is it? Does it have a color or colors?

   - Is your mind identical with your thoughts, or does it abide as the ground or space in which your thoughts arise and pass away?

   - Where is your mind located? Is it inside or outside your body? Does it have a beginning or an end?

   - Does your mind have substance like the earth, or is it empty and spacious like the sky? Is it blank and dark, or is it bright and clear?

6. **Rest for a few minutes in the nature of your mind before getting up and going about your day.**

Asking "Who am I?"

For as long as they've had the capacity to reflect on their experience, human beings have asked, "Who am I?" Zen masters, Sufi sheikhs, Indian sages, Jewish rabbis, and teachers of virtually every other spiritual tradition have used this question to help their disciples see beyond their accustomed identities to a deeper realization of their essential nature.

When you first ask this question, you may come up with the usual answers: "I'm a woman," "I'm a father," "I'm an attorney," "I'm a runner." As you probe further, you may get more spiritual answers, such as "I'm love incarnate" or "I'm a child of God." But if you just set these aside and continue to inquire, you'll eventually have a direct intuition of a more fundamental identity that has nothing to do with who you think you are.

Practice the following exercise with a partner, if possible. (One person begins by questioning, the other by asking.) If you don't have a partner handy, you can do it alone facing a mirror:

1. **Sit comfortably facing your partner, gazing at one another in a relaxed and natural way.**

2. **Allow the questioner to begin by asking, "Who are you?" Then the other person responds by saying whatever comes to mind.**

3. **After a pause, the questioner asks again, "Who are you?" and the other person again responds.**

   Of course, if you're doing it alone, you get to play both roles.

4. **Continue in this way for 15 minutes, then switch places for an equal amount of time.**

   If you're the questioner, don't critique or judge the answers in any way. Just listen, pause, and ask again.

   If you're the respondent, gently look for an answer, then respond. If you can't find one and have nothing to say for a moment or two, just sit with the silence and the not knowing. You may become flustered or confused, start to laugh or cry, or have moments of deep stillness.

   Accept whatever arises, relax into the process, and keep going. Even a brief glimpse of who you really are can completely transform your life.

5. **When you're done, sit for a few minutes with your experience before getting up and going about your day.**

How to Find a Teacher — and Why You May Want to Bother

If you'd like to play tennis but don't know how, what do you do? To begin with, you can watch other people play, maybe buy a book or two, and then head out to the court yourself and start practicing. But once you've mastered the basics, you may want to take a class or get some personal instruction to help you refine your stroke or eliminate the mistakes you've picked up along the way. Sure, self-taught prodigies do occasionally make it to the pros — but most good tennis players who want to improve their game eventually find a teacher.

The same holds true for meditation. You can practice the exercises provided in this book for weeks, months, or even years and reap the benefits without additional instruction. But at a certain point, you may encounter difficulties you don't know how to handle by yourself (see Chapters 11 and 12). Or you may start having spiritual experiences that give you glimpses of a greater reality and whet your appetite for further exploration. To continue to move forward and refine your meditation practice, you need to find yourself a teacher.

Choosing the right kind of teacher

Before you can find a teacher, however, you need to know what kind of teacher you want. Most meditation teachers have a particular spiritual affiliation — they're yogis or Zen Buddhists or Christian contemplatives, for example — and the instruction they offer comes packaged with a particular orientation toward the spiritual journey as well as particular teachings and terminology. No problem if that's what you're looking for — but if you want your instruction straight, without any spirituality, you may have a more difficult time finding a teacher.

Some hatha yoga teachers offer basic meditation instructions with a minimum of Sanskrit words, and they may even know the territory well enough to help you if you get stuck. More and more adult ed programs, community colleges, and local churches are offering generic meditation or stress-reduction classes, but you may want to look over the teacher's credentials first — he or she may be no further along in practice than you are.

If you practice the mindfulness meditations provided in this book (see Chapter 6), you might check out the Vipassana tradition of Buddhism, also known as *insight meditation.* Jon Kabat-Zinn, author of the bestseller *Wherever You Go There You Are,* long-time teacher of Vipassana, and founder of the mindfulness-based Stress Reduction Clinic at the University of Massachusetts Medical Center, has developed a program that offers rigorous training to prospective instructors of basic mindfulness practices. Or you could just take a class in Vipassana, use what you find meaningful and helpful, and leave the rest. Many teachers go light on the Buddhism, especially in introductory courses.

If you're drawn to a particular spiritual tradition or path, you should have less trouble finding a teacher. But you still may want to consider beforehand what kind of teacher you need. Here are four major categories of teachers, based on the content of their teachings and their relationships with their students. (The terms I use here won't necessarily show up on a teacher's resume or brochure; they're just my way of making sense of the different roles teachers play. Some teachers may be a combination of several or all four.)

- ✔ **Instructor:** Teaches you techniques, offers good advice on how to implement them, and helps you troubleshoot or fine-tune. May be a friend or peer.

- ✔ **Mentor:** Gives you personal encouragement and support in your practice, offers guidance for getting unstuck, and provides a role model of someone who's been there before you. Usually teaches techniques as well.

- ✔ **Pandit:** Transmits knowledge by articulating and explaining spiritual teachings and texts. May be a scholar as well as a meditator.

- ✔ **Master:** Embodies the essence of the spiritual teachings. Helps you break through your stuck places and facilitates the process of expanding or dissolving the self. May (or may not) have an intense or challenging relationship with students.

Why you may need a teacher

As I mentioned earlier, a meditation instructor can help you refine your practice and deal with basic questions that arise along the way. But if you want to deepen your practice and use it as a means to spiritual ends (as described earlier in this chapter), you'll definitely want to find a spiritual mentor or master.

First of all, you may encounter difficulties and challenges like the ones described in Chapters 11 and 12. For example, you may have trouble dealing with intense recurring emotions like anger or fear. Or you may come up against roadblocks like doubt or procrastination and not know how to move forward on your own. Or perhaps you start having powerful currents of energy running up and down your spine and don't know how to make them stop. Suddenly you're in need of a teacher — pronto!

As you continue on your journey, you may encounter genuine spiritual insights and experiences that you don't know how to revisit or sustain. In fact, the process of spiritual unfolding more often resembles the confusing, trackless outback than a "path," as it is euphemistically called. The truth is, you never know what you're going to encounter when you practice intensively. As you experiment with expanding or dissolving your self in your meditation, for example, you may meet with powerful opposition from the forces of your psyche that don't want you to change. After all, we're talking radical transformation here — and most of us resist even the most minor changes in our lives.

Your spiritual teacher may coach and support you through the transformational process and even accelerate it by confronting the ways in which you resist or hold back. Some teachers act more like *spiritual friends,* treating you with the camaraderie and equality you expect from a peer, while also sharing their wealth of understanding. Others act more like *traditional gurus,* transmitting their understanding directly to you while actively pushing against your stuck places. (Of course, many teachers lie somewhere between these two extremes and combine a little of both styles.)

Whatever their approach, however, all good teachers help create and sustain, through their relationship with you, a sacred vessel or space in which the difficult, wondrous, and ultimately liberating process of spiritual transformation can take place inside you.

What to look for in a teacher

Before I suggest what to look for in a teacher, I'd like to encourage you to examine your expectations and preconceptions. When you think of a spiritual teacher, what images or ideas come to mind? Perhaps you envision a cloistered monastic dressed in earth-colored robes who gives you spiritual counsel in hushed tones and then returns to his cell to continue his practice. Or maybe you think of a joyful, expansive being who lives in the world and radiates love and light wherever she goes.

Some people idealize the teacher and expect him to be perfect — and become disillusioned when it turns out he's not. Others go to the other extreme and have difficulty treating anyone with reverence or letting go long enough of their staunchly held opinions to allow the wisdom of others to enter. In the West, we tend to distrust authority and believe, like our pioneer and cowboy predecessors, that we can do it all ourselves. Besides, look at all those preachers, priests, and self-styled gurus, you may say, who get caught with their pants down. While a healthy dose of skepticism can do wonders, too much can make you shy away from teachers (and hence from spiritual practice) entirely.

Consulting the guru inside you

Before you go searching for a spiritual teacher, you may want to check out your own inner source of guidance and wisdom. Ultimately, it's the only thing you can really trust, and a good teacher will help you locate it. Yes, that's right, even *you* have a guru inside you. As Jesus said, "Seek and you shall find; knock and the door will open to you." Well, here's an exercise for seeking and finding:

1. **Begin by sitting quietly, closing your eyes, and taking a few slow, deep breaths, relaxing a little with each exhalation.**

2. **Take a few minutes to imagine yourself in a safe, comfortable, relaxing, peaceful place, using all your senses to make the experience as vivid as possible.**

3. **As you explore this peaceful place, you may begin to sense the presence of a wise and compassionate being.**

   Know that this being represents your higher self or deepest truth. (Feel free to use whatever words you prefer to name this being.) You may sense this presence somewhere in your body, or you may just intuit that it's there. If you don't immediately sense this presence, continue to enjoy your peaceful place as you invite this presence to appear to you.

4. **Imagine yourself settling down in a particular spot and gazing out in front of you, relaxed and open.**

5. **Gradually, this wise and compassionate being materializes in the space in front of you.**

   Notice how it appears to you. It may take the form of a wise old man or woman or a Zen master or Christian contemplative, or it may appear as a rose or a tree or (if

you're not visually inclined) merely a feeling in your belly or heart. Or it may just be an older, wiser version of you.

6. **Take whatever form appears to you and treat it with the respect and reverence you would reserve for a spiritual teacher.**

   Note: If this being seems critical or punitive in any way, it's not the one you're looking for, so ask it to step aside and allow the real one to appear.

7. **Spend a few minutes of silence in the presence of this wise and compassionate being.**

   You might imagine it radiating light and love in all directions as you silently receive what it has to offer.

8. **Take a few minutes or longer to ask any question you have and receive answers.**

   Don't worry if this exchange seems strange or awkward at first; with practice, you'll find that this being develops a voice of its own.

9. **Before you say good-bye, you might ask this being to give you a gift that represents exactly the qualities you're needing right now.**

10. **When you feel complete, thank this being for spending time with you today.**

    Tell it that you would like to meet again in the future and say good-bye for now.

11. **Gradually shift your awareness to your sensate experience and open your eyes.**

12. **Take some time to reflect on your experience and the answers and gifts you received.**

Whatever your expectations and preconceptions, you may need to set them aside when you look for a teacher because he or she may appear in a guise you don't anticipate. At the same time, you may want to compare your prospective teacher against the following checklist of qualities that the best teachers embody — in my humble estimation, at least. (I've based this list on my own observation over more than 25 years of spiritual practice.) Not all teachers will have every one of these characteristics, of course, but the more, the better:

- ✔ They're humble, ordinary, down-to-earth, not arrogant or inflated. In Zen monasteries, the head monk cleans the toilets.

- ✔ They're honest, straightforward, and clear, not evasive or defensive. As people gain spiritual maturity, they become increasingly free of psychological baggage.

- ✔ They encourage independent thinking and open inquiry in their students, rather than blind obedience to a particular dogma or ideology.

- ✔ They're primarily concerned with the spiritual development of their students, not with fame, power, influence, or the size of their organization.

- ✔ They practice what they preach, rather than considering themselves exempt from the moral and ethical guidelines that others must follow.

- ✔ They embody the highest spiritual qualities, such as kindness, patience, equanimity, joy, peace, love, and compassion.

How to find a teacher

Now that I've explained the importance of teachers and described what to look for, let me tell you a secret: The process of finding a teacher can be as mysterious as the spiritual journey itself. For some people, it's a lot like finding a lover or a mate — it involves a complex mixture of luck, availability, and chemistry. For others, it's simply a matter of following the counsel of a friend or showing up at the right place at the right time. I met my first teacher after looking up "Zen" in the local phone book. Other people I know met their teachers in dreams before encountering them in the flesh. In the words of a popular Indian expression, "When the student is ready, the teacher appears."

Ultimately, you need to trust your intuition, your own inner knowing, when choosing a teacher — it's the only reliable equipment you have for navigating in this flawed phenomenal universe of ours. The best advice I ever received from a teacher came from a Tibetan lama, who touched my chest near my heart and said, "The true guru is inside you." (For instructions on how to meet your inner teacher, see the sidebar "Consulting the guru inside you.")

Discovering the sky of mind

Here's a brief meditation that you can do anytime you're outdoors to give you a taste of the vastness of your own essential nature, which the Zen folks call, appropriately enough, "big mind."

1. **Preferably on a clear day, sit or lie down and look up at the sky.**

   Set aside your analytical mind for now and all you think you know about the sky.

2. **Take a few minutes to contemplate the vastness of the sky, which appears to stretch endlessly in every direction.**

3. **Gradually allow your mind to expand to fill the sky — up and down, north and south, east and west.**

let go of all sense of personal boundaries as you fill the sky with your awareness.

4. **Become the sky completely and rest in the experience for a few minutes.**

5. **Gradually return to your ordinary sense of yourself.**

   How do you feel? Has your awareness changed in any way?

   Once you get the knack of this exercise, you can do it for brief moments at any time of the day to remind you who you are – for example, walking tour dog in the morning or gazing out your window on a break at work.

I've found myself drawn to teachers intuitively because of the qualities of being they seem to radiate. On the other hand, I've also stumbled on teachers unexpectedly through a serendipitous sequence of events. Be open but not gullible, skeptical but not cynical. Feel free to ask questions, expect good answers, and take your time. According to the Dalai Lama, Tibetan students may spend years checking out teachers to make sure they embody the teachings they espouse. Just as you wouldn't rush into a marriage, you shouldn't rush into anything as intimate and deep as a relationship with a spiritual teacher.

Chapter 14

Developing a Practice That Works for You

- -

- -

As you may have noticed if you've flipped through some of the other chapters, I've filled this book with meditation techniques drawn from a variety of different spiritual and secular sources. Maybe I'm just greedy, but I wanted to make sure I covered all the bases and offered meditations that would appeal to just about everyone.

Needless to say, you can't practice all these techniques — nor would you want to. So I'm going to show you how to choose the ones that are appropriate for your purposes and cobble together a meditation practice that's well suited for your particular needs. You can also pick up a few tips on how to find other people to meditate with — and how to design your own little monastic retreat for a day.

Fitting the Puzzle Pieces Together

In centuries past, ordinary folks didn't have the opportunity to thumb through a copy of *Meditation For Dummies,* pick and choose their favorite meditation techniques, and then sample them like tourists at a wine tasting. Instead, they considered themselves extremely fortunate if they happened upon a teacher willing to impart some secret method. Then they took it home and practiced it single-mindedly for the rest of their lives.

But times have changed, and you and I live in a veritable meditation superstore, with a different technique down every aisle. So, what's a poor guy or gal to do? Well, you need to know yourself, what you like or don't like, and what you're hoping to get out of your meditation. Next, you need to take a sip here and there, trust your taste buds, and eventually settle on a particular approach. Then you can use this approach as the centerpiece around which you construct a regular practice — just as, say, a wonderful meal can be constructed around an especially fine wine. But so much for epicurean metaphors!

Here are the principal pieces of a complete meditation practice as they're presented in this book. As you can see, I've included both meditations themselves and related practices:

- ✔ Mindfulness meditation (Chapter 6)
- ✔ Mantra meditation (Chapters 3 and 13)
- ✔ Body scan and relaxation (Chapter 6)
- ✔ Walking meditation (Chapter 15)
- ✔ Lovingkindness meditation (Chapter 10)
- ✔ Compassion meditation (Chapter 10)
- ✔ Working with your emotions and habitual patterns (Chapter 11)
- ✔ Devotional meditation (Chapter 13)
- ✔ Insight practices like self-inquiry (Chapter 13)
- ✔ Healing meditation (Chapter 16)
- ✔ Mindfulness in action (Chapter 15)
- ✔ Using a meditation altar (Chapter 8)
- ✔ Chanting and/or bowing (Chapter 13)
- ✔ Dedicating your practice (Chapter 13)

How do you know which practices to include in your own custom-tailored routine? To begin with, you're better off starting out simple: Choose one technique and stick with it for a few months — or even years. Then, when you feel confident in your ability to concentrate reasonably well, you may want to consider how traditional meditators combine different practices.

In the Buddhist tradition, for example, they generally mix meditations designed to cultivate wisdom with those that have the power to elicit compassion or love. Then they season the basic ingredients as needed with others like self-inquiry or healing meditations. Next, they throw in some walking meditation (to act as a bridge between sitting meditation and everyday life). Finally, they frame the whole routine by first reminding themselves why they're meditating and then, when they're done, by dedicating the virtue or power of the meditation to the benefit of others. (Of course, this mixture of ingredients is no casual hodge-podge but has evolved over several thousand years.)

Maybe you're not as methodical as all that and would rather just use your intuition and do what feels right. If so, then go for it! Ultimately, the process of choosing a set of meditation techniques may be as personal and mysterious as the process of choosing a mate. But before you make your choices, here are a few pointers for checking your motivation, balancing your practice, and trusting your intuition.

Different pieces for different folks

Just as you wouldn't take a hacksaw to a stick of butter or use your toothbrush to scrub your floor, you don't need to meditate three hours a day if you're just looking for a little stress-reduction, and you wouldn't want to limit yourself to ten minutes if you're determined to get enlightened by the end of next week. In Chapter 4, I describe five principal motivations for meditation:

- ✔ Improving your life
- ✔ Understanding and accepting yourself
- ✔ Realizing your true nature
- ✔ Awakening others
- ✔ Expressing your innate perfection

Knowing which of these best describes you can help you determine both how and how much you meditate. (Needless to say, most people fall into the first three categories; the other two are generally reserved for seasoned meditators.) Mindfulness meditation (explained in detail in Chapter 6) makes a great foundation practice, no matter what your motivation, and can be extended to every moment of your life (see Chapter 15). But the rest is up to you.

For example, if you want to help heal a chronic ailment, you can add one or more of the healing meditations from Chapter 16. If you want to get to know yourself better or deal with difficult emotions or behaviors, you might want to pursue some of the techniques offered in Chapter 11. And if you're headed straight for the top of the meditation mountain (as described in Chapter 1), you can experiment with meditations from Chapter 13 for getting closer to God or gaining direct insight into your essential being.

Just remember that this book is merely an introduction; if you want to go deeper in any direction, you're going to need other books and ultimately, perhaps, a living teacher. (For a listing of books you might want to read after this one, see the appendix. For more on choosing a teacher, check out Chapter 13.)

Play to your strengths or fill in the gaps?

In addition to motivation, you may want to know a little more about your general tendencies and personality traits and how they influence your meditation choices. For example, some people tend to be more cerebral and get attracted to meditation because they seek greater clarity or understanding. Others identify more with their feelings and may be drawn to meditation out of a deep desire to feel God's love or express their devotion or compassion or work closely with a particular teacher. Still others focus more on their bodies and turn to meditation for physical healing or energy or power. These three types — people who are oriented toward their heads, their hearts, and their bodies — are described in a number of the great meditative traditions and in the Western scientific tradition as well. Take a few moments to check out your predominant orientation.

The *head types* immediately gravitate to the insight practices, the *heart types* to the devotion and compassion practices, and the *body types* to the relaxation exercises and healing meditations. But the truth is, we all have a heart, a mind, and a body, and we need to develop and cultivate all three in our meditation practice if we're going to evolve into complete, well-rounded human beings.

So notice your tendencies, and indulge them as much as you like. After all, you need to do what feels right — and often what feels right are the practices that fit your type. But you may also want to consider filling in the gaps by including meditations or other practices that stretch you in directions you don't ordinarily go. For example, do insight practices, but preface them with some devotional chanting or bowing (or, even better, do them with an attitude of kindness and compassion). Focus on compassion practices or working with your emotions, but also relax your body or be mindful of your sensate experience. Ultimately, any of the basic meditations will help develop the different parts of you — heart, mind, and body — but be aware of your tendency to favor one over the others, or even to sidestep one entirely.

Also, life has an uncanny tendency to reveal your Achilles heel and show you precisely what qualities you need to develop, so pay attention. If you keep drawing "overly emotional" people into your life or your partner's "intellectualizing" drives you crazy, perhaps you're being shown the very qualities you most need to add to your own repertoire.

Experiment, trust your intuition, and then settle down

You can't really tell how a particular meditation will affect you until you practice it regularly for a period of time. Just reading about it in a book like this one won't tell you much, and practicing it once or twice may give you a taste and show you whether it's worth pursuing, but you won't get the impact the meditation was designed to evoke.

So do begin by shopping around and sampling the meditations that catch your eye. Notice how you feel when you try them out. Then trust your intuitive sense of what's right and appropriate for you, and commit yourself to actually do the practice regularly for a period of time — I'm talking months or even years here. (For more on discipline, effort, and commitment, see Chapter 9.) That's right, I said "commit" — the dreaded C word. Simply put, you have to do the same meditation again and again if you want to reap the benefits. I know this advice runs counter to the quick-fix orientation of our culture, but you won't find any shortcuts or get-enlightened-quick schemes in the world of meditation. As the Nike ad puts it, "Just do it" — preferably with kindness, gentleness, patience, and compassion, but ultimately you have to do it, again and again!

The downside of being a dilettante

In every area of interest, from baseball to investing, you can amass a wealth of information to impress your family and friends without getting your hands dirty actually doing what you know so much about. (For example, you can memorize the stats for every player in the Major Leagues without ever learning how to throw a baseball.) The same holds true for meditation. As they say in Zen, "Painted cakes won't satisfy your hunger" — and reading all the best meditation books in the world won't reduce your stress or calm your busy mind one iota. (You'll just end up becoming what one Buddhist teacher called a "spiritual materialist.") You need to roll up your sleeves and apply what you've read.

In the same way, you won't make any progress by dabbling in different techniques. ("Mmm, it's Tuesday; it must be time for mindfulness.")

You need to choose one (or two) and stick with it. (Remember the old adage, "Jack of all trades and master of none"? Well, your goal is to master the art of meditation, not amass a few new tricks to add to your collection.)

When you encounter restlessness or boredom (or any of the other "obstacles" described in Chapter 12), don't immediately conclude you've made a mistake. Instead, use your resistance and other difficult emotions and mind-states as grist for the mill of your meditation. (For instructions on how to do that, see Chapters 11 and 12.)

Create a regular practice

Now that you have a few guidelines for putting the various pieces together, you can fashion a practice that you can do day after day. Remember to keep it simple — after all, the point of meditation is to relax your body and ease your busy mind, not make your life more complicated. Here are the basic stages for creating a regular practice that works for you:

- ✔ **Choose a core technique:** If you do nothing else, you've still created a viable meditation practice that will serve you quite well. I recommend mindfulness meditation because it teaches skills you can translate to every activity and moment of your life, but some people prefer mantra meditation or concentration on a particular object.

- ✔ **Round out your practice:** As I suggest in the previous section, you may want to add another practice or two that cultivates different qualities of mind, body, or heart. But if you have only a snippet of time each day, stick with your core technique, rather than get too complex.

- ✔ **Decide how much and how often:** Depending on your motivation and your reasons for meditating, you're going to sit longer or shorter periods more or less frequently. Your interest in meditation may also wax and wane somewhat with the cycles of your life. For example, you may have times when you focus more on outward achievement or family life, and times when you pay more attention to inner unfolding. For guidelines on scheduling your meditation, see Chapter 8.

- ✔ **Keep it regular:** I can't say this too often. Whatever else you do (and whatever the cycles of your life), stand by your core technique as you would your loved one or your kids — through thick and thin, ups and downs, feast and famine, and any other clichés you can muster.

- ✔ **Add practices as needed, but stick with them:** For example, if you get sick, by all means add a healing meditation. If you want to open your heart some more, then add a lovingkindness meditation. But don't sacrifice your core technique, and stick with your new one as well.

- ✔ **Know when to go deeper:** If you find yourself hungering for more time on your meditation cushion, then by all means pencil it in. The more you do, the deeper you'll go — and you'll know intuitively when you're ready. Better to wait until you want to, rather than pushing yourself because you think you "should." (For suggestions on doing a meditation retreat, see the section "Whenever Two or More of You: Meditating with Others.")

- ✔ **Seek help when you need it:** You can venture only so far into unknown terrain alone. If you start encountering problems in your meditation or experiences that confuse or scare you (or you just want to make sure you're doing it right), then you may want to look for a teacher. (For an overview of meditation problems and pitfalls, check out Chapter 12. For advice on finding a teacher, turn to Chapter 13.)

Respecting the cycles of practice

I generally don't like to talk about progress in meditation. I'd rather remind you that you've always been where you're headed, which is right here and now. If anything, meditation involves stripping away the veils that keep you from seeing what's been true all along.

It's especially important to realize that meditation doesn't entail linear development or improvement. Every day's a new day, and every meditation differs from the last. One day your mind may seem extraordinarily clear and still, like the proverbial forest pool, leading you to conclude that you finally have this meditation stuff down cold. The next day, without warning, your mind may seem as turbulent as the ocean during a hurricane. So much for linear improvement!

Instead of a line, I like to use the image of a spiral that keeps circling around and around but gradually rises. You may go through times when challenging life circumstances like career changes, losses, or separations stir up difficult emotions and patterns that pervade your meditation. Then you may go through more tranquil periods when your concentration deepens and your mind settles down. If you keep meditating patiently, without becoming overly discouraged or elated, you'll find that you gradually expand to include more and more of who you are — the ups and downs, the highs and lows, the rough spots and the smooth. In the process, you become more joyful and peaceful — but not in the measurable, linear way you might have expected.

Whenever Two or More of You: Meditating with Others

All the great meditative traditions agree: Meditating with others confers extraordinary benefits that enhance your individual practice and accelerate your personal and spiritual unfolding. Buddhists regard the community of practitioners as one of the three jewels or treasures of practice, along with the awakened teacher and the truth itself. Jews believe that God really listens when ten of His faithful convene together in prayer. And Jesus himself put it quite elegantly: "Whenever two or more of you are gathered in my name, there is love."

Besides, researchers like Dean Ornish have found that a sense of belonging or connectedness with others not only improves the quality of life but also increases longevity. In one study, people who answered yes to the questions "Do you draw strength from your religious faith?" and "Are you a member of any organization that meets regularly?" were seven times more likely to survive open-heart surgery than those who answered no. In another study, women being given the same conventional treatments for metastatic breast cancer were divided into two groups — one that met together once a week for mutual support and one that didn't. After five years, the women who met had lived twice as long as the ones who didn't.

On a more practical level, you may simply find encouragement from other meditators to persist at what may sometimes seem like a tedious pursuit. And you can discuss your practice and get useful suggestions based on others' experiences — they may already have solved the problems or traversed the terrain that you're just encountering.

You may wonder how you can find others to meditate with. Well, you have several options: You can seek out a group or class that's already meeting, form a group yourself, or attend a weekend workshop or group retreat.

Joining or forming a meditation group

Now that meditation has become a more mainstream pursuit, it's becoming easier to find meditation classes at readily accessible venues like local churches or synagogues, community centers, adult ed programs, and community colleges. The problem is, you may not be drawn to the technique they're teaching, or you may already know how to meditate and simply want the support of other warm bodies.

You could ask friends who meditate or check local bulletin boards or classified ragsheets for ads announcing the formation of leaderless groups. Or you could take the initiative and form such a group yourself! Participants don't have to practice the same technique or hold the same spiritual or religious beliefs — they just have to be willing to sit quietly in the same room together doing whatever they do. You could begin with a reading from the world's spiritual literature, if everyone seems amenable, and you might end with discussion or a Quaker-style silence in which people offer whatever the spirit moves them to share. Or you can just convene, sit quietly, smile at one another, and leave. The form is up to you.

Attending your first workshop or retreat

If you're feeling adventurous or simply want more in-depth instruction and guidance, you can sign up for an extended period of group meditation. Many of the organizations listed in the appendix of this book have regional centers that offer individual instruction and workshops, groups, or retreats. Or you can head for the main monastery, community, or ashram itself and get a taste of what it's like to live with a group of people whose primary focus is the practice of meditation.

Be sure you know in advance what you'll be doing on your retreat, and be wary of the tendency among groups to proselytize for their own particular faith or ideology — unless, of course, you happen to be interested.

Also, no matter how relaxed the atmosphere or gentle the approach of the retreat, you may feel a little scared at first because extended periods of silent meditation don't provide any of the usual diversions, such as phone calls or TV, that keep you from facing yourself. So don't be surprised if you sign up and then conjure all kinds of great reasons for canceling at the last minute, from sick kids to business emergencies. My suggestion: Stick with your original intention and go anyway. You'll be glad you did.

Here are a few other reasons you might come up with for putting off your first workshop or retreat, with some answers:

- ✔ **"I'm not good enough yet."** Understandably, you may shudder at the prospect of sitting quietly for three or four or even more hours each day when you've had difficulty mustering the patience for even 15 minutes. But don't let your reservations stop you — you'll be surprised and pleased by how deep your concentration can go and how long you can sustain it when you have the support of a teacher and a group of like-minded people.

- ✔ **"I have back or knee problems."** If you have serious physical limitations, you may need to take special precautions and even follow a modified schedule, but don't be daunted or deterred. Just be sure to let the retreat leaders know beforehand so they can help you get comfortable. (If you merely suffer from the usual aches and pains that accompany sitting, you may be pleased to discover that they actually improve or become less distracting during the course of your retreat.)

- ✔ **"I don't have the time."** What do you mean, exactly? Are you suggesting that every spare moment between now and next Christmas is booked up in advance? Or do you really mean that you'd rather do other things with your time? Well, no problem. But if you do decide you'd like to attend a retreat, I can guarantee that the time will materialize like magic. And who knows? You may find that the insight and peace of mind you bring back buys you more time than you spent.

Monk for a day: Creating your own solitary retreat

If you've been meditating regularly for a few weeks or months (or years) and feel inspired to practice for an extended period of time but would rather do it on your own (or don't have easy access to a group), you can design and follow your own retreat schedule. You'll need the time (even a half day will do at first), the place (you're better off leaving the distractions of home, even if you live alone), and an extra dose of motivation and self-discipline.

Be sure to block out periods for both sitting and walking meditation (so you can spell your tired knees and back), leave some open, unstructured gaps in the program for just being or walking in nature or listening to the birds, and use the schedule as a guideline, rather than as a rigid form that squeezes the life out of your practice. If you need to adapt it as inspiration or physical limitations dictate, please do. And be sure to maintain the spirit of meditation and the practice of mindfulness throughout your day, whether you're meditating or napping or going to the bathroom.

Here's a suggested schedule for a one-day retreat that a beginner should be able to manage without strain:

8:00-8:45	Breakfast (eating meditation)
8:45-9:00	Contemplation (of your deeper intention or motivation for doing this retreat)
9:00-9:30	Sitting meditation
9:30-9:45	Walking meditation
9:45-10:15	Sitting meditation
10:15-10:30	Walking meditation
10:30-11:00	Sitting meditation
11:00-12:30	Inspirational reading
12:30-1:30	Lunch (eating meditation)
1:30-3:30	Siesta, walk, or more inspirational reading
3:30-4:00	Sitting meditation
4:00-4:15	Walking meditation
4:15-4:45	Sitting meditation
4:45-5:00	Walking meditation
5:00-5:30	Sitting meditation
5:30-5:45	Dedication (of the value of this retreat to the benefit of all)
5:45-7:00	Dinner (eating meditation)

Optional

7:00-7:30	Sitting meditation
7:30-7:45	Walking meditation
7:45-8:15	Sitting meditation
8:15-8:30	Walking meditation
8:30-9:00	Sitting meditation
9:00-9:15	Dedication

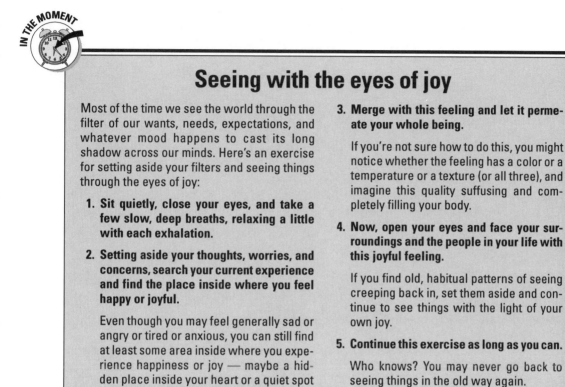

Seeing with the eyes of joy

Most of the time we see the world through the filter of our wants, needs, expectations, and whatever mood happens to cast its long shadow across our minds. Here's an exercise for setting aside your filters and seeing things through the eyes of joy:

1. **Sit quietly, close your eyes, and take a few slow, deep breaths, relaxing a little with each exhalation.**

2. **Setting aside your thoughts, worries, and concerns, search your current experience and find the place inside where you feel happy or joyful.**

   Even though you may feel generally sad or angry or tired or anxious, you can still find at least some area inside where you experience happiness or joy — maybe a hidden place inside your heart or a quiet spot at the back of your head.

3. **Merge with this feeling and let it permeate your whole being.**

   If you're not sure how to do this, you might notice whether the feeling has a color or a temperature or a texture (or all three), and imagine this quality suffusing and completely filling your body.

4. **Now, open your eyes and face your surroundings and the people in your life with this joyful feeling.**

   If you find old, habitual patterns of seeing creeping back in, set them aside and continue to see things with the light of your own joy.

5. **Continue this exercise as long as you can.**

   Who knows? You may never go back to seeing things in the old way again.

Part IV
Meditation in Action

The 5th Wave   By Rich Tennant

"The kids love it when Chuck meditates."

In this part . . .

You discover how to extend your meditation into every area of your life. After all, what's the point of sitting calmly for half an hour, then stressing yourself out for the rest of the day? When you can stay present and mindful and keep your heart open even when you're arguing with your partner or driving in rush hour traffic or dealing with a screaming child or an angry boss, you've learned how to meditate no matter where you are. You also pick up some great techniques in this section for using the power of meditation to facilitate healing and enhance performance.

Chapter 15

How to Meditate in Everyday Life

*E*lsewhere in this book, I compare meditation to a laboratory in which you experiment with paying attention to your experience and discovering how to cultivate qualities like peace, love, and happiness. Well, the discoveries you make in the controlled environment of a lab have only limited value until you can apply them to real-life situations and problems — and the skills, insights, and peaceful feelings you have on your meditation cushion won't get you far unless you do the same. In fact, that's the whole point of meditation — to help you live a happier, fuller, more stress-free life!

As you become more adept at being mindful during formal meditation, you naturally get better at paying mindful attention to everything you encounter, both on and off the cushion. Still, you may find it helpful to pick up a few tips on how to extend the practice of mindfulness so you can stay open, present, and attentive from moment to moment, even in the midst of challenging circumstances like driving a car in heavy traffic, running errands, doing chores, taking care of the kids, or dealing with stressful situations at work. In addition, you can find out how to use meditation to improve the quality of your family life and your intimate relationships, including the most intimate encounter of all — making love.

Being Peace with Every Step: Extending Meditation in Action

Here's a quote that expresses the spirit of meditation-in-action better than anything I could possibly say. It comes from the book *Peace Is Every Step* by the Vietnamese Buddhist monk Thich Nhat Hanh.

Every morning, when we wake up, we have twenty-four brand-new hours to live. What a precious gift! We have the capacity to live in a way that these twenty-four hours will bring peace, joy, and happiness to ourselves and others. . . . Every breath we take, every step we make, can be filled with peace, joy, and serenity. We need only to be awake, alive in the present moment.

The person who wrote these words is neither a recluse nor a Pollyanna; he's had experience practicing mindfulness in extraordinarily difficult times. During the Vietnam War, he worked tirelessly for reconciliation between the warring factions in his homeland and created and headed the Buddhist Peace Delegation to the Paris Peace Talks. For his efforts, Martin Luther King nominated him for a Nobel Peace Prize. Since then Thich Nhat Hanh has actively taught a blend of mindful living and social responsibility, and wherever he goes he embodies the peace he espouses.

As Nhat Hanh suggests, you need to be awake and alive in the present moment — after all, it's the only moment you have. Even memories of the past and thoughts of the future occur right now, in the present. If you don't wake up and smell the flowers, taste your food, and see the light in your loved ones' eyes, you'll miss the beauty and preciousness of your life as it unfolds. Says Thich Nhat Hanh: "Each thought, each action in the sunlight of awareness becomes sacred."

On a more practical level, you can only reduce stress by getting out of your head (where all the stressful thoughts and emotions vie for your attention) and showing up for what's happening right now. Once you learn how to be present in your meditation, you need to *keep* being present again and again, moment after moment — otherwise, you'll just fall back into your old stressful habits. Besides, mindful awareness of what you're doing and experiencing can confer tremendous benefits, including the following:

- Greater focus, efficiency, and precision in what you do
- An experience of effortlessness, flow, and harmony
- Reduced stress because the mind is not distracted by its habitual worries and concerns
- Increased enjoyment of the richness and fullness of life
- Greater availability or presence and the capacity to open your heart and be touched or affected by others
- Deeper connections with loved ones and friends
- An openness to the spiritual dimension of life

Now, you don't have to be a Buddhist monk to practice mindfulness — you can wake up and be mindful in the midst of the most mundane activities. But you can certainly take advantage of some of the techniques and tricks that the great meditation teachers have devised, which I describe in the following sections.

Coming back to your breath

Sometimes you feel like you're just moving too quickly and dealing with too many matters at once to know how (or where) to be mindful. "Where do I place my attention," you may wonder, "when things are happening so fast?" Just as you can begin the formal practice of mindfulness meditation by counting or following your breaths (see Chapter 6), you can always return to the direct and simple experience of breathing, even in the most complicated circumstances. No matter how many other things you may be doing, you're always breathing — and the physical experience of inhaling and exhaling provides a reliable anchor for your attention in stressful times. Then, once you've begun to pay attention to your breath, you can gradually expand to include mindful awareness of your other activities.

Besides, gently paying mindful attention to your breath gradually calms your mind by shifting awareness away from your thoughts and slowing your mind down to the pace and rhythms of your body. With your mind and body in synch, you start to feel a natural ease and an inner harmony and tranquillity that external circumstances can't easily disturb.

You can begin by stopping whatever you're doing for a moment or two and tuning in to the coming and going of your breath. Your attention may be drawn to the rise and fall of your abdomen as you breathe, or to the feeling of your breath as it enters and leaves your nostrils. Be mindful of these sensations for four or five breathing cycles, enjoying the simplicity and directness of the experience. When you breathe with awareness, you're consciously awake and alive in the present moment. Then resume your normal activities while continuing to be mindful of your breath. (If you find this multidimensional awareness too confusing or complicated, you can just remember to come back to your breath every now and then.)

Listening to the bell of mindfulness

Monasteries traditionally use bells and gongs to remind the monks and nuns to stop whatever they're doing, drop their thoughts and daydreams, and gently return their attention to the present moment. Since you and I don't live with bells, Thich Nhat Hanh suggests that we use the recurring sounds of our environment to gently remind us to wake up and be mindful.

For example, you can set the beeper on your alarm watch to sound every hour, and when it does you can stop, enjoy your breathing for a minute or two, and then resume your normal activities (with greater awareness, of course). Or you can hear the mindfulness bell in the ring of your telephone or the sound of your computer booting up or the buzzer that goes off in your car before you fasten your seatbelt. Just remember to stop, enjoy your breathing, and keep going with greater awareness and aliveness.

Enjoying your meal with mindful eating

Did you ever finish a meal and wonder what happened to the food? You can remember enjoying it at first, and then suddenly you notice that your plate is empty, and you can't recall a single bite in between. Perhaps you spent the time talking with a friend or reading a newspaper or worrying about your bank account or your relationship.

Here's a meditation to help you be mindful of what you're putting into your mouth. Not only will you enjoy your food as never before, but mindful eating will facilitate your digestion by reducing any tension or stress you bring to the table. (You probably won't want to eat as meditatively as this all the time, but you can still apply a little mindfulness to every meal, no matter how informal.)

1. **Before you begin eating, take a few moments to appreciate your food.**

   You may want to reflect Zen-style on the earth and the sunshine that gave life to this food and the people and effort that brought it to your table. Or you can express your thanks to God or spirit — or simply sit silently and feel grateful for what you have. If you're eating with others, you might want to hold hands, smile at one another, or connect in some other way.

2. **Bring your awareness to your hand as you lift the first bite of food to your lips.**

   You can experiment with the custom in certain monastic traditions of eating more slowly than usual. Or just eat at your usual speed, but be as mindful as you can.

3. **Be fully aware as the first morsel of food enters your mouth and floods your taste buds with sensations.**

   Notice the tendency of the mind to judge the flavor: "It's too spicy or salty," or "It's not what I expected." Notice any emotions that might get stirred up: disappointment, relief, irritation, joy. Be aware of any ripples of pleasure or warmth or other physical sensations. Enjoy your food!

4. **If you talk while you eat, notice how the talking affects you.**

   Do certain topics cause you to tense up or give you indigestion? Does the talk take you away from the enjoyment of your meal, or can you have both?

5. **Stay mindful of each mouthful as you gradually eat your meal.**

   This part is probably the hardest because most people have a tendency to space out once they know how their food tastes. But you can continue to enjoy the taste freshly, bite after bite. (If you get distracted, you can stop and breathe for a moment or two before starting to eat again.)

6. **To facilitate your mindfulness, you may want to eat in silence every now and then.**

   It may feel strange or uncomfortable at first, but you may gradually find that a quiet meal can provide a nourishing respite from the pressures of life.

Even nonsounds make great reminders. Whenever you encounter a red light in traffic, for example, instead of indulging your frustration or anxiety, you can remember to tune in, breathe consciously, and let go of your tension and speed. Or you can allow moments of beauty to help you wake up — a beautiful flower, the smile on a child's face, sunlight through your window, a warm cup of tea. Then again, you can always buy a traditional meditation bell and strike it every now and then as a special reminder.

Freeing yourself from the tyranny of time

Many people feel that their appointment books run their lives and leave them no room for connecting with themselves or the people they love. But you don't have to let your time clock control you. You may not be able to free up your schedule, but you can definitely free up your relationship to time.

Here are a few pointers for doing just that (adapted from the book *Full Catastrophe Living* by Jon Kabat-Zinn):

✔ **Remember that time is a useful convention created by our minds to help organize our experiences.** It has no absolute reality, as Einstein discovered. When you're enjoying yourself, time just flies by; when you're bored or in pain, minutes seem to last forever.

✔ **Live in the present moment as much as possible.** Since time is created by thought, you drop into a timeless dimension when you bypass the thinking mind and settle your attention in the here and now. As soon as you start planning for the future or regretting the past, you're immediately bound by the pressures of time once again.

✔ **Take some time to meditate each day.** Meditation teaches you how to be present and provides the most effective entree into the realm of the timeless. As Jon Kabat-Zinn puts it, "Just making the commitment to practice non-doing, to let go of striving, to be non-judgmental . . . nourishes the timeless in you."

✔ **Simplify your life.** When you fill up your life with trivial pursuits and habits that squander time, it's no wonder you don't have enough for the things that really matter to you. Take stock of what you do with your day, and consider letting go of a few activities that don't feed your deeper intention to slow down and connect with yourself.

✔ **Remember that your life belongs to you.** Even though you may have a family to take care of or a job that requires your attention, keep in mind that you have the right to apportion your time as you choose. You're not cheating the other people in your life if you take a half hour for yourself each day to meditate.

Repeating a phrase to help you be mindful

The Jewish tradition has special prayers for just about every occasion, from seeing a bolt of lightning to eating a piece of bread, that are designed to remind the faithful that God is constantly present. Buddhists use short verses to encourage them to come back to the unadorned simplicity of being in each moment. Christians say grace before meals, at bedtime, and on other auspicious occasions. Unlike mantras — words or brief phrases repeated again and again (described in Chapter 13) — these verses or prayers differ from one situation to the next and have a unique message to impart.

For example, Thich Nhat Hanh suggests silently intoning the following verse to enhance your mindfulness and turn your conscious breathing into an opportunity to relax and enjoy your life:

> Breathing in, I calm my body.
> Breathing out, I smile.
> Dwelling in the present moment,
> I know this is a wonderful moment.

Coordinate the first line with the inhalation, the second line with the exhalation, and so forth — and be sure to do what you're saying. That is, calm your body, smile to yourself (see the sidebar "Practicing a half smile" later in this chapter), and appreciate this present moment. Once you get the knack, you can simply say, "Calming, smiling, present moment, wonderful moment." If you don't cotton to Nhat Hanh's terminology, feel free to make up verses of your own for everyday situations like breathing, eating, bathing, working, even talking on the phone or going to the bathroom.

Noticing how situations affect you

Once you begin to expand your formal mindfulness practice from your breathing to the full range of your sensory experience (see Chapters 6 and 11), you can bring this inner awareness to your other activities as well. Instead of losing touch with yourself as you watch TV or drive your car or work at your computer, you can maintain what one of my teachers calls *dual awareness* — that is, simultaneous awareness of what's going on around you and of how the situation or activity affects you.

Gradually you may start to notice that driving too fast makes you tense, or watching certain TV shows leaves you nervous or agitated, or talking for hours on the phone just saps your energy rather than enlivening you. You don't need to make any judgments or formulate any improvements based on what you discover. Just gently take note. If you're highly motivated to reap the benefits of the meditation you practice so diligently, you'll find yourself naturally moving away from situations (like habits, leisure pursuits, people, and work environments) that stress you out and gravitating to situations that support you in feeling calm, relaxed, harmonious, and connected with yourself and others.

When your suffering and stress are based on your own habitual patterns and difficult emotions (see Chapter 11), you can use dual awareness to notice your reactivity and create space inside to experience and make friends with it, instead of acting it out in relation to others.

Taking meditation to work with you

With tight deadlines, performance reviews, and the threat of downsizing, today's highly competitive work environment places extraordinary pressures on employees and managers alike. Even practitioners of traditionally stable occupations like teaching and medicine are experiencing unprecedented work stress with the advent of larger class sizes and HMOs. But whatever your job situation, you can reduce your stress by following these tips for meditating while you work:

✔ Each morning before you leave, you can reinforce your resolve to stay as calm and relaxed as possible. If you can, meditate briefly before you head out the door to set the tone of the day.

✔ By being mindful of your experience, you can discover the situations that really stress you out — and then avoid or change them as much as possible. Work can be demanding enough without taking on more than you can handle.

✔ Notice how your mind adds to stress — for example, by feeding you negative self-statements like "I'm a failure" or "I don't have what it takes" or by imagining that you're about to get canned or that your

boss and coworkers are plotting against you. Gently set these fabrications aside and return to paying mindful attention to whatever you're doing.

✔ Instead of hanging around the coffee machine and adding caffeine to your long list of stressors, use your breaks to meditate quietly in your office or cubicle. You'll get up feeling more relaxed and refreshed.

✔ Have lunch with people you like — or have a quiet lunch alone. You can also take a walk or do some other kind of exercise during your break — a great way to relieve your stress.

✔ Every hour take a few moments to stop what you're doing, take some deep breaths, follow your breathing, and get up and stretch or walk around.

✔ Practice using a half smile to radiate well-being to yourself and your coworkers. When you have contact with others, do it with a warm and friendly attitude. One meditator I know reported that he singlehandedly reversed the negative mood in his office by deliberately smiling and generating good-will.

Applying meditation to familiar activities

Anything you do or experience can provide you with an opportunity to practice mindfulness. But you may want to begin with some of your usual activities — the ones you may be doing now on automatic pilot while you daydream, space out, or obsess. The truth is, even the most routine tasks can prove enjoyable and enlivening when you do them with wholehearted care and attention. Here's a list of common activities with a few suggestions for infusing them with mindfulness:

✔ **Washing the dishes:** If you set aside your judgments, which may insist you should be doing something more meaningful or constructive with your time, and instead simply wash the dishes — or sweep the floor or scrub the tub — you may find that you actually enjoy the activity. Feel the contours of the plates and bowls as you clean them. Notice the smell and the slipperiness of the soap, the sounds of the utensils, the satisfying feeling of removing the old food and leaving the dishes clean and ready for use.

✔ **Working at your computer:** As you become engrossed in the information flashing across your screen, you may find yourself losing touch with your body and your surroundings. Pause every now and then to follow your breathing and notice how you're sitting. If you're starting to tense up and crane your head forward, gently straighten your spine (as described Chapter 7) and relax your body. During recurring gaps in the flow of your work, come back to your body, breathe, and relax.

✔ **Driving your car:** What could possibly be more stressful than navigating an automobile through heavy traffic? Besides the constant stop and go, you need to be aware of potential problems in every direction, any one of which could pose a threat to your safety. Yet, you add to the stress of driving when you hurry to get to your destination faster than you realistically can and then get angry and impatient in the process.

As an antidote to the stress, you can practice mindfulness while you drive. Take a few deep breaths before you start and return to your breathing again and again as you consciously let go of tension and stress. Feel the steering wheel in your hands, the pressure of your feet against the pedals, the weight of your body against the seat. Notice any tendency to criticize other drivers, to space out, to become angry or impatient. Pay attention to how the music or talk shows you listen to affect your mood as you drive. When you wake up and pay attention, you may be surprised to realize that you and the people around you are actually piloting these two-thousand-pound chunks of plastic and steel with precious, vulnerable beings inside. And you may feel more inclined to drive mindfully and safely as a result.

TRADITIONAL WISDOM

Attention, attention, attention!

With its emphasis on hard work and its appreciation of the ordinary, the Zen tradition has many stories that extol the benefits of mindful awareness in everyday activities. Here are two of my favorites.

In the first, a businessman comes to see a famous master and asks him to draw the Japanese characters that most precisely express the spirit of Zen. The master draws just one word: Attention.

"But there must be more to Zen than this," the businessman complains.

"Yes, you're right," the master replies, and he draws the same character beneath the first: Attention, attention.

Now the businessman becomes angry. "You're just putting me on," he fumes, his face turning red.

Silently, the master adds a third character and shows it to his volatile guest. Now the scroll reads: Attention, attention, attention.

In the second story, a wandering monk arrives at a famous monastery and starts climbing the path that leads up the mountain when he notices a lettuce leaf floating down the mountain stream. "Hmm," he muses to himself, "any master who lets his disciples prepare the food so carelessly doesn't merit my time and attention."

Just as he's turning around to leave, he sees the head cook himself, robe fluttering in the breeze, hurrying down the path to retrieve the wayward leaf.

"Ah," the visiting monk thinks as he changes direction once again, "perhaps I should stop here and study for a while after all!"

✔ **Talking on the phone:** As you engage in conversation, stay connected with your breathing and notice how you're affected. Do certain topics bring up anger or fear or sadness? Do others bring up pleasure or joy? Do you become reactive or defensive? Notice also what moves or motivates you to speak. Are you attempting to influence or convince this person in some way? Do you have a hidden agenda of jealousy or resentment — or possibly a desire to be loved or appreciated? Or are you simply open and responsive to what's being said in the moment, without the overlay of past or future?

✔ **Watching TV:** Just as when you work at a computer, you can easily forget you have a body when you tune in to the tube. (For more on meditation and TV, see Chapter 8.) Take a break during commercials to turn down the sound, follow your breathing, and ground your awareness in the present moment. Walk around, look out the window, connect with your family members. (Like many people, you may use food to ground you in your body while you're watching TV, but it won't work unless you're mindful of what you're eating — and besides, mindless eating has its price, as any couch potato can tell you.)

✔ **Working out:** Physical exercise offers you a wonderful opportunity to shift your awareness from your mind to the simple, repetitive movements of your body. Unfortunately, many people just put on the headphones, switch on the Walkman, and space out. The next time you hit the exercise equipment or attend an aerobics class, make a point of following your breathing as much as you can. (Even if the routine is a challenging one, you can still keep coming back to your breath.) Or simply be mindful of your body as you move — the flexing of your muscles, the contact with the equipment (or the floor), the feelings of warmth or pleasure or strain. Notice also what takes you away. Do you worry about your body image or obsess about your weight? Do you fantasize about your new physique and so forget to be present for what's happening right now? Just notice, and then return to your experience. You may start enjoying your body so much that you stop caring how others see it.

The Family That Meditates Together: Partners, Children, and Other Loved Ones

If you're a budding meditator, family life poses a twofold challenge. On the one hand, you may feel inclined to invite, encourage, or even coerce your loved ones to meditate with you. On the other, you may find that the people closest to you disturb your fragile, newfound peace of mind in ways that no one else can.

For example, only your spouse or partner may know precisely the words that can pique your anger or evoke your hurt. And your children may have a unique capacity to try your patience or challenge your attachment to having situations be a certain way. (If you've ever tried to relax and follow your breathing while your toddler throws a tantrum or your teenager tries to explain why he came home at 2 a.m. the night before, you know what I'm talking about.)

You can definitely find ways of incorporating the formal practice of meditation into your closest relationships, as long as your loved ones are responsive to your efforts. But whether or not they have any interest in meditation, you can still use the ties that bind you to them as an exceptional opportunity to pay mindful attention to your habitual patterns of reacting and behaving. (For more on how to do this, see Chapter 11.) Ultimately, in fact, family life has the capacity to open your heart as no other circumstance can.

Meditating with kids

Once you become enthusiastic about meditation yourself, you may want to pass on the benefits to your children (or grandchildren or godchildren or nephews and nieces). Or they may simply notice that you're spending time every day sitting quietly, and they may become interested in joining you. (Younger kids especially will imitate just about anything their parents do.) If your children express curiosity, by all means give them *brief* instructions and invite them to meditate with you — but don't expect them to stick with it. Younger children have limited attention spans, and older ones may have other interests they find more compelling.

As you may have noticed, children under the age of six or seven already spend much of their time in an altered state of wonder and delight (when they're not screaming at the top of their lungs, of course). Instead of teaching them how to meditate, join them where they are as much as you can. Draw their attention to the little, wondrous details of life and encourage them to observe without interpretation. Pick up a leaf and examine it closely with them, watch the ants on the ground, gaze together at the stars in the night sky. To protect the development of their natural capacity to meditate, limit TV and video time, which stifles curiosity and fantasy, and avoid pushing them to develop their intellects too soon.

If older kids show interest, feel free to introduce formal meditation practices such as following the breath or reciting a mantra, but keep them light and fun as much as possible — and let the kids do the practices or not, as they feel moved. Meditation will actually have its greatest impact on your children by making *you* calmer, happier, more loving, and less reactive. As they watch you change for the better, your kids may naturally be drawn to meditation because they want to reap the same benefits for themselves.

Meditating with partners and family members

Like prayer, meditation can draw a family closer. (By family, I'm also referring to partners and spouses.) When you sit together in silence, even for a few minutes, you naturally attune to a deeper level of being, where differences and conflicts don't seem so important. You can also practice specific techniques in which, for example, you practice opening your hearts and sending and receiving love to and from one another (see the following sidebar "Connecting more deeply with a partner or friend"). If your family members are willing, you can incorporate meditative practices into your usual routine — for example, by sitting quietly together for a few moments before dinner or by reflecting before bed on the good things that happened during the day.

Hugging wholeheartedly

Instead of practicing formal meditation with your children, you can turn the simple, everyday act of hugging into an opportunity to breathe and be present. The next time you hug your kids, notice how you hold them. Do you tense up or keep them at a distance? Do you hold your breath or space out or withhold your love because you're irritated or upset? Do you rush through the hug so you can get on with other, "more important" things? You may be surprised by what you discover. (Of course, you may be quite happy with the way you hug, in which case feel free to ignore the rest of this sidebar!)

Instead of judging yourself, you may want to practice a different way of hugging. The next time you embrace your kids (or your partner or friends or other family members), pause while you hold them, relax your body, and breathe in and out with awareness three or four times. If you're so inclined, you can rest your awareness in your heart and consciously send them your love. (For more on opening your heart and extending love, see Chapter 10.) You may find that you enjoy hugging more — and that your kids feel more loved and nurtured in the process.

Family rituals offer a wonderful opportunity to practice mindfulness together and to connect in a deeper, more heartful way. If you invite your family members to join you as you cook a meal or work in the garden mindfully, they may begin to notice the quality of your attention and follow your lead. Of course, you can always suggest cooking or eating or working in a new and different way (you may prefer to use words like "love" and "care," rather than "mindfulness"), but your example will have a greater impact than the instructions you give. You can also practice eating meditation with your family occasionally (see the sidebar "Enjoying your meal with mindful eating" earlier in this chapter) — but be sure to keep it playful, loving, and relaxed.)

Meditative lovemaking

"Why would I want to meditate while I make love?" you may wonder. "My partner and I have a great time already — what could we possibly add to the experience?" Well, I have an appealing answer for you: You can enhance your lovemaking enormously by giving it your wholehearted and undivided attention. Many people make love with their minds — they fantasize about sex not only when they're alone but when they're having sex with their partner as well. But the real lovemaking happens in the here and now, touch after touch, sensation after sensation. When you're spacing out or daydreaming, you miss the best part — and reduce your pleasure and satisfaction in the process.

Connecting more deeply with a partner or friend

If your partner knows how to meditate, you may enjoy scheduling some regular time to practice side by side. Then, if you feel adventurous and want to connect more deeply, you can experiment with the following exercise. (You can also do it with a close friend, if you like.) If your partner doesn't meditate but is open to learning how, this exercise can serve as an excellent introduction:

1. **Sit facing one another with your knees close together. Place your hands in front of you and join them with your partner's — right hands facing up, left hands facing down.**

2. **Close your eyes, take a few deep breaths, and relax as much as possible on the exhalation.**

3. **Attune yourself to your partner's breathing and gradually synchronize your inhalation and exhalation with hers.**

   In other words, start breathing in and out together. Allow yourself to enjoy the deeper harmony and connectedness this shared rhythm evokes.

4. **After several minutes, begin to alternate your inhalations and exhalations.**

   Breathe out love or light or healing energy and send it to your partner; breathe in the love and energy he sends you and take it into your heart. Continue this phase of the exercise for as long you both feel inclined. To intensify the connection, gaze with soft focus into one another's eyes and allow the love to flow back and forth through your gaze.

5. **When you feel complete, imagine the love that you've generated between you expanding to include everyone you love — and ultimately enveloping and enlivening all beings everywhere.**

6. **End the meditation by bowing to one another or embracing.**

   You may want to follow up with a shared massage or, if you're lovers, a hot bath or shower together or some meditative lovemaking.

People who make love meditatively report greater responsiveness and more intensely satisfying, whole-body orgasms. Men in particular say that they can last longer, and women that they can reach orgasm more frequently. Perhaps even more important, wholehearted, mindful awareness helps you infuse more love into your lovemaking, allows you to connect more deeply with your partner, and can actually transform sex into a spiritual experience.

Here are a few guidelines for making love in a meditative way. By all means, share them with your partner if he or she is interested — but remember that just applying them as much as possible yourself can improve the quality of your sexual connection and may even entice your partner to follow your lead.

- ✔ **Connect with the love between you.** Before you make love, take a few minutes or more to connect in a heartful, loving way. You may want to gaze soulfully into one another's eyes or give one another a nurturing massage or whisper sweet words of love (or do the exercise in the sidebar "Connecting more deeply with a partner or friend") — whatever helps you to drop your defenses and open your heart.

- ✔ **See the Divine in your partner.** In the traditional meditative sexual practices of India and Tibet, the partners visualize one another as god and goddess, the embodiment of the divine masculine and feminine. Maybe you're not prepared to go quite so far, but you can certainly reconnect with the feelings of reverence and devotion you felt for your partner when you first fell in love.

- ✔ **Be present — and come back when you drift off.** Once you've established the connection between your genitals and your heart, you can begin to touch one another lovingly, with as much awareness as you can muster. When you start fantasizing or spacing out, gently return to the present moment. If unresolved feelings such as resentment or hurt prevent you from connecting wholeheartedly with your partner, don't pretend — just stop and talk things through until you reconnect.

- ✔ **Slow down and tune in.** Notice any tendency you may have to switch to automatic pilot, especially when the passion builds. Instead, slow down the pace and tune in to the full range of your sensations, rather than just focusing on your genitals. You'll enjoy your lovemaking more, and you'll find that you have greater control over your energy. Be sure to tune in to your partner as well — and feel free to ask your partner how he or she wants to be touched.

- ✔ **Remember to breathe.** In the throes of passion, most people have a tendency to hold their breath. Unfortunately, this response can suppress your pleasure and hurry your climax (if you're a man) or inhibit your orgasm (if you're a woman). Conscious, mindful breathing can ground you in the present moment, relax your body, and deepen your enjoyment immeasurably.

- ✔ **When the energy starts to peak, stop for a few moments, breathe together, and relax.** This step may seem counterintuitive (most people tend to speed up when they get excited), but it's actually the secret doorway to a new world of sexual fulfillment. By letting go of your active, goal-directed orientation and just relaxing and breathing together, you deepen your heart connection and open yourselves to a higher frequency of pleasure, akin to what the mystics call ecstasy. When you feel your passion begin to wane, you can make love actively again — but feel free to stop and breathe once more when your energy peaks and then return to active lovemaking.

IN THE MOMENT

Practicing a half smile

If you look closely at the classical statues of the Buddha or at the faces of Renaissance madonnas, you'll notice a half smile that signifies a blend of tranquillity and joy. The Vietnamese Buddhist teacher Thich Nhat Hanh suggests that you can actually lift your mood and restore your innate happiness by smiling consciously, even when your spirits are low. "A tiny bud of a smile on our lips nourishes awareness and calms us miraculously," he writes in *Peace Is Every Step.* " It returns us to the peace we thought we had lost."

Contemporary scientific research agrees, indicating that smiling relaxes muscles throughout the body and has the same effect on the nervous system as real joy. Besides, smiling encourages others to smile and be happy.

Here are a few brief instructions for practicing the half smile that Thich Nhat Hanh recommends:

1. **Take a few moments right now to form your lips into a half smile.**

   Notice how other parts of your body respond. Does your belly relax? Does your back naturally straighten a little? Does your mood change in subtle ways? Notice also if you have any resistance to smiling when "you don't really feel like it."

2. **Maintain this half smile for at least ten minutes.**

   Do you notice a shift in how you act or respond to others? Do others respond to your smile by smiling back?

3. **The next time you feel your spirits sagging, practice this half smile for half an hour and notice how you feel.**

Chapter 16

Using Meditation for Healing and Performance Enhancement

. . . .

In This Chapter

▶ Benefiting from recent advances in mind-body medicine

▶ Exploring the many ways that meditation supports the healing process

▶ Using light, imagery, sound, and breath to facilitate healing

▶ Checking out the meditation skills that help you do your personal best

▶ Meditating your way to more successful performance

. . . .

*I*f you practice the basic meditations taught elsewhere in this book (especially Chapter 6), you may begin to notice that your health gradually improves (even if you think you're already healthy), your energy and vitality increase, and you find it easier and less stressful to do (and do effectively) the things that used to stress you out. In fact, Western researchers have corroborated the findings of traditional healers and teachers that meditation has an extraordinary capacity to help strengthen and heal your body and enhance your performance by training your mind and opening your heart. (If you don't believe me, check out the detailed list of meditation's benefits in Chapter 2.)

But what if you want to deal with a particular health problem, or transform your tennis game, or put in a better showing at work? Does meditation have some specialized techniques to offer? Sure it does! Healers both ancient and modern have concocted some great meditations for facilitating the healing process (which you get to sample in this chapter), and in recent years sports gurus and corporate trainers have been applying the principles of meditation to enhance performance both on the field and in the office.

I know I say somewhere else in this book that you shouldn't be goal-oriented when you meditate. Well, here you get to cheat a little and apply the skills you picked up in earlier chapters — or if you haven't read any other chapters, you can pick them up here!

Meditation Has the Power to Help Heal Your Body Too

The link between meditation and healing is a venerable one indeed. Take the world's great spiritual teachers — many were renowned for their healing abilities as well as their wisdom and compassion. Jesus, for example, first revealed his spiritual maturity by helping the lame to walk and the blind to see. The Jewish mystic known as the Baal Shem Tov had a reputation as a miracle worker and healer, and the historical Buddha is traditionally likened to a physician because the practices he taught help alleviate suffering. Even the English language reflects the sacred dimension of healing: The word "heal" derives from the same root as "whole" and "holy"!

Perhaps more important for ordinary folks like you and me, these teachers passed down special meditation techniques that make it possible for practitioners to influence their bodily functions to an extraordinary degree. Ever hear about the yogis who stop their heart and live for hours without any breathing or measurable metabolism? Or the Tibetan monks who generate so much internal heat that they dry wet blankets on their bodies in subzero temperatures? These people do exist — and their exceptional feats have been measured by Western researchers.

In fact, the emerging field of mind-body medicine developed in the 1970s when scientists studying the abilities of Eastern-trained meditators began to realize that the mind can have an extraordinary effect on the body — or even more precisely, that the body and the mind are inseparable. (Of course, the link between type A behavior and heart disease dates back even earlier, to the 1960s.) More recently, researchers studying immune response have shown that the immune system and the nervous system are inextricably intertwined and that psychological and emotional stress can suppress immune functioning and encourage the growth or spread of immune-related disorders such as cancer, AIDS, and autoimmune diseases. (For more on the mind-body connection and the health benefits of meditation, see Chapter 2.)

These days, most physicians recognize the relevance of psychological factors and the importance of relaxation and stress reduction in maintaining health. There's even a joke making the rounds of the medical field. Instead of offering the old saw about aspirin, the contemporary mind-body physician advises: "Take two meditations and call me in the morning."

The good news is, you don't have to control your heartbeat or your metabolism to benefit from the healing power of meditation. You just have to sit still, focus your mind, and practice some of the exercises provided in this section. Of course, it helps to have some meditation experience — which you can get by turning to Chapter 6 — but you're welcome to begin here, if you're strongly motivated, and learn as you go.

What healing really means

As I suggest at the start of this section, healing involves returning to an intrinsic state of wholeness and well-being, which our language, in its wisdom, links with the sacred. Take a cold, for example. When you get better, you don't end up feeling like a different person — you just go back to being the way you were before you got sick. That's why people often say, when the cold goes away, "I finally feel like myself again!"

Meditation by its very nature provides healing of the deepest kind. The disease it helps heal is perhaps the most painful one of all — an epidemic human disorder known as *separation* (or, even worse, *alienation*) from our own being and from other beings and things. (For more on this "disease," see Chapter 2.) When you meditate, you heal this separation by gradually reconnecting in the here and now with your feelings, your sensate experience, and other aspects of yourself you may have previously disowned. That is, you become more whole!

Most important, perhaps, you reconnect with your basic nature — *pure being* itself — which is complete and perfect just the way it is. Stephen Levine, whose numerous books have pioneered the use of meditation in healing, calls this "the healing we took birth for."

The more you reconnect with your essential wholeness and well-being, the more you suffuse your body-mind with life energy and love. (As I mention in Chapter 5, the wellspring of being inside you is the source of all positive, life-affirming qualities and feelings.) And, as researchers have proven again and again, this life-giving energy mobilizes your body's healing resources, bolsters your immune system, and naturally facilitates the process of repair and renewal. In other words, as you heal your separation, you contribute to the healing of your body as well.

But even if you have some chronic ailment and can never heal your body completely, you can still do the healing you were born to do. You don't have to consider yourself a failure if you don't get well (as some alternative healing approaches suggest you should). After all, you can encourage your healing with meditation — but illness is a mysterious process you and I can't really understand. Who knows? You may be sick because you need to slow down, reevaluate your priorities, and reconnect with yourself. Like few other life circumstances, illness can be a powerful messenger urging you to change your life in significant ways.

How meditation heals

Besides overcoming separation, the basic meditation practices provided in this book (especially Chapters 6 and 10) contribute to the healing process in a number of essential ways:

✔ **Love and connectedness:** As Dean Ornish, M.D., reveals in his ground-breaking research (described in Chapter 10), love is more important than any other factor in the healing process, including diet and exercise. To heal your heart, he discovered, you need to open your heart — and his findings have been corroborated in studies of cancer, AIDS, and other life-threatening illnesses. By putting you in touch with the love in your heart (which, as I mention elsewhere, is not just an emotion, but a direct expression of being itself), meditation nourishes not only your internal organs but your entire body-mind organism.

✔ **Relief of tension and stress:** By teaching you how to relax your body and calm your mind (see Chapter 6), meditation helps you to avoid getting sick in the first place by alleviating stress, a major cause of many ailments, from heart disease and stroke to gastrointestinal disorders and tension headaches. In particular, Jon Kabat-Zinn (author of the bestseller *Wherever You Go There You Are*) has developed a stress-reduction program based on Buddhist mindfulness meditation that teaches participants not only how to reduce stress while they're meditating, but also how to extend the benefits of mindfulness to every area of their lives. (For more on Kabat-Zinn's work, see Chapter 2.)

✔ **Restoring alignment and balance:** Traditional healing practices such as *ayurveda* (the traditional medicine of India involving herbs and diet) and Chinese medicine, as well as more mainstream approaches like chiropractic and osteopathy, suggest that the body gets sick when it becomes unbalanced or misaligned. Meditation slows the mind down to the speed of the breath, which restores balance and harmony to the body and facilitates healing. Besides, sitting up straight (see Chapter 7) aligns the spine and encourages the unimpeded flow of life-giving energy through the body, which promotes both physical and psychological well-being.

✔ **Opening and softening:** If you're like many people, you tend to get impatient or upset with yourself when you're sick or hurting. You may even have strong judgments, as though it's a bad or blameworthy thing to be ill. Unfortunately, these negative emotions may compound your suffering — and even amplify your illness — by causing you to tense up and contract. When you meditate regularly, you develop the skill of opening to your experience, however unpleasant, and softening around it instead of judging it or pushing it away.

✔ **Creating space for all your emotions:** As you accept your experience in meditation, you create a welcoming environment in which your feelings can bubble up and release, rather than be suppressed or acted out. (For more on meditating with emotions, see Chapter 11.) Research suggests that unexpressed feelings locked in the body form focal points of tension and stress that may eventually contribute to the development of life-threatening illnesses such as cancer and heart disease. Besides, you naturally feel more enlivened — and therefore more healthy — when you can feel your feelings fully.

✔ **Harmony, joy, and well-being:** Positive qualities like happiness, joy, peace, and well-being don't originate outside you, in some other person or thing. Instead, they well up inside you naturally and spontaneously, like water bubbling up from a spring — you simply have to create the right internal environment, as you do when you meditate. (Of course, you can always cultivate positive emotions like love and compassion, as I describe in Chapter 10.) Western researchers have shown that these positive qualities correlate with a host of life-enhancing bodily responses, from lowered blood pressure and improved immune response to the release of natural painkillers called *beta-endorphins*. (For more on the health benefits of meditation, see Chapter 2.) As the *New Jerusalem Bible* puts it, "Gladness of heart is life to anyone; joy is what gives length of days." (Eccles. 30:5)

✔ **Freedom from self-clinging and habitual patterns:** Ultimately, it's the illusion (which we all share) of being a separate, isolated individual cut off from others and the rest of life that lies at the heart of all suffering and stress. According to the Tibetan scholar and meditation master Tulku Thondup, author of *The Healing Power of Mind,* "living in peace, free from emotional afflictions, and loosening our grip on 'self' is the ultimate medicine for both mental and physical health." As you gradually begin to penetrate and let go of habitual patterns (which have deep roots in the body as well as the mind), you become less emotionally reactive (which reduces stress) and more positively (even joyfully) responsive to life as it unfolds. (For more on working with habitual patterns, see Chapter 11.)

✔ **Awakening to a spiritual dimension:** Herbert Benson, M.D., a professor at Harvard Medical School, developed the technique known as the Relaxation Response (see Chapter 2) on the basis of studies of people who repeated a simple word or phrase, known as a *mantra*. But over the years, he discovered that the more meaningful the mantra, the more effective the technique in relaxing the body and promoting healing. "If you truly believe in your personal philosophy or religious faith," he reported in *Beyond the Relaxation Response,* "you may well be capable of achieving remarkable feats of mind and body that [we] may only speculate about." In other words, you enhance the healing powers of meditation when you expand your awareness to include a spiritual dimension of being.

Meditation at the edge of life

Many teachers have written about the powerful role meditation can play in helping people bridge the chasm between life and death. In fact, some traditions, like Zen Buddhism, teach that one of the primary purposes of meditation practice is to prepare you for the ultimate transition.

Certainly, most traditions would agree that how you live helps to determine how you die. (For example, if you tend to be fearful or angry in your life, then you're likely to be filled with fear or anger when you die. And if you tend to be calm or loving or joyful, then these qualities will probably suffuse your being at death.) And many traditions believe that the moment of death itself can be a crucial factor in determining what happens next. (Of course, they tend to part company when it comes to describing what the next step might be!)

If you're concerned about the way you may die, you can prepare for death by using meditation to help you bring more peace and harmony into your life right now. In addition, the meditations presented throughout this book teach skills that will definitely come in handy when you approach the threshold between life and death.

Here are a few of the ways that meditation can help you (and those you love) die a more loving, conscious death. (*Remember:* Meditation may help make death more comfortable and less frightening, but there's no right or wrong way to do it. Everyone lives and dies in their own unique way.)

✔ **Staying present:** Needless to say, fear, regret, and other negative feelings may get magnified a thousandfold when you approach the ultimate unknown. By bringing your awareness back to your breath or some other object, you can help calm your mind and keep it from spiraling down into negativity.

✔ **Welcoming whatever arises:** The weeks, days, and moments leading up to death may be filled with painful sensations and difficult emotions and mind-states. When you've developed the capacity through meditation to be with your experience, whatever it may be, you're better prepared for this challenging time.

✔ **Opening your heart:** If you practice opening your heart to yourself and others (see Chapter 10), you'll be ready to access the love when you need it — and when could you possibly need it more! Many traditions teach that love helps bridge the chasm between this life and the next. Besides, people who die in love bestow the immeasurable legacy of love on those they leave behind.

✔ **Letting go:** When you keep returning to your breath or some other object of meditation, you become accustomed to letting go of your thoughts, emotions, preoccupations, likes and dislikes — and ultimately, perhaps, even letting go of who you think you are. In Zen, they say that when you become adept at dying this way on your meditation cushion, the real death poses no problem at all. Or, as Stephen Levine puts it in *Healing into Life and Death,* "To let go of the last moment and enter wholeheartedly the next is to die into life, is to heal into death."

✔ **Trusting the deathless:** As you deepen your connection with *being* (as opposed to thinking or doing) through the practice of meditation, you may awaken to a spiritual or sacred dimension that infuses this life with meaning but at the same time transcends it. Whether you call this dimension true self or essential nature, God or spirit, or simply the One, you now know (rather than simply believe) that something far greater than your separate existence informs your life and survives your death. As you can imagine, this realization makes death far easier to face.

Besides preparing you to face your own demise, meditation can teach you how to be a source of support for your loved ones and friends as they approach death. Just apply the principles listed here to the time you spend with them, either by sharing what you've discovered in your meditation (if they're open to hearing it) or by being present with them with as much love, awareness, trust, openness, and letting go as you can muster. (You can also ease their letting go by practicing the "Ahh breath" with them. To find out more about meditation and the process of dying, read *Healing into Life and Death* by Stephen Levine or *The Tibetan Book of Living and Dying* by Sogyal Rinpoche.)

The healing power of imagery

In her book *Staying Well with Guided Imagery,* psychotherapist and guided imagery pioneer Belleruth Naparstek cites extensive research that establishes three basic principles behind the healing power of imagery. These principles help explain the effectiveness of the meditations provided in this chapter, which use imagery extensively. (Incidentally, imagery may or may not involve visual images; if you're more kinesthetic or auditory, for example, you may hear or feel the "images," rather than see them.)

- ✔ **Your body responds to sensory images as though they were real.** If you're not sure what I mean, just recall the last time you had a sexual fantasy or reminisced about a vacation and had all the emotions and sensations of the actual event. In one study cited in Naparstek's book, for example, 84 percent of subjects exposed to poison ivy had no reaction when, under hypnosis, they imagined the plant to be harmless. In other words, their bodies believed the images their minds evoked and didn't break out in a rash! Other studies have shown that patients can use positive imagery to measurably increase the numbers of immune response cells (for example, white blood cells and neutrophils) in their bloodstream.

- ✔ **In the meditative state, you can heal, change, learn, and grow more rapidly.** Naparstek uses the term *altered state,* which refers (in her usage) to a calm, relaxed, but focused state of mind — precisely the state you cultivate in meditation. This principle also applies to problem-solving and performance enhancement: You can explore new behaviors, improve existing ones, and make tactical breakthroughs far more easily in a meditative state than you can in your ordinary frame of mind. (For more on meditation for performance enhancement, see the section "Meditation Can Enhance Your Performance at Work and Play" later in this chapter.)

✔ **Imagery gives you a sense of mastery in challenging circumstances, which reduces your stress and bolsters your self-esteem.** When you're struggling with a health problem or a difficult assignment at work, you may feel flustered and helpless if you believe you can't do anything to control the outcome. But if you know that you can use imagery to help your body heal or enhance your performance, you can regain your confidence and your hope in the future. Numerous studies have shown that people feel better and perform more effectively when they believe they have some control over their lives.

In addition to these principles, Naparstek adds that emotion amplifies the power of imagery. When you allow yourself to feel the images intensely as well as experiencing them fully in all your senses, you give them more power to heal and transform you.

Six healing meditations

As I mention at the beginning of this chapter, you don't have to do any special exercises to enjoy the health benefits of meditation — just develop a consistent practice based on the instructions provided elsewhere in this book. But if you're struggling with a chronic health problem (or just want to improve your overall state of health), you may want to experiment with one or more of the meditations that follow. You can add them to your regular practice or do them exclusively for a period of time. With one exception, they use guided imagery to help you relax your body, reduce your stress, ease your suffering, enhance your sense of self-mastery, and mobilize your healing resources. (To find out more about how to use meditation to facilitate healing, read *Healing into Life and Death* by Stephen Levine or *The Healing Power of Mind* by Tulku Thondup.)

Peaceful place

Because this meditation relaxes the body quickly and easily, it can be used by itself to help facilitate healing, or it can be practiced as a preliminary exercise before the other healing visualizations provided in this section.

1. **Begin by sitting comfortably, closing your eyes, and taking a few deep breaths.**

2. **Imagine yourself in a safe, protected, peaceful place.**

   It may be a place you know well (a place in nature, for example, such as a meadow, a forest, or a beach), a place you've visited once or twice before, or simply a place in your imagination.

3. **Take as much time as you need to imagine this peaceful place as vividly as you can, in all your senses.**

   Notice the colors, the shapes, the sounds, the light, the feeling of the air against your skin, the contact of your feet against the ground. Explore this special place to your heart's content.

4. **Allow yourself to rest in the feelings of comfort, safety, and tranquillity this special place evokes.**

5. **Spend as much time here as you wish.**

   When you're done, gradually return to the present moment and open your eyes, while continuing to enjoy the pleasant, positive feelings.

Inner smile

By smiling into your internal organs, you can infuse them with the healing energy of love. "In ancient China, the Taoists taught that a constant inner smile, a smile to oneself, insured health, happiness, and longevity," writes Mantak Chia in his book *Awakening Healing Energy Through the Tao.* "Smiling to yourself is like basking in love: you become your own best friend." Try the following meditation, which is adapted from Chia's book.

1. **Begin by closing your eyes, forming a half smile with your lips, and smiling into your eyes.**

   Feel the smile shine through your eyes. Taoists believe that relaxing the eyes calms the entire nervous system.

2. **When you feel your eyes filled with the vibrant energy of your smile, you can begin to send this energy down through your body.**

   If you're not sure how to "send energy," don't worry. Just imagine the energy moving, and it will! (Incidentally, the Taoists call this energy *chi,* as in the well-known martial arts *t'ai chi* and *chi kung,* and equate it with the life force.)

3. **Smile down into your jaw and tongue.**

   Like most people, you probably hold tension in your jaw — and when your jaw relaxes, you may notice your whole body relaxing as well.

4. **Smile into your neck and throat and dissolve any tension there.**

5. **Let the relaxing energy of your smile flow down into your heart, filling it with love.**

6. **From your heart, allow the love to flow into your other internal organs in the following order, relaxing, softening, and rejuvenating them as it moves:**

   lungs; liver (beneath your ribcage on the right side); kidneys (just below the ribcage in back, on either side of the spine); pancreas and spleen (in the center of your abdomen).

   When you finish sending love to these organs, rest your smile in your *t'an t'ien* (a point about two inches below your navel and an inch and a half inside your body).

7. **Smile again into your eyes and then into your mouth.**

8. **Gather some saliva, swallow it, and allow your smile to follow it through your digestive system, spreading relaxation into your esophagus, stomach, small intestines, and colon.**

9. **Once again return your smile to your eyes and smile down the center of your spine, one vertebra at a time, until you reach your tailbone.**

Be sure to have your back straight as you do this exercise.

REMEMBER

Working with pain

Like death, pain is a complex topic that definitely deserves a chapter (or even a book) of its own. Most of us never simply experience physical pain just the way it is — a set of intense physical sensations. Instead, we tend to react to our pain — to tighten and contract around it, to struggle to get rid of it — and weave a story about it that we superimpose on the experience: "Why me? What did I do to deserve it?" or "I can't stand it. I won't be able to make it through." In the process, we prolong our pain and turn it into suffering. (For more on the difference between pain and suffering, see Chapter 5.)

The secret to coping with pain is to soften around it, rather than resist it, and to expand your awareness (and your heart) to include it, rather than tighten and contract. After all, if you can't actually get rid of the pain or block it out of your mind, you may as well welcome it — and even (dare I say) make friends with it. But you can't do this readily without considerable practice, which is why the meditations taught throughout this book provide the best preparation for working with pain. (You might begin with deep relaxation as described in Chapter 6. For more suggestions on dealing with pain, see Chapter 7.)

You can begin by opening and softening in relation to the small aches and pains you experience when you sit in meditation and gradually work up to the larger pains, such as a bad headache or a sore throat or a back in spasm.

You can also do the moment-to-moment work of challenging the story your mind keeps telling you and returning to the bare sensation of the pain itself — which is inevitably more bearable than the worst-case scenario your mind keeps fabricating. In his book *Full Catastrophe Living,* Jon Kabat-Zinn, who works with people in chronic pain at the Stress-Reduction Clinic at the University of Massachusetts Medical Center, suggests going directly into the sensations of the pain and asking yourself the question, "How bad is it right now, in this very moment?" Most of the time, he counsels, you will find that the pain is tolerable after all.

Intense pain also has a tendency to flush out the unresolved issues and unfelt emotions of a lifetime, so don't be surprised if you need to turn to Chapter 11 for some guidance on how to work with difficult mind-states. Ultimately, pain can be a powerful teacher, forcing you to deepen your meditation and open to the present moment as never before.

10. **When you finish with your spine, rest your smile in your t'an t'ien again and notice how your body feels now.**

    Rest in this feeling for a few minutes before resuming your normal activities. Once you get the knack of this exercise, you can do it in just a few minutes, if you wish.

Good medicine

If you have an illness that requires you to take medication, you may find yourself swallowing the pills with a certain distaste, a certain judgment or aversion to being sick in the first place, as though you were somehow flawed or at fault for allowing your body to suffer. When you take your pills (or your injection or surgery) with awareness, you can send love to your body along with the remedy and contribute immeasurably to its healing effect. (Even if you're not sick, you can take your vitamins or herbs with the same attitude.) The Sioux know this well: They call any act of love "good medicine." (The following meditation is adapted from the book *Healing into Life and Death* by Stephen Levine.)

1. **Begin by closing your eyes and holding the pills in your hand for a few moments.**

   Notice how they feel — their weight, their texture.

2. **Consider that these pills have the power to help your body heal.**

   You may even feel some gratitude welling up in your heart. You are one of the fortunate ones: You have access to medical care, and you have a health professional who prescribed these pills for you.

3. **Notice whether you feel any resistance to taking these pills — any fear or shame or self-blame.**

   Allow these feelings to arise in your awareness, and meet them with kindness and compassion.

4. **Relax and soften your body as you prepare to receive these pills.**

5. **Gently and with awareness, put the pills into your mouth and wash them down with liquid.**

   Feel them moving down your esophagus into your stomach and radiating their healing potential there like the glow of a warm fire. Open your body to receive them.

6. **Imagine the medicine entering your bloodstream and reaching the parts that cry out for healing.**

   Send love and compassion to these parts along with the medicine.

7. **Feel the love and the medicine suffusing and healing these parts.**

   Imagine all disease and resistance dissolving. Let yourself be healed.

8. **Continue to sit quietly for a few minutes as you allow the medicine and the love to help you heal.**

Healing with light

Just as you can help to purify and eliminate habitual patterns by invoking the power of spiritual beings or energies (see Chapter 11), you can access the same source of power and light to help your body heal. After all, physical illness and emotional suffering are just different facets of the same basic problem — just different ways you contract away from your essential wholeness and health. Here's an exercise for directing the light to the places inside your body that cry out for healing.

1. **Begin by sitting down and meditating in your usual way for several minutes.**

   If you don't have a usual way, you can find one in Chapter 6 — or just sit quietly, take a few deep breaths, and allow your body to relax a little on each exhalation.

2. **Imagine a sphere of white light suspended about a foot above your head and slightly in front of you.**

   As you look more closely, you may notice that this sphere takes the form of a being who embodies all the positive, healing energy you need. Perhaps it's a spiritual figure, like Jesus or Mother Mary or the Dalai Lama, or possibly it's a being or object from nature, such as the sun, the moon, the wind, the ocean, a tree, a flower, or a mountain.

3. **Imagine this sphere radiating light in all directions to the farthest corners of the universe.**

   As it does so, it draws the energy of all the benevolent forces that support your healing back into the sphere.

4. **Imagine this positive, healing energy shining from the sphere like the light of 1,000 suns streaming down through your body.**

   Imagine the light eliminating all toxicity and stress, all disharmony and disease, and replacing them with radiance, vitality, and health. In particular, you can imagine directing this light like a beacon to all the places you know to be involved in your illness or distress. Imagine the light dissolving any contractions, replacing them with openness and ease, and flooding any weakness with power and strength.

5. **Continue to imagine this powerful, healing light infusing every cell and molecule of your being, leaving you healthy, peaceful, and strong.**

6. **Imagine this luminous sphere gradually descending into your heart, where it continues to radiate this powerful, healing light.**

7. **Imagine yourself as a luminous being with a sphere of light in your heart that constantly radiates health, harmony, peace, and vitality — first to every cell and particle of your own being and then, through you, to every other being in every direction.**

   You can carry the feeling of vitality and strength that this exercise evokes throughout the rest of your day.

Ahhh breath

If you're looking for a way to support a loved one in his or her healing process, beyond buying flowers, cooking a meal, or helping with chores, you might try this partner meditation, drawn from the work of Stephen Levine, whose many books have helped thousands of people to live (and die) with greater love and awareness. In *Healing into Life and Death,* he writes: "This is one of the simplest and most powerful exercises we know to give confidence that the ever-healed is never far away — to sense the heart we all share, the one mind of being." You can also use it to bring greater intimacy to your relationships with parents, children, partners, and friends. (If the other person feels up to it, take some time to receive the ahhh breath as well as give it.)

1. **Before you begin, describe the exercise to your partner and make sure she feels comfortable doing it with you.**

   Let her know that she can end it at any time by simply raising her arm.

2. **Begin by having the person receiving the ahhh breath lie down on the floor or a bed.**

   You sit at her side, near her torso but not touching her.

3. **Encourage the other person to relax and breathe comfortably while you observe the coming and going of her breath.**

   Now drop all verbal communication until the exercise is over.

4. **Begin to synchronize your breath with her breath.**

   When she inhales, you inhale. When she exhales, you exhale. Remain attuned to the ever-changing rhythm of her breath and adjust your own rhythm accordingly.

5. **After eight or ten breaths breathed in this way, start making the sound ahhh on the exhalation, softly and gently but audibly.**

   With each repetition, allow the sound to come from an even deeper place in your body until the ahhh originates in the bottom of your belly. Inhale together in silence, then intone ahhh on the exhale. (Your partner need not repeat the sound.)

6. **Continue this shared meditation for as long as you both feel comfortable.**

   When you're done, take some time to talk with your partner about your experiences. This shared practice may elicit any number of responses. Some people relax more deeply than ever before. Others notice some fear of letting go or getting so close to another person. Still others glimpse a deep peace beneath all the usual turmoil and concern. Whatever you or your partner experience, you can welcome it (as much as possible) with openness and nonjudgmental acceptance.

Great Mother

Many meditative traditions feature an archetypal feminine figure who nurtures and heals and carries the pain of others. In the Christian tradition, she's Mary, mother of sorrows. In Buddhism, she's called Kuan Yin, who hears and responds to the cries of the world. Patterned after the good mother who loves her children unconditionally, the Great Mother can be invoked in whatever form feels most comfortable for you. She has the capacity to ease your pain with her compassion and to help you heal into wholeness.

1. **Begin by sitting comfortably, closing your eyes, and taking a few deep breaths, relaxing a little with each exhalation.**

   Allow your belly to soften.

2. **Bring your attention to your heart and notice any pain or suffering you may be holding there.**

   Gently breathe with awareness into this painful place in your heart.

3. **Imagine the presence of an infinitely compassionate feminine figure — the Great Mother.**

   Feel her arms surrounding you and holding you in her warm, supportive, nurturing embrace. You can let go completely and relax into her arms. No need to hold yourself up anymore.

4. **With each inhalation, breathe her love into your heart in the form of warm, liquid light.**

   With each exhalation, breathe out all your suffering and disease in the form of black soot, which she naturally receives and transforms into light.

5. **If you feel moved to share your pain with her in the form of words or tears, go ahead.**

   Her infinite heart is filled with compassion; she welcomes your suffering as though it were her own.

TRADITIONAL WISDOM

Making Great Waves

As I was thumbing through an old Zen text, I came across a true story that exemplifies the power of meditation for performance enhancement. It seems that a sumo wrestler named Great Waves was so powerful and adept that he could defeat even his teacher, but in public he lost both his confidence and his matches. He decided to seek out a local Zen master for guidance.

After listening to the wrestler's story, the master told him to spend the night in the temple in meditation, imagining himself to be the "great waves" of his name. "Imagine sweeping everything before you with your power," advised the master. "Then you will be the great wrestler you were destined to be."

Throughout the night, Great Waves focused his attention on the image of the powerful water. Gradually, his mind became one-pointed, and by morning he had become the indomitable ocean itself. From then on, the story concludes, no one in all of Japan could defeat him.

6. **Continue to surrender yourself into her arms and receive her love into your heart as you let go of your suffering and sorrow.**

   With each breath, you feel more complete, more whole, more healed. Gradually, you feel your own heart dissolve into hers.

7. **Spend as much time as you need in the presence of the Great Mother.**

   When you're done, imagine her entering you and filling you with her presence. You are the Great Mother (whether you're a man or a woman) — her heart is your heart. From this heart, you can radiate out the warm light of compassion and healing to all beings everywhere. May all beings be happy, peaceful, and free from suffering.

Meditation Can Enhance Your Performance at Work and Play

For many of the same reasons that meditation helps to facilitate healing, it also enhances performance. It relaxes your body and reduces stress and anxiety, which allows you to function more effectively. It promotes positive mind-states, such as love, joy, and well-being, and encourages the flow of life-energy through the body, which in turn promotes self-confidence and a sense of power and effectiveness. And it awakens a deeper connection with a source of meaning and purpose, which inspires and uplifts you in whatever you do.

Meditation also teaches you how to cultivate certain other qualities and skills that naturally contribute to making you better at your favorite endeavor, whether it's sports or business, gardening or studying, or simply washing the dishes or sweeping the floor. Here's a brief list — if you think of any more, just let me know:

- **Increased focus and concentration:** This one's a no-brainer: As you become adept at staying on task as you follow your breaths or recite your mantra, you can easily transfer this skill to working at your computer or playing ball with friends. For the benefits of focus, just look at great athletes like Michael Jordan, Mark McGwire, and Steffi Graf!

- **Minimal distractions:** This little benefit is the flip side of the preceding one: The more regularly you meditate, the more quickly distractions fade into the background as your mind settles down and becomes one-pointed. Needless to say, you work or play more effectively without a million irrelevant thoughts chattering away inside your head. As Yogi Berra once said about baseball, "How can you think and hit at the same time?"

- **Being in the moment, free from expectations:** Even though you may have a particular goal in mind — for example, winning the race, completing the project, landing the ball in a tiny cup 300 yards away — the paradox is that you're more likely to succeed if you set aside your expectations and keep your attention focused on the precise movements or tasks you need to execute right now. Former Chicago Bulls coach Phil Jackson calls it "trusting the moment."

- **Enhanced mental and perceptual clarity:** One of the fortuitous side effects of keeping your mind on the moment is that your senses become sharper and your mind quicker and more attuned to subtle details — which, needless to say, comes in quite handy when you're trying to do something well.

- **Greater endurance and longer attention span:** As you gradually increase the length of your meditations from 10 to 15 to 20 minutes or more, you gradually build your power to pay attention longer. As a result, you may find that you don't get so easily burned out or discouraged when you turn your attention to an extended work project or other demanding activity.

- **Flow experience:** In sports they call it "the zone": moments or extended periods when you feel totally in synch with your body and your surroundings. Time seems to slow down, feelings of well-being and enjoyment increase, you see everything clearly as (or even before) it transpires, and you know exactly what you need to do next. By cultivating your powers of concentration in meditation, you develop the ability to enter the flow more easily in every situation. (For more on flow, see Chapter 1.)

✔ **The ability to see things multidimensionally:** In meditation, you practice witnessing or observing your experience without getting lost in the details. This more expanded, global awareness naturally allows you to step back and see the whole picture, which can be extraordinarily useful when you're trying to solve a problem or scope out the opposing team (in sports or business) or just evaluate and improve your performance. Some great athletes even report that they can see the whole game as though from above when they're playing.

✔ **Mindfulness of self-defeating behaviors:** When you expand your awareness in your meditation to include sensations and mental processes, you begin to notice repetitive patterns of thinking and feeling that cause you stress or inhibit your full self-expression (see Chapter 12). By extending this mindfulness to your performance (at work or play), you can catch self-defeating patterns and then replace them with more productive, effective alternatives.

✔ **Self-acceptance and freedom from self-criticism:** Nothing dampens enthusiasm and inhibits effective performance more than the tendency most of us have to put ourselves down, especially under pressure. Through regular meditation, you practice accepting yourself the way you are and noticing the judgments as they arise. Then, when the going gets tough, you can use your meditation skills to gently defuse the self-criticism as you focus on doing your personal best.

✔ **Compassion and teamwork:** In his best-selling book *Sacred Hoops,* Phil Jackson describes how he forged a world-champion basketball team based on the principles and lessons he learned in his study of Zen meditation. In addition to focus, mindfulness, and the other factors listed here, Jackson emphasizes the role of compassion (which can be deliberately cultivated in meditation; see Chapter 10). "As my [meditation] practice matured," he writes, "I began to appreciate the importance of playing with an open heart. Love is the force that ignites the spirit and binds teams together."

Besides the benefits of a regular meditation practice listed here, you can also do meditations that are specifically designed to improve performance. In particular, you can use guided imagery to help you create a positive mindstate and rehearse performances before they occur. (For more on guided imagery, see the previous section.)

In her book *Staying Well with Guided Imagery,* Belleruth Naparstek calls the first kind of guided imagery *feeling-state imagery* and the second *end-state imagery.* (In the sidebar "Making Great Waves" earlier in this chapter, the sumo wrestler uses a third, called *metaphoric imagery,* which actually incorporates elements of the other two.)

Encouraging your creativity

Creative people often report that they enter an altered or meditative state when they envision or create. Meditation naturally feeds creativity by helping you to bypass your analytical mind and tap into a deeper wellspring of energy, vitality, and intuition. Ideas and images may spontaneously bubble up in meditation as though from some collective source.

In addition to doing the basic meditations provided elsewhere in this book, you can encourage your creative juices to flow with a meditation called the "morning pages," adapted from the book *The Artist's Way* by Julia Cameron. It's designed to engage what Cameron calls artist-brain — the playful, creative, holistic part of your mind — and evade the "Censor," the inner critic who dampens or even ridicules your creative impulses.

The meditation itself is actually quite simple: First thing every morning, preferably right after you roll out of bed, sit down and write by hand three pages of whatever comes into your mind. It doesn't have to be good or grammatical; it doesn't even have to make sense — it just has to fill three pages. By writing without double-checking or trying to be logical or smart, you're bypassing the Censor, while

clearing your brain of all the cobwebs that accumulated overnight. You're also showing yourself that you don't have to feel good or be in a great mood to create. You can scribble down complaints or dreams or things you need to do, whatever — you can't do it wrong. Just write!

Cameron does suggest a few guidelines for getting the most out of your morning pages:

- ✔ **Do them every day without fail.** You can decide in advance how many weeks you're going to do them, and then follow through on your intention. Like meditation itself, the morning pages may become a habit you don't want to break.

- ✔ **Don't show them to anyone else — and don't read them yourself for the first few weeks at least.** Cameron actually suggests not reading them for the first eight weeks, but don't be too concerned if curiosity overtakes you.

- ✔ **Remember that the negative opinions of your Censor aren't true.** You can include your Censor's judgments in your morning pages, if you like — but don't believe them!

You've no doubt read about the Olympic and professional athletes who use both feeling and end-state imagery in their training regimen. In the following two sections, you have an opportunity to practice first a generic feeling-state performance meditation and then a meditation designed to help you execute your performance successfully.

Enjoying past success

Here's a meditation that will relax your body, lift your spirits, and put you in a positive frame of mind for an upcoming performance. If possible, begin practicing it several days or a week or more before the performance so that you have ample time to prepare.

1. **Begin by doing the "Peaceful place" meditation described in the previous section.**

   Or you can just sit comfortably, close your eyes, and take a few deep breaths, relaxing a little on each exhalation. Spend several minutes breathing and relaxing in this way.

2. **Recall a time when you successfully completed the same or a similar performance.**

   If you've never done anything like this before, just remember a time when you did something especially well and successfully.

3. **Take some time to remember this successful performance as vividly and with as much sensory detail as you possibly can.**

   Where were you? What were you wearing? What exactly were you doing? How did your body feel? Who else was there? What kinds of feelings did this successful performance evoke?

4. **When you're fully immersed in the memory and your positive feelings reach their peak, find a physical gesture that underscores these feelings.**

   For example, you might touch two fingers together or rest your hand on your belly.

5. **Gradually, let go of the memory, return to ordinary consciousness, and open your eyes.**

6. **Practice this meditation several times between now and the actual performance, each time repeating the physical gesture.**

7. **As you begin the actual performance, close your eyes for a moment and repeat the physical gesture.**

   You'll be amazed to discover that the positive feelings return in a flash.

Rehearsing peak performance

It's one thing to be in a positive frame of mind when you perform, but quite another to know exactly what you're doing. Once you're feeling relaxed, you can apply the principles of meditation to fine-tune your performance beforehand so you're peaking when you step up to the proverbial plate.

Here's a meditation similar to the exercises athletes use. To quote Jack Nicklaus from his book *Golf My Way:* "I never hit a shot, not even in practice, without a very sharp, in-focus picture of it in my head." Again, be sure to give yourself plenty of time to practice before the actual performance.

1. **Begin by doing the "Peaceful place" meditation described in the previous section.**

   Or you can just sit comfortably, close your eyes, and take a few deep breaths, relaxing a little on each exhalation. Spend several minutes breathing and relaxing in this way.

2. **Imagine yourself executing your performance perfectly from beginning to end.**

   Imagine it as vividly and with as much sensory detail as you possibly can. If you're rehearsing a tennis match, for example, feel the racket in your hand and your shoes against the court; feel your arm lifting, reaching back, and arcing forward as you serve; feel the contact of the ball against the racket; and so on.

   Studies have shown that kinesthetic rehearsals (in which you feel your body going through the motions) are nearly as effective as actual practice in improving performance in sports and other physical activities. If you're rehearsing a presentation at work, imagine standing in front of the group, speaking articulately and cogently, getting the important points across, and so on.

3. **Include a feeling-state dimension by noticing how good you feel as you move through the performance.**

   You may feel exhilaration, excitement, power, or enjoyment. If you notice any fear or apprehension, just pause for a moment, take a few deep breaths, do whatever you usually do to allay your fear, and then resume your rehearsal.

4. **Take as much time as you need to imagine yourself executing the performance perfectly.**

   If you notice any mistakes, stop and correct them and then repeat the performance correctly. At first, your rehearsal may take as long as the actual performance. Once you've clarified all the details, you can abbreviate subsequent rehearsals if you have only limited time.

5. **Be sure to practice this exercise at least several times before the actual performance.**

   Immediately before the performance, stop for a moment, close your eyes, and run through an abbreviated rehearsal.

IN THE MOMENT

Enjoying the dance of yes

For the next ten minutes, notice the subtle (and not so subtle) ways your mind keeps saying *no* to life — suppressing your feelings and impulses, judging or even rejecting other people, refusing to accept the way things actually are. For example, you may feel sadness arising but push it away and refuse to feel it. Or you may look in the mirror but edit what you see, either by criticizing yourself for your appearance or refusing to see your imperfections. Or perhaps you close your heart to your loved ones because they don't live up to your expectations.

You may be amazed to discover how much energy your mind consumes by refusing to accept what's actually happening right in front of you.

Instead, for the next ten minutes, just say yes. Whatever you experience, whomever you meet, however life presents itself to you, notice your tendency to resist or deny and instead say yes. Yes to your feelings, yes to your partner or your kids, yes to your body and your face, yes to your life. As much as possible, keep an open, spacious, attentive mind. Of course, you're welcome to change what you don't like, but take a moment to say yes to it first.

You may be so accustomed to saying no that you don't know how to say yes at first. So feel free to experiment. Repeating the word "yes" to yourself can help get you started. Maybe you'll end up enjoying the dance of yes so much that you extend it to every area of your life. Yes, yes, yes!

Part V
The Part of Tens

The 5th Wave   By Rich Tennant

"I know it's not as exciting as bungee jumping, but this might be the time to take up meditating as a pastime."

In this part . . .

This is the place to turn for quick answers and brief meditations. The next time you're stumped when Aunt Sally or Cousin Dave asks a question about meditation, the next time you come up with a few questions yourself, the next time you're in the mood to meditate but don't want to thumb through the rest of this book — check out the gems in this part.

Chapter 17

Answers to Ten Commonly Asked Questions about Meditation

● ●

*W*hen most folks first consider taking up the practice of meditation, they usually have a few questions they need to have answered — and once they get started, they come up with a few more. Well, here are some brief answers to ten of the most popular questions. For more detailed answers, check out the rest of this book.

Will meditation make me too relaxed or spaced out to succeed at work or school?

Many people still associate meditation with impractical alternative life-styles and fear they might get morphed into a hippie or a navel-gazing yogi if they dare to sit quietly for a few minutes. The truth is, however, that medita-tion actually teaches you how to focus your mind and minimize distractions so you can get things done more effectively. Besides, when you're tense, you can't do anything particularly well — and meditation helps you relax your body and reduce your stress so you can make better (and more enjoyable) use of your time.

As I explain in more detail in Chapter 1, most meditation practices are a blend of concentration and receptive awareness. With concentration, you discover how to stabilize your attention on a particular object, such as your breath or some other bodily sensation. Eventually, you can extend this concentration to work or sports or any other activity. In fact, psychologists have a word for the total absorption that comes with intense concentration; they call it *flow,* a state of mind in which time slows down, distractions fall away, and activity becomes effortless and supremely enjoyable.

With receptive awareness, you practice expanding your attention to include the full range of your experiences, both inner and outer. The two together — concentration and receptive awareness — combine to create the kind of relaxed alertness you see in great performers, athletes, and martial artists. Now, you couldn't accuse them of being spaced out or ineffectual, could you?

How can I find the time to meditate in my busy schedule?

Ah yes, the perennial issue: time! Well, the great thing about meditation is that it doesn't really take all that much time. Once you pick up the basics (by reading this book, of course), you can begin by practicing for five or ten minutes each day. Mornings are generally best, at least to start. You may want to sandwich a little quiet time between brushing your teeth and taking a shower. Or if you're an early bird, you can enjoy the precious moments of stillness before the rest of the family wakes up.

Whatever time slot works best for you, the most important thing is to meditate regularly — every day if possible, give or take a day here or there (and some time to sleep late on Sundays). The reason for this recommendation is not to turn you into an automaton, but rather to give you an opportunity to enjoy the wonderful benefits of meditation, such as reduced stress and greater focus. Like lifting weights or practicing a musical instrument, meditation doesn't really have an impact unless you keep it up and keep it regular.

As you meditate consistently over the days and weeks, you may begin to notice little changes in your life — moments of ease or peace or harmony you may not have experienced since childhood, if ever. And the more you benefit from your meditation practice, the more you're going to feel motivated to carve out the time — and perhaps even extend the niche from five or ten minutes to fifteen or twenty.

Since I can't sit on the floor and cross my legs, can I meditate in a chair or lying down instead?

Yes, absolutely. In fact, traditional meditation postures include sitting, standing, walking, lying down, and moving in particular patterns (for example, t'ai chi or Sufi dancing). Basically, any position that you can comfortably sustain is appropriate for meditation. (To find a posture that works for you, check out Chapter 7.) Of course, lying down has its downside (so to speak): You're more likely to fall asleep. So, you may have to make a special effort (without getting tense about it, that is) to stay alert and focused. Also, you're better off lying on a mat or carpet, rather than on your bed — for obvious reasons!

More important than whether you sit, lie, or stand for meditation is what you do with your back. Slumping forward or tilting to the side, so your body fights against gravity, may eventually prove painful and make it difficult to sustain your practice over the weeks and months. Instead, you can get into the habit of extending your spine (as explained in Chapter 7), which contributes to good posture in your other activities as well.

What should I do about the restlessness or discomfort I feel when I try to meditate?

To begin with, you might find it comforting to realize that you're not alone. Everyone experiences agitation or discomfort in their meditation from time to time — or even often. In fact, meditation acts like a mirror that reflects you back to you. Believe it or not, that's one of its virtues. When you stop your busy life for a few minutes and sit quietly, you may suddenly notice all the nervous energy and frenzied thinking that have been stressing you out all along. Welcome to the world of meditation!

Initially, meditation involves focusing your attention on some object (like your breathing or a word or phrase known as a *mantra*) and gently bringing your attention back like a mischievous puppy whenever it wanders off. (For basic meditation instructions, see Chapter 6.) Gradually, you may notice that your restlessness and discomfort begin to settle down by themselves.

Once your concentration deepens, you can expand your awareness to include first your sensations, and then your thoughts and emotions. At this stage, you can begin to explore, make friends with, and ultimately even accept your restlessness and discomfort. Though this process may not be an easy one, it has broad implications because it teaches you the resilience and peace of mind to accept unavoidable difficulties in every area of your life. (For more on making friends with your experience, see Chapter 11.)

What should I do if I keep falling asleep while I meditate?

Like restlessness, sleepiness is a common roadblock on the journey of meditation. (For more on roadblocks, see Chapter 12.) Even the great meditators of the past reported struggling with sleep — and some of them devised extreme measures for staying awake, like tying their hair to the ceiling or meditating on the edge of a cliff. Talk about determination!

Ordinary folks like you and me have the option of using gentler means to keep ourselves awake and alert while we meditate. First, you may want to explore the sleepiness a little. Where do you experience it in your body? Is it just mental dullness, or are you physically tired as well? Perhaps you should be napping rather than meditating!

If you decide to keep going, you can try opening your eyes wide and sitting up as straight as possible to rouse your energy. If you still feel sleepy, get up and walk around or splash some cold water on your face. In any case, sleepiness doesn't necessarily have to prevent you from meditating — after all, sleepy meditation is better than no meditation at all.

How can I tell if I'm meditating the right way? How do I know if my meditation is working?

These two questions (actually flip sides of the same question) reflect the goal-oriented perfectionist in each of us, who monitors our activities to make sure we're doing them right. The great thing about meditation is that you can't do it wrong, short of not doing it at all. (In fact, it's the perfectionist that causes most of your stress — and the point of meditation is to reduce stress, not intensify it.)

When you meditate, just set aside the perfectionist (as much as you can) and keep gently returning to your focus in the here and now. (For detailed meditation instructions, check out the other chapters in this book, especially Chapter 6.)

The experiences that may arise as you meditate — sleepiness, busy thoughts, physical discomfort, restlessness, deep emotion — don't indicate that you're going astray. Quite the contrary, they're the grist for the mill of your meditation, the old habits and patterns that get transformed as you deepen your practice. (For more on transforming old patterns, see Chapter 11.)

As for knowing when your meditation is "working," you probably won't notice any flashing lights or sudden jolts of energy. Instead, you may recognize subtler shifts — for example, your friends or loved ones may remark that you seem less irritable or stressed out than before, or you may find that you're feeling happy or peaceful at times for no apparent reason. Again, don't look for results, or, like the proverbial watched pot, your meditation may never boil over. Just trust in the process and let the changes take care of themselves.

Can I meditate while I'm driving my car or sitting at my computer?

Although you can't practice formal meditation while you're engaged in ordinary activities, you can practice doing things meditatively. (For more on how to meditate in everyday life, see Chapter 15.) During your daily periods of silent meditation, you discover how to stay present as much as possible amidst the welter of distracting thoughts, emotions, and sensations. Then, when you slip behind the wheel of your car or sit down in front of your computer, you can apply at least some of the same mindful, attentive presence to negotiate rush-hour traffic or prepare a report. You'll find that you accomplish the activity with less effort and strain and enjoy yourself more.

It's like practicing a sport — say, tennis. First, you need to work on your backhand again and again. Then, when you get into a match with a friend, you know exactly what to do, even though the situation is more challenging and complex.

Do I have to give up my religious beliefs in order to meditate?

Definitely not. In fact, as many contemporary Christian and Jewish contemplatives have discovered, you can apply the basic principles and techniques of meditation (as taught in this book) to any spiritual or religious tradition or orientation. Meditation just involves pausing in your busy life, taking a few deep breaths, sitting quietly, and turning your attention inward. What you discover is not Zen or Sufi or TM (Transcendental Meditation), but *you* — complete with all your beliefs, affiliations, and personality traits!

Like William Johnston in his book *Christian Zen* (see Appendix), many people also find that meditation methods with Eastern roots actually deepen their connection to their own Western faith by supplementing prayer and belief with some direct experience of the love and presence of God.

What should I do if my partner or other family members don't support me in my meditation practice?

I must admit that I don't have an easy answer for this one, especially if your loved ones are openly antagonistic. But if they're merely resistant or tend to interrupt you at inopportune moments or demand your attention when you're just about to get quiet, you may want to talk with them and explain your interest in meditation. Reassure them that you don't love them any less just because you're spending five or ten minutes in silence each day. Show them this book — or even lend them a copy so they can read about meditation for themselves.

Once you've been practicing for a while, they may begin to notice that you're more enjoyable to be around — more relaxed, more attentive, less distracted and stressed out — and their resistance may gradually melt away. Who knows? One day they may decide to join you and give meditation a try themselves.

Can meditation actually improve my health?

Yes, it can. Researchers have published hundreds of studies investigating the health benefits of meditation, and the results consistently indicate that people who meditate regularly have better health than those who don't. In particular, the meditators have lower blood pressure, cholesterol levels, and heart rate; slower brain waves (which correlates with increased relaxation); deeper, slower breathing; quicker recovery from stress; and less pain. (For more on the health benefits of meditation, see Chapter 2.)

By bringing your mind and body into harmony and increasing your overall level of peace, relaxation, and well-being, regular meditation facilitates the release of life-enhancing chemicals into the bloodstream and bolsters the immune response. You can also practice specific techniques developed over the centuries by the great meditators of the past (and adapted for contemporary Westerners) that are especially designed to stimulate the healing process. (To find out more about meditation and healing, check out Chapter 16.)

Chapter 18

Ten Favorite All-Purpose Meditations (Plus Two)

● ●

*H*ere are ten of my all-time favorite meditations, drawn from the pages of this book. I've chosen them not only because I enjoy them, but also because they provide a range of different practices for you to sample, from elaborate visualizations to basic mindfulness techniques. (For more on mindfulness, see Chapter 6.) Feel free to experiment with these meditations straight off the page, if you're so inclined. With regular practice, they offer a taste of the meditative experience. If you start hungering for the whole meal — well then, go ahead and thumb through the rest of the book.

Practicing relaxation

To reduce your stress and reap the other benefits of relaxation, try practicing this simple exercise for 15 or 20 minutes each day. Known as the *Relaxation Response,* it was developed in the 1970s by Herbert Benson, M.D., a professor at Harvard Medical School, based on research into the benefits of Transcendental Meditation (TM).

1. **Find a spot where you can sit quietly and undisturbed.**

   For more on how to create an environment conducive to meditation, see Chapter 8.

2. **Sit in a position that you can comfortably maintain for the duration of your meditation.**

   For a complete discussion of sitting posture in meditation, including diagrams, see Chapter 7.

3. **Choose an object to concentrate on.**

   This "object" can be a visual symbol (such as a geometric shape) or a special syllable, word, or phrase, known as a *mantra,* that you repeat again and again. (For more on mantras, see Chapters 3 and 13.) Objects with deep personal or spiritual meaning are especially effective. As much as possible, keep your attention focused on this object; when you get distracted, come back to your focus. (If your object is internal, close your eyes.)

4. **Maintain a receptive attitude.**

   Let thoughts, images, and feelings pass through without trying to hold or interpret them. Resist the temptation to evaluate your progress; just gently bring your attention back when it wanders.

With regular practice, you may gradually begin to notice that your body is more relaxed and your mind is more peaceful — just a few of the many benefits of meditation.

Following your breath

Drawn from the mindfulness tradition of Buddhism, this basic meditation practice develops concentration and uses the breath to teach you how to stay present from moment to moment, no matter where you are or what you may be doing. For more complete instructions (and more about mindfulness), see Chapter 6.

1. **Begin by finding a comfortable sitting position that you can hold for 10 or 15 minutes.**

   Then take a few deep breaths and exhale slowly. Without trying to control your breath in any way, allow it to find its own natural depth and rhythm. Always breathe through your nose unless you can't for some reason.

2. **Allow your attention to focus either on the sensation of your breath coming and going through your nostrils or on the rising and falling of your belly as you breathe.**

   Although you're welcome to alternate your focus from one session to the next, it's best to stick with a single focus for the entire meditation — and eventually you're better off using the same focus each time you meditate.

3. **Give your full attention to the coming and going of your breath.**

   Do it the way a mother tracks the movements of her young child — lovingly yet persistently, softly yet precisely, with relaxed yet focused awareness.

4. **When you realize that your mind has wandered off and you're engrossed in planning or thinking or daydreaming, gently but firmly bring your mind back to your breath.**

   Thoughts and images will almost certainly continue to skitter and swirl through your mind as you meditate, but don't worry. Just patiently and persistently keep coming back to your breath. If you find it virtually impossible to follow your breath, you may want to begin with counting your breaths (see Chapter 6).

5. **Continue this simple (but not easy!) exercise for the duration of your meditation.**

   With repeated practice, you may find that your mind settles down more quickly — and that you're more present and focused in other areas of your life as well.

Walking meditation

If you don't feel like sitting still, you can try meditating while you walk. A time-honored technique that's practiced in monasteries and meditation centers throughout the world, it's a great way to discover how to translate the focus you learn on your cushion or chair to the ordinary world of movement and activity. If the weather allows, by all means walk outside. Or you can just walk back and forth in your house, if you like.

1. **Begin by walking at your usual pace, following your breath as you walk.**

2. **Coordinate your breathing with your walking.**

   For example, you can take three steps for each inhalation and three steps for each exhalation — which, as you may notice, is considerably slower than most people walk. If you want to change the speed of your walking, just change the number of steps per breath. But maintain the same pace each time you walk. (If your inhalations and exhalations are different lengths, just adapt your walking accordingly.)

3. **In addition to your breathing, be aware of your feet and legs as you lift and move them.**

   Notice the contact of your feet with the ground or floor. Gaze ahead of you, with your eyes lowered at a 45-degree angle. If you find it too complicated to follow your breathing and be aware of your feet at the same time, just choose one focus and stick with it. Be relaxed, easy, and comfortable as you walk.

4. **Enjoy your steady, mindful walking for as long as you wish.**

If your attention wanders or you start to hurry, gently bring your attention back to your walking.

Mindful eating

Did you ever finish a meal and wonder what happened to the food? Well, here's a meditation for paying attention to what you're putting into your mouth. Not only will you enjoy your food as never before, but mindful eating will facilitate your digestion by reducing the tension or stress you bring to the table. (You probably won't want to eat as meditatively as this all the time, but you can still apply a little mindfulness to every meal, no matter how informal.)

1. **Before you begin eating, take a few moments to appreciate your food.**

You may want to reflect on the earth and the sunshine that gave life to this food and the people and effort that brought it to your table. Or you can express your thanks to God or spirit — or simply sit silently and feel grateful for what you have. If you're eating with others, you may want to hold hands, smile at one another, or connect in some other way.

2. **Bring your awareness to your hand as you lift the first bite of food to your lips.**

You can experiment with the custom in certain monastic traditions of eating more slowly than usual. Or just eat at your usual speed, but be as mindful as you can.

3. **Be fully aware as the first morsel of food enters your mouth and floods your taste buds with sensations.**

Notice the tendency of your mind to judge the flavor: "It's too spicy or salty," or "It's not what I expected." Notice any emotions that get stirred up: disappointment, relief, irritation, joy. Be aware of any ripples of pleasure or warmth or other physical sensations. Enjoy your food!

4. **If you talk while you eat, notice how the talking affects you.**

Do certain topics cause you to tense up or give you indigestion? Does the talk take you away from the enjoyment of your meal, or can you have both?

5. **Stay mindful of each mouthful as you gradually eat your meal.**

   This part is probably the hardest because most people have a tendency to space out once they know how their food tastes. But you can continue to enjoy the taste freshly, bite after bite. (If you get distracted, you can stop and breathe for a moment or two before starting to eat again.)

Finding the beauty

Even in the most chaotic and unappealing situations, you can attune yourself to a quality or dimension of beauty, if you try. It's like one of those figure-ground puzzles. At first, you can't even perceive the shape in the background. But once you've seen it, you just need to shift your awareness to see it again. The next time you find yourself in a mildly unpleasant place or circumstance, do the following meditation.

1. **Take a moment to look for the beauty.**

   You may notice a patch of green grass in the distance, or a bouquet of flowers on a table, or the laughter of a child, or an aesthetically pleasing piece of furniture. Or you may just notice a warm feeling in your belly or heart.

2. **Take a deep breath, shift your attention from your stress or discomfort, and enjoy the beauty.**

   Allow yourself to resonate with it for a few moments as you would with a favorite piece of music or a walk in the woods.

3. **Shift your focus back to the situation at hand and notice whether your attitude has changed in any way.**

   Know that you can shift your awareness to see the beauty whenever you feel inclined.

Cultivating lovingkindness

Here's a meditation for opening your heart and initiating a flow of unconditional love (also known as *lovingkindness*) to yourself and others. You may want to begin with five or ten minutes of some basic meditation, such as the Relaxation Response or following your breath, to deepen and stabilize your concentration. (For a more complete version of this meditation, turn to Chapter 10.)

1. **Begin by closing your eyes, taking a few deep breaths, and relaxing your body.**

2. **Remember a time when you felt deeply loved.**

   Spend a few minutes dwelling on this memory and allowing your heart to respond. Notice the gratitude and love that arise for the person who loved you.

3. **Allow these loving feelings to overflow and gradually suffuse your whole being.**

   Allow yourself to be filled with love. You may also want to express the wishes and intentions that underlie this love. For example, you might say to yourself, as the Buddhists do, "May I be happy. May I be peaceful. May I be free from suffering." Feel free to use whatever words seem right for you. As the recipient, be sure to take in the love as well as extend it.

4. **When you feel complete with yourself for now, imagine extending this lovingkindness to a loved one or dear friend, using similar words to express your intentions.**

   Don't hurry; allow yourself to feel the love as much as you can, rather than merely imagine it.

5. **Extend this lovingkindness from your heart to all your loved ones and friends.**

   Again, take your time.

6. **Extend this lovingkindness to all people and all beings everywhere.**

   May all beings be happy. May all beings be peaceful. May all beings be free from suffering.

Softening your belly

Stephen Levine, an American meditation teacher who has written extensively on healing and dying, counsels that the state of your belly reflects the state of your heart. By consciously softening your belly again and again, you can let go and open to the tender feelings in your heart. (The following meditation is adapted from his book *Guided Meditations, Explorations and Healings*.)

1. **Begin by sitting comfortably and taking a few deep breaths.**

2. **Allow your awareness to settle into your body.**

3. **Allow your awareness to descend to your belly as you gently soften this area of your body.**

    Consciously let go of any tension or holding.

4. **Allow your breath to enter your belly.**

    When you inhale, your belly rises. When you exhale, your belly falls.

5. **With each breath, continue to soften your belly.**

    Let go of any anger, fear, pain, or unresolved grief you may be holding in your belly.

6. **As you continue to soften your belly, notice how your heart responds.**

7. **After five minutes or longer of this soft-belly meditation, open your eyes and go about your day.**

    Every now and then, check in with your belly. If you notice that you're tensing it again, gently breathe and soften.

Healing with light

Many meditation traditions suggest that physical illness and emotional suffering are just different facets of the same basic problem — just different ways we contract away from our essential wholeness and health. Here's an exercise for directing the life-giving power of light to the places inside your body and mind that cry out for healing.

1. **Begin by sitting down and meditating in your usual way for several minutes.**

    If you don't have a usual way, you can find one in Chapter 6 — or just sit quietly, close your eyes, and take a few slow, deep breaths, relaxing a little on each exhalation.

2. **Imagine a luminous sphere of white light suspended about a foot above your head and slightly in front of you.**

    Like a sun, this sphere embodies and radiates all the positive, healing, harmonious qualities you most want to manifest in your life right now. (You may want to be specific at first — strength, clarity, peace, love; eventually, you can just flash on the light.) If you find it helpful, you can imagine a spiritual being such as Jesus or Buddha in place of (or inside) the sphere.

3. **Imagine yourself soaking up all these qualities with the healing light as though you were sunbathing.**

4. **Imagine this light radiating in all directions to the farthest corners of the universe and drawing the energy of all the benevolent forces that support your growth and evolution back into the sphere.**

5. **Visualize this positive, healing energy shining from the sphere, like the light of a thousand suns streaming down through your body and mind.**

   Imagine the energy eliminating all negativity and tension, darkness and depression, worry and anxiety and replacing them with radiance, vitality, peace, and all the other positive qualities you seek.

6. **Continue to imagine this powerful, healing light flooding every cell and molecule of your being, dissolving any contractions and stuck places you may be aware of and leaving you clean, clear, and calm.**

7. **Visualize this luminous sphere gradually descending into your heart, where it continues to radiate this powerful light.**

8. **Imagine yourself as a luminous being with a sphere of light in your heart that constantly radiates clarity, harmony, and purity — first to every cell and particle of your own being and then, through you, to every other being in every direction.**

   You can carry the feelings and images this exercise evokes throughout the rest of your day.

Grounding into the earth

When you're feeling scattered or spaced out and you've lost touch with your connection to the earthly plane of existence, you may find it helpful to use the following meditation to ground you.

1. **Begin by sitting quietly, closing your eyes, and taking a few slow, deep breaths.**

   If possible, sit on the ground, with your back relatively straight (see Chapter 7 for more on sitting positions).

2. **Focus your awareness on your lower abdomen, at a point about 2 inches below your navel and $1^1/_2$ inches inside your body.**

   Martial artists call this area the *t'an t'ien* and believe it's a focal point for life energy, or *chi*. Explore this area with mindful attention, noticing how it feels.

3. **Direct your breath into this area, expanding it when you inhale and contracting it when you exhale.**

   Consciously and deliberately breathe into your t'an t'ien for five minutes or more, allowing your awareness and your energy to concentrate there. Notice how your center of gravity shifts from the upper part of your body to your t'an t'ien.

4. **Continuing to breathe with your t'an t'ien, imagine that you're a tree with roots that go deep into the earth.**

   Both feel and visualize these roots originating in the t'an t'ien and growing down through the base of your spine into the ground, spreading through the soil as far down as you can imagine.

5. **Feel and visualize these roots drawing energy up from the earth into your t'an t'ien on the inhalation, and feel the energy spreading down through the roots on the exhalation.**

   Continue to feel and visualize this circulation of energy — up on the inhale, down on the exhale, for five or ten minutes.

6. **Once your t'an t'ien feels charged and strong, you can get up and go about your day.**

   Every now and then, remind yourself to breathe with your belly again for a minute or two.

Sky of mind

Here's a brief meditation that you can do anytime you're outdoors to give you a taste of the vastness of your own essential nature, which the Zen folks call, appropriately enough, "big mind."

1. **Preferably on a clear day, sit or lie down and look up at the sky.**

   Set aside your analytical mind for now and all you think you know about the sky.

2. **Take a few minutes to contemplate the vastness of the sky, which appears to stretch endlessly in every direction.**

3. **Gradually, allow your mind to expand to fill the sky — up and down, north and south, east and west.**

   Let go of all sense of personal boundaries as you fill the sky with your awareness.

4. **Become the sky completely and rest in the experience for a few minutes.**

5. **Gradually, return to your ordinary sense of yourself.**

How do you feel? Has your awareness changed in any way? Once you get the knack of this exercise, you can do it for brief moments at any time of the day to remind you of your skylike nature — for example, walking your dog in the morning or gazing out your window on a break at work.

Practicing a half smile

The Vietnamese Buddhist teacher Thich Nhat Hanh suggests that you can actually shift your mood and restore your innate happiness by smiling consciously, even when your spirits are low. Contemporary scientific research agrees, indicating that smiling relaxes hundreds of facial muscles and has the same effect on the nervous system as real joy. Besides, smiling encourages others to smile and be happy as well.

1. **Take a few moments right now to form your lips into a half smile.**

   Notice how other parts of your body respond. Does your belly relax? Does your back naturally straighten a little? Does your mood change in subtle ways? Notice also if you have any resistance to smiling when "you don't really feel like it."

2. **Hold this half smile for at least ten minutes as you engage in ordinary activities.**

   Do you notice a shift in how you act or respond to others? Do others respond to your smile by smiling back?

3. **The next time you feel your spirits sagging, practice this half smile for at least half an hour and notice how you feel.**

Peaceful place

This simple meditation relaxes the body quickly and easily and can be used to help facilitate healing. It's also a kind of inner monastery or refuge that you can escape to when you're feeling threatened, unsafe, or stressed out.

1. **Begin by sitting comfortably, closing your eyes, and taking a few deep breaths.**

2. **Imagine yourself in a safe, protected, peaceful place.**

   It may be a place you know well (a place in nature, for example, like a meadow, a forest, or a beach), a place you've visited once or twice before, or simply a place in your imagination.

3. **Take as much time as you need to imagine this peaceful place as vividly as you can, in all your senses.**

   Notice the colors, the shapes, the sounds, the light, the feeling of the air against your skin, the contact of your feet against the ground. Explore this special place to your heart's content.

4. **Allow yourself to rest in the feelings of comfort, safety, and tranquillity this special place evokes.**

5. **Spend as much time here as you wish.**

   When you're done, gradually return to the present moment and open your eyes, while continuing to enjoy the pleasant, positive feelings this exercise evoked.

Part VI
Appendix

In this part . . .

1f this book whets your appetite for further inspiration and instruction, here's an annotated list of resources to sustain you. You can find organizations and centers specializing in a variety of techniques and spiritual orientations, as well as books by some of the best contemporary meditation teachers, both Eastern and Western.

Appendix

Meditation Resources

• •

*O*nce you've read this book, you may have a hankering to hook up with other people who meditate, to do some in-depth training, to check out other styles and approaches, or to read books on particular aspects of meditation. So here's a listing of organizations and centers and a brief, annotated bibliography of some good meditation books to complement this one.

Organizations and Centers

With the rapid spread of meditation in the West, centers and organizations devoted to the practice have sprung up in every major city — and plenty of small towns too! Needless to say, I couldn't possibly list them all in these pages (even if I *could* track them down, which would be no small feat, given that meditation comes in countless styles and spiritual affiliations). So, I offer you an annotated catalogue of major national organizations and (in the case of traditions like Zen, where no centralized organization exists) representative centers. If you just want something nearby and don't particularly care about style or affiliation, you may want to consult your local phone book, alternative newspaper, or New Age periodical. Otherwise, check out the following list. If an organization appeals to you, contact them directly for more information.

Note: Meditation instruction in these organizations often comes packaged with a set of spiritual beliefs, which may or may not interest you. Also, some organizations offer free instruction, whereas others charge for the opportunity. Finally, although most have been providing meditation instruction for many years (or even decades), I haven't personally checked them out and so can't offer my double-your-money-back satisfaction guarantee.

Jewish, Christian, and Sufi Meditation

The World Community for Christian Meditation
c/o Carla Cooper
National Coordinator (USA)
3727 Abbeywood
Pearland, TX 77584
281-412-9803
www.wccm.org

Dedicated to the practice of Christian meditation as taught by John Main, a Benedictine monk who rediscovered the "pure prayer" (mantra recitation) of the desert fathers, this organization boasts more than a thousand local groups in over 40 countries worldwide — and you don't have to be a Catholic (or even a Christian!) to join.

Unitas
1475 Pine Ave. W.
Montreal, Quebec, Canada H3G 1B3
514-849-2728; 514-281-0173 (fax)
unitas@total.net (e-mail)
www.total.net/~unitas/

A residential retreat center in the heart of old Montreal, Unitas offers a variety of programs encouraging inner reflection and renewal, including classes and workshops devoted to Christian meditation, as well as the opportunity for self-directed retreats.

Chochmat HaLev
2525 Eighth Street, #13
Berkeley, CA 94710
510-704-9687
chochmat@best.com (e-mail)
www.chochmat.org

Specializing in Jewish "meditation and spirituality training and practice," this organization offers classes and year-long intensive programs and hosts regular conferences that draw well-known leaders in the Jewish meditation renaissance, including rabbis Rami Shapiro, David Cooper, and Zalman Schachter.

International Association of Sufism
25 Mitchell Blvd. Suite #2
San Rafael, CA 94903
415-472-6959; 415-472-6221 (fax)
ias@ias.org (e-mail)
www.ias.org

Established to introduce Sufism to the public and to foster dialogue between different Sufi schools, this ecumenical organization publishes a quarterly journal, *Sufism: An Inquiry,* and sponsors the annual Sufi Symposium that features Sufi teachers from around the world. If you want to find out more about Sufi meditation, their Web site is a great place to start.

Hindu and Yoga Meditation

Self-Realization Fellowship
3880 San Rafael Avenue, Dept.8W
Los Angeles, CA 90065-3298
323-225-2471; 323-225-5088 (fax)
www.yogananda-srf.org

Founded in 1920 to further the teachings of the Hindu spiritual teacher Paramahansa Yogananda, SRF teaches Kriya Yoga, a set of "scientific techniques of concentration and meditation that lead to a deepening interior peace and awareness of God's presence." The organization has meditation and retreat centers around the world.

The Expanding Light
14618 Tyler Foote Rd.
Nevada City, CA 95959
800-346-5350
info@expandinglight.org (e-mail)
www.expandinglight.org

Established in 1968 by a disciple of Paramahansa Yogananda, "the first great Indian master of yoga to make his home in the West" (see preceding entry for Self-Realization Fellowship), this community teaches meditation and yoga through more than 70 affiliated centers worldwide.

Kripalu Center for Yoga and Health
Box 793
Lenox, MA 01240
800-741-7353 or 413-448-3152
www.vgernet.net/kali/

Located in the Berkshire mountains, this "spiritual retreat and program center" offers classes and workshops focusing on yoga, holistic health, and spiritual development. Because it draws teachers from a variety of different disciplines, Kripalu is a good place to begin exploring yoga-based meditation practices.

International Sivananda Yoga Vedanta Centers
1746 Abbot Kinney Blvd.
Venice, CA 90291
310-822-9642
www.sivananda.org

Founded in 1959 and featuring nearly 80 centers worldwide, this organization provides instruction in traditional yoga meditation and hatha yoga based on the teachings of the Indian master Swami Sivananda and his disciple Swami Vishnu-devananda. Ask for a listing of yoga teachers and centers near you.

Yogaville Ashram and Integral Yoga Institutes
Rt. 1, Box 1720
Buckingham, VA 23921
800-858-9642 or 804-969-3121
iyi@yogaville.org (e-mail)
www.yogaville.org

Established by Swami Satchidananda (the bearded sage who gave the invocation at Woodstock in 1969), Yogaville offers traditional meditation and hatha yoga through its community and retreat facility in Virginia, through Integral Yoga Institutes worldwide, and through an extensive network of yoga teachers and centers.

SYDA Foundation (Siddha Yoga)
371 Brickman Road, PO Box 600
South Fallsburg, NY 12779-0600
914-434-2000, ext. 2202
www.siddhayoga.org

This organization offers initiation into Siddha Yoga meditation, a devotional practice designed to awaken the fire of divinity within. Founded by the Indian guru Swami Muktananda and currently headed by his female successor, Swami Chidvilasananda, SYDA boasts six ashrams (in the U.S., England, and Australia) and more than 600 centers worldwide.

Vedanta Society of Southern California
1946 Vedanta Place
Hollywood, CA 90068
323-465-7114
info@vedanta.org (e-mail)
www.vedanta.org

Based on the teachings of the nineteenth-century Indian sage Ramakrishna and his successors, the Vedanta Society offers an integrated approach to realizing the divinity within, including meditation, devotion, insight into the oneness of God and all creation, and selfless service. Features 16 independent centers in the United States, Europe, and South America.

The Transcendental Meditation Program
639 Whispering Hills Road, Suite 704
Boone, NC 28607
888-532-7686 (automatically connects you to the nearest Maharishi Vedic
University, school, or center)
www.tm.org

Perhaps the best known of all the meditation organizations (the Beatles
popularized it in the 1970s), TM is also the most expensive, with brief
introductory courses costing many hundreds of dollars. But proponents
claim that the technique is far superior to any other and therefore well
worth the price of instruction.

Taoist Meditation

Healing Tao International
PO Box 20028
New York, NY 10014
888-432-5826
healingt@loxinfo.co.th (e-mail)
www.healing-tao.com

This organization is a loosely knit association of teachers and centers
offering Taoist meditation and healing techniques in the style of Mantak
Chia, whose popular books include *Awaken Healing Light of the Tao* and
Taoist Secrets of Love.

Zen Meditation

San Francisco Zen Center
300 Page Street
San Francisco, CA 94102
415-863-3136
sf-zen@pacbell.net (e-mail)
http://bodhi.zendo.com/~sfzc

Founded in the 1960s by Zen master Shunryu Suzuki (see *Zen Mind, Beginner's
Mind* in the "Books" section later in this appendix) and popularized in the '70s
by *The Tassajara Bread Book* by resident monk Ed Brown, this organization
offers traditional Zen meditation instruction and retreats at its city center and
also at Green Gulch Zen Farm in nearby Marin County. (For intensive training,
seasoned practitioners head to Tassajara Zen Mountain Center, a monastery
in the wilderness near Big Sur, California.)

Zen Buddhist Temple (Chicago)
1710 West Cornelia Avenue
Chicago, IL 60657
773-528-8685

Located in a former Pentecostal church, this center offers meditation
instruction to the general public, provides a supportive community for
ongoing practice, and hosts monastic training for monks and nuns. Ven.
Samu Sunim, the resident teacher, is a Korean Zen master.

Zen Mountain Monastery (New York)
PO Box 197
Mt. Tremper, NY 12457
914-688-2228
zmmtrain@zen-mtn.org (e-mail)
www.zen-mtn.org/zmm

Set in the scenic Catskill Mountains, this traditional Zen center offers
meditation instruction, ongoing practice, and intensive retreats. It hosts
programs on Zen and related topics, including the arts, the environment,
and academic studies. The center also features affiliate centers in Vermont,
New York City, and New Zealand.

Community of Mindful Living
PO Box 7355
Berkeley, CA 94707
510-527-3751
www.parallax.org

Established in 1983 to support the work of Vietnamese Zen master Thich
Nhat Hanh (see *Peace Is Every Step* in the "Books" section), the center offers
mindfulness meditation instruction and retreats and publishes and distrib-
utes books and tapes. Contact them for a list of affiliate centers throughout
the U.S.

Tibetan Buddhist Meditation (Vajrayana)

Rigpa U.S. National Headquarters
449 Powell Street, Suite 200
San Francisco, CA 94102
415-392-2055; 415-392-2056 (fax)
www.rigpa.org

An international network of centers under the guidance of Tibetan teacher
Sogyal Rinpoche, author of *The Tibetan Book of Living and Dying* (see "Books"
section), Rigpa offers meditation instruction and retreats in the Buddhist
Vajrayana tradition. The organization also provides a special spiritual
training program for caregivers who work with the dying.

Shambhala International
1084 Tower Road
Halifax, NS (Canada) B3H 2Y5
902-425-4275
info@shambhala.org (e-mail)
www.shamhala.org

Founded in the early 1970s by Chogyam Trungpa Rinpoche, an Oxford-educated Tibetan meditation master who articulated the traditional teachings for his Western audience in a fresh and accessible way, Shambhala features over 100 meditation centers worldwide (including six rural retreats) and North America's only Buddhist-inspired accredited college, Naropa Institute in Boulder, Colorado.

Insight Meditation (Vipassana)

Spirit Rock Meditation Center
PO Box 909
Woodacre, CA 94973
415-488-0170
www.spiritrock.org

Based on traditional Buddhist mindfulness practices as taught in Southeast Asia (commonly known as *Vipassana,* or insight meditation), Spirit Rock offers a variety of practice options, from basic instruction and weekly meditation groups to intensive retreats of ten days or longer. An active family program also provides practice opportunities for parents and children. Teachers from Spirit Rock (who are Westerners) lead retreats throughout the United States.

Insight Meditation Society
1230 Pleasant Street
Barre, MA 01005
978-355-4378
www.dharma.org

Founded in 1975 by Westerners trained in Southeast Asia, IMS, which is located in rural Massachusetts, offers intensive insight meditation (Vipassana) practice, including both short- and long-term retreats led by Western teachers. Features an annual three-month Vipassana course and regular retreats focusing on the cultivation of lovingkindness.

Vipassana Meditation Center
PO Box 24
Shelburne Falls, MA 01370
413-625-2160; 413-625-2170 (fax)
info@dhara.dhamma.org (e-mail)
www.dhamma.org

Affiliated with over 30 sister centers and many associations in 35 countries worldwide, VMC conducts intensive silent retreats in the tradition of the Indian Vipassana teacher S. N. Goenka. Retreats are free of charge; expenses are covered by previous participants who wish to give others the same opportunity. Contact VMC for a retreat schedule or an affiliate group near you.

Other Organizations

Stress-Reduction Clinic
Center for Mindfulness in Medicine, Health Care, and Society
University of Massachusetts Medical Center
419 Belmont Avenue, 2nd Floor
Worcester, MA 01604
508-856-2656

Founded by Jon Kabat-Zinn, author of *Wherever You Go There You Are,* the clinic teaches mindfulness-based stress reduction (MBSR) in an eight-week nonresidential format. The Center for Mindfulness also offers a professional training program and sponsors research into the benefits of mindfulness. Call the clinic to find an MBSR program near you.

Dr. Dean Ornish's Program for Reversing Heart Disease
Preventive Medicine Research Institute
900 Bridgeway
Sausalito, CA 94965
800-775-7674
www.ornish.com

This ground-breaking meditation-based program is now being offered in hospitals throughout the United States. Contact PMRI for the name of the program nearest you or for information about their week-long residential retreats.

Meditation for Beginners
Workshops and Retreats
PO Box 45
Fairfax, CA 94978
415-451-7133
info@meditationsource.com (e-mail)
www.meditationsource.com

Taught by yours truly and offered in different parts of the country, this enjoyable, easy-going introduction to the practice of meditation offers a taste of the real thing without all the spiritual trappings. Highly recommended.

Books

As you'll discover if you check out your local alternative bookstore (or one of the online megastores like amazon.com), meditation books abound — though none, in my humble estimation, is as comprehensive or as user-friendly as this one. Here's a brief annotated list of some of my favorite titles. Many focus on one particular technique or tradition; others emphasize the application of meditation for healing, peak performance, or spiritual development.

Christian Zen. William Johnston. Fordham University Press, 1997.

Written by one of a series of Catholic contemplatives to study with Zen masters in Asia (several even became Zen masters themselves!), this book provides an illuminating introduction to the application of Zen teachings and techniques to the Christian spiritual journey.

Dr. Dean Ornish's Program for Reversing Heart Disease. Dean Ornish, M.D. Ballantine, 1991.

Though meditation is only one aspect of the Ornish program (along with yoga, exercise, lowfat diet, and group support), this ground-breaking book is a must-read for heart patients and their families — and a sobering reminder for overachievers and other type-A personalities. The simple but powerful message: To heal your heart, you have to open your heart.

Full Catastrophe Living: Using the Wisdom of Your Body and Mind to Face Stress, Pain, and Illness. Jon Kabat-Zinn. Dell, 1990.

Don't be put off by the rather negative title — this book details the highly successful mindfulness-based stress-reduction program developed by the author at the University of Massachusetts Medical Center. Also highlights scientific research revealing the mind-body impact of stress and the healing power of meditation.

Healing into Life and Death. Stephen Levine. Anchor/Doubleday, 1987.

The author, who trained and taught extensively with Elizabeth Kubler-Ross, has pioneered an approach to serious illness and dying that applies insights and techniques drawn from the Buddhist tradition. A lucid, heartful book designed to help bring love and healing to the most challenging and painful life circumstances.

The Healing Power of Mind: Simple Meditation Exercises for Health, Well-Being, and Enlightenment. Tulku Thondup. Shambhala, 1996.

A skillful distillation of Buddhist teachings on healing by a Tibetan meditation master and scholar, this eminently readable book offers not only a wealth of basic healing practices, but also deep insights into the nature of mind and the true source of suffering.

Jewish Meditation: A Practical Guide. Aryeh Kaplan. Schocken, 1995.

Deeply rooted in tradition (the author was an Orthodox rabbi) yet informed by the wisdom and practices of other faiths, this little book provides an accessible, comprehensive overview of Jewish meditation, including stories and examples drawn from Kabbalah and the Talmud.

Lovingkindness: The Revolutionary Art of Happiness. Sharon Salzberg. Shambhala, 1995.

Written by a founding teacher at the Insight Meditation Society in Barre, Massachusetts, this book provides a series of exercises for increasing your happiness and peace of mind by cultivating the qualities of lovingkindess, equanimity, compassion, generosity, and sympathetic joy.

The Meditative Mind: The Varieties of Meditative Experience. Daniel Goleman. Tarcher/Putnam, 1988.

By the author of *The New York Times* bestseller *Emotional Intelligence,* this book explores the psychology of meditation, including a detailed description of the inner terrain that meditators may encounter, and provides a helpful overview of different approaches to meditation, from Hindu and Buddhist to Sufi, Jewish, and Christian. Be prepared for some rather complex spiritual terms and ideas.

A Path with Heart: A Guide Through the Perils and Promises of Spiritual Life. Jack Kornfield. Bantam, 1993.

Based on the author's experience as a Buddhist meditator and meditation teacher for more than 25 years, this book provides a detailed roadmap for the spiritual journey that can be applied to any tradition. Filled with the wise counsel and touching stories that have made Kornfield such a popular presenter at conferences around the country.

Peace Is Every Step: The Path of Mindfulness in Everyday Life. Thich Nhat Hanh. Bantam, 1991.

By the Vietnamese Buddhist monk who was nominated for a Nobel Peace Prize by Martin Luther King, this gentle, compassionate book teaches how to extend the practice of mindful awareness to every moment of life. Filled with inspiring examples and informed by the author's commitment to social justice and ecological awareness.

Sacred Hoops: Spiritual Lessons of a Hardwood Warrior. Phil Jackson. Hyperion, 1995.

Written by the former coach of the Chicago Bulls, this fascinating autobiography tells how Jackson used the skills and principles he learned in the practice of Zen meditation to forge a world-champion basketball team. A must-read for sports fans!

The Tibetan Book of Living and Dying. Sogyal Rinpoche. HarperCollins, 1992.

Although this book transmits the traditional Tibetan Buddhist teachings about death, dying, and rebirth (which you may or may not find appealing), it's also filled with heartwarming stories and powerful practices that can be applied not only to help with the dying process, but also to bring more love and compassion into your life right now!

Yoga For Dummies. Georg Feuerstein and Larry Payne. IDG Books Worldwide, 1999.

If you enjoyed the yoga poses in Chapter 7 and feel hungry for more, check out this book. You'll find expert instruction in dozens of poses, from easy to more challenging, designed to keep your body and mind flexible and fit, plus illuminating insights into the spirit of yoga from Georg Feuerstein, one of America's premier yoga scholars.

The Way of a Pilgrim. Anonymous. Shambhala, 1996.

First made popular in the West by J. D. Salinger, this little book tells the true story of a simple nineteenth-century Russian peasant who wanders the countryside reciting the Jesus prayer ("Lord Jesus Christ, have mercy on me!") and discovering love and joy wherever he goes. An inspiring tale of the power of Christian mantra meditation.

Zen Mind, Beginner's Mind. Shunryu Suzuki. Weatherhill, 1970.

Not an instruction manual, exactly, but a prolonged meditation on the nature of meditation (and life) by one of the best-loved Zen masters of our time, this book seamlessly weaves together profound insights and practical guidance. A spiritual classic that is also eminently accessible.

Index

• S •

Notes

Notes

YOUR ONLINE RESOURCE

WWW.DUMMIES.COM

Discover Dummies™ Online!

The *Dummies* Web Site is your fun and friendly online resource for the latest information about *...For Dummies*® books on all your favorite topics. From cars to computers, wine to Windows, and investing to the Internet, we've got a shelf full of *...For Dummies* books waiting for you!

Ten Fun and Useful Things You Can Do at www.dummies.com

1. Register this book and win!
2. Find and buy the *...For Dummies* books you want online.
3. Get ten great *Dummies Tips*™ every week.
4. Chat with your favorite *...For Dummies* authors.
5. Subscribe free to *The Dummies Dispatch*™ newsletter.
6. Enter our sweepstakes and win cool stuff.
7. Send a free cartoon postcard to a friend.
8. Download free software.
9. Sample a book before you buy.
10. Talk to us. Make comments, ask questions, and get answers!

Jump online to these ten fun and useful things at
http://www.dummies.com/10useful

SURF THE NET

WWW.DUMMIES.COM

For other technology titles from IDG Books Worldwide, go to
www.idgbooks.com

Not online yet? It's easy to get started with *The Internet For Dummies*,® 5th Edition, or *Dummies 101*®: *The Internet For Windows*® *98*, available at local retailers everywhere.

IDG BOOKS WORLDWIDE

Find other *...For Dummies* books on these topics:
Business • Careers • Databases • Food & Beverages • Games • Gardening • Graphics • Hardware
Health & Fitness • Internet and the World Wide Web • Networking • Office Suites
Operating Systems • Personal Finance • Pets • Programming • Recreation • Sports
Spreadsheets • Teacher Resources • Test Prep • Word Processing

IDG BOOKS WORLDWIDE
BOOK REGISTRATION

Register This Book and Win!

We want to hear from you!

Visit **http://my2cents.dummies.com** to register this book and tell us how you liked it!

✔ Get entered in our monthly prize giveaway.

✔ Give us feedback about this book — tell us what you like best, what you like least, or maybe what you'd like to ask the author and us to change!

✔ Let us know any other *...For Dummies*® topics that interest you.

Your feedback helps us determine what books to publish, tells us what coverage to add as we revise our books, and lets us know whether we're meeting your needs as a *...For Dummies* reader. You're our most valuable resource, and what you have to say is important to us!

Not on the Web yet? It's easy to get started with *Dummies 101*®: *The Internet For Windows*® *98* or *The Internet For Dummies*®, 5th Edition, at local retailers everywhere.

Or let us know what you think by sending us a letter at the following address:

...For Dummies Book Registration
Dummies Press
7260 Shadeland Station, Suite 100
Indianapolis, IN 46256-3945
Fax 317-596-5498

BESTSELLING BOOK SERIES